Process Thought
and Roman Catholicism

Religion and Borders

Series Editor: Alexander Y. Hwang, Holy Family University, PA

Traditional borders and boundaries are challenged, tested, defended, and redefined in unprecedented ways. Our current crises can be seen as a consequence of conflicting interpretations of the meaning and purpose of borders and boundaries—tribal, political, national, theological, religious, social, familial, sexual, gender, and psychological, among others. The crises of immigration, refugees, famine, disease, poverty, wars, misogyny, sexism, and the environment originate from reified misunderstandings of borders and boundaries. Borders and boundaries define who we are and are not; they divide those who suffer and perish from those who flourish and survive. Religion, itself based on "holiness," or separateness, plays a vital role—both as object and subject—in better understanding borders and boundaries. Religion and Borders interrogates and reconceptualizes the nature and function of borders and the role that religion plays in enforcing or overturning barriers. This series welcomes different scholarly approaches that examine the connection between religion and borders/boundaries, broadly defined. It aims to illuminate how religion—as a socio-cultural phenomenon and a discipline—constitutes itself on the premise of borders, while containing within itself the resources, instincts, and practices to resist boundaries and enclosures.

Volumes in the series explore the methodological and theoretical dimensions of the discipline, but will engage with salient social and political issues, particularly the various crises that are deeply embedded in religious discourse (e.g., migration, environment, public health, sexuality, poverty, war/violence). Projects that engage and draw upon comparative theology, comparative religion, multi-religious sources, interreligious engagement, and interdisciplinary perspectives are especially welcome.

Titles in the Series

Process Thought and Roman Catholicism

Challenges and Promises

Edited by
Marc A. Pugliese and John Becker

LEXINGTON BOOKS
Lanham • Boulder • New York • London

Published by Lexington Books
An imprint of The Rowman & Littlefield Publishing Group, Inc.
4501 Forbes Boulevard, Suite 200, Lanham, Maryland 20706
www.rowman.com

86-90 Paul Street, London EC2A 4NE, United Kingdom

British Library Cataloguing in Publication Information Available

Library of Congress Cataloging-in-Publication Data available

ISBN 978-1-7936-2778-0 (cloth : alk. paper)
ISBN 978-1-7936-2779-7 (electronic)

♾ ™ The paper used in this publication meets the minimum requirements of American National Standard for Information Sciences—Permanence of Paper for Printed Library Materials, ANSI/NISO Z39.48-1992.

Contents

Introduction

Catholic Theology

John B. Cobb, Jr.

This is a truly impressive collection of theological papers. It reminds me of what I have often thought. Catholics have a far better understanding of the task of theology than Protestants. In reaction to what they felt to be an excessive influence of alien philosophies on Catholic thought, the classical Reformers called for theology to be *sola scriptura*. Like many slogans, this one has its use and importance. The ways of thinking expressed in scripture are very different from those that expressed the thinking of Greek philosophers, and it makes sense for theologians to give priority to the former.

But the slogan cannot survive examination. The scriptural texts are themselves not developed in the way called for, so that one is deriving one's method from a source other than scripture. The idea that people of a later generation and culture can avoid being influenced by the beliefs of their own time is simply not true. Further, within the scriptures the same event is often described in multiple ways all of which cannot be strictly accurate. Some ancient texts reflect cultural assumptions that are strongly rejected in later writings.

A sophisticated version of *sola scriptura* can be found in a hermeneutical theology that develops in the context of critical study of the Bible. Obviously, that critical study is not *sola scriptura*. But explicit appeal to the authority of science or philosophy can be avoided, and this still occurs in much Protestant theology. But I am not attracted. I believe that as a Christian I should seek truth wherever it can be found. In doing that I believe I am faithful to the founder of my denomination, John Wesley. We speak of the Wesleyan quadrilateral: scripture, tradition, experience, and reason.

As a Wesleyan theologian, I should accept truth wherever I find it. But theology cannot just be a list of true sentences. As a Christian, I find the organizing principle for life and thought in my discipleship to Jesus. That is still very tricky. Wesley, as a member of the Church of England, got his fourfold authority from Catholicism. Catholic theologians locate themselves in a history of ordered development of ideas that guides them without dictating. For them the theological tradition is a coherent process that provides the background for further steps forward. We Wesleyans are freer to look where we wish, but that leaves the overall theological situation among us chaotic. Again, I am a bit jealous.

Most of the chapters in this book deal with topics on which the authors think that process philosophy throws light. They display again the rich potentialities to be found in Whitehead. I can only rejoice.

One chapter provides a series of challenges to this whole movement. These are well formulated and sensitively argued. And since the structure of the book did not offer the writers who make use of Whitehead an opportunity to respond, I will comment at some length. What is now needed is a book in which those who favor use of Whitehead and those who oppose it could interact.

Although David Burrell's formulations leave an impression of opposition, there is really much agreement. Positively, he is arguing that the problems with classical philosophical theology have already been dealt with adequately. I think he agrees that the philosophies available to the classical theologians were in tension with the highly relational Christian faith. And perhaps some theologians were too much affected by these philosophies. But we critics do not appreciate the ways in which the theologians pressed these philosophies into use in highly relational formulations of theology. The creeds, for example, are in tension with the philosophies they used on just these points.

No doubt some of us Protestant process theologians have so emphasized the influence on theologians of nonrelational substance philosophy that we have wrongly accused classical theologians of believing what they have in fact skillfully avoided. *Mea culpa.* But Whitehead himself is not so oblivious to the reality. He saw that in the doctrine of the Trinity the church recognized its need to understand the deep relationship that allows for both distinctness and unity. Their solution *perichoresis*, he wrote, was a major metaphysical breakthrough. He saw in it the relation that binds all things together without reducing their autonomy. He only regretted that philosophy did not pick up on the achievement of the theologians. He considers that he is doing so.

I think Burrell will agree that it is easy to read a good deal of classical theology and think that the authors suppose that the God they ask us to worship is, like the divine substances of classical philosophy, impassible and immutable. If it is important to know that this is a mistaken impression, that there is no tendency in this direction among classical theologians because of the philosophy they used, then at least some credit should be given to process theology for ending this tragic misreading. Burrell hints some agreement with me on this. If process philosophy provides a way of thinking that agrees with classical theologians rather than being in tension with them, however, the failure of many Protestant process theologians to do justice to classical theologians is not a sufficient reason for Christians to ignore the positive contribution of process philosophy.

Burrell not only believes that Catholic theology has no need of process theology but also that this philosophy pulls away from the personalistic thinking achieved by traditional Catholic theology. His main argument here is that Whitehead develops his ideas in the study of nature rather than human persons. One might say that if he is wrong about this, then much of his criticism crumbles. And he is wrong.

One senses, perhaps incorrectly, that Burrell begins with a dualism between the human and the natural that Whitehead rejects. Human beings are for him part of nature and the picture of nature derived from Descartes and still widely held by scientists is simply wrong. If humans are part of nature, the rest of nature must have many of the same characteristics as human beings. So, we seek an understanding of the world that includes such complex things as mathematicians and saints as well as slime molds and plasma.

To do that, Whitehead does not begin with elementary beings. The simplest actual entities are "physical purposes." But these are introduced late in *Process and Reality*. He begins with occasions of human experience and shows that the occasions of experience of unicellular organisms are like these human occasions in important respects.

So is God. But just as there are important differences between human occasions of experience and the occasions of experience of a bacterium, so also there are important differences, even metaphysical differences, between the experience of humans and of God. Here he differs from Hartshorne. But in neither case can it be said that God is a principle rather than a person. In both cases, God is fully actual. God acts and is acted on. Principles are neither causes nor effects.

There are other process thinkers who think of God in other ways. Positing process instead of substance as the deepest nature of things does not decide all questions about God. A theologian who finds help in process relational philosophy is not immediately bound to all the ideas of any one process thinker. I am myself one who follows Whitehead's formulations closely. I feel myself called forward, but often resistant, and Whitehead's analysis of the initial and final subjective aim fits my experience. It also fits the biblical idea that God "calls" people in quite particular ways remarkably well. To me it seems a very personal relationship. But "person" and "personal" are understood in a variety of ways. Some seem applicable only to the human realm. I understand Catholic theologians, like Whitehead, to teach that God is very different from a human being.

Burrell is also concerned that process theology does not clearly affirm either the resurrection of the body or the immortality of the soul. He is right. If Burrell is looking to philosophy rather than theology to settle these questions, process philosophy is not for him. Hartshorne thought that our attention should be entirely on this life which God preserves forever. Whitehead thought that the question of ongoing personal experience after physical death should be decided empirically. My colleague, David Griffin, approached this topic skeptically, but spent a sabbatical studying evidence. He was convinced that personal experience does not end with physical death. This became an important part of his theology. I myself feel quite sure that he is right. I have written on the resurrection of the soul.

Many moderns are committed to atheism, and Whitehead's rejection of atheism is a main reason that, as noted by Burrell, Whitehead's philosophy has not been accepted by most philosophers. Indeed, it has been excluded from study in most American universities. I, on the other hand, do not think that the rejection of Whitehead and Hartshorne by contemporary atheists should exclude their thought from consideration by theologians.

Having considered Burrell's challenges and offered my response, I will now comment on each constructive chapter but return to another critical chapter later.

Ilia Delio offers us a profound study of Duns Scotus. My first reaction was to recuse myself from comment on the grounds of ignorance. But my assumption can be instead that what she finds in Duns Scotus is there to be found. She then engages in comparisons with Whitehead that show remarkable similarities. This strongly undercuts the tendency of Whiteheadian scholars to speak of scholasticism on the whole as opposed to Whitehead. The majority of scholastics may indeed have held to views with which Whitehead disagreed. But this chapter shows that in the medieval discussions some of Whitehead's most distinctive and important insights are anticipated.

I found of special interest the univocity of "being" in relation to the creatures and to God. This is extremely important for Whitehead. It does not exclude fundamental differences. For Whitehead, God is like every other being in such a way that God can rightly be called an actual entity. But all other actual entities are also actual occasions. They occur momentarily. God is not temporal in this sense. There are differences, but the similarity is also striking.

Also, although the understanding of "being" may not be the same, I gather that Whitehead's understanding of it as "creativity" is not altogether different from Scotus. Although Scotus does not avoid the notion of substance altogether, the typical view of Whiteheadians that medieval thought was based on fundamental assumptions of the ultimacy of substance rather than event may miss the mark at least in part. Whiteheadians suppose that the medieval notion of substance cuts against any appreciation of the radical character of relationality among all things. Scotus apparently did not allow his idea of substance to have this consequence.

Occasionally what Delio writes seems to imply that Duns Scotus's work prepared the way for Whitehead's. I am doubtful that there is much historical relation. But the fact that one of the greatest medieval theologians had similar insights as a result of entirely independent reflection is not unimportant. That this thinker was a devoted follower of Saint Francis adds interest and importance. May this chapter liberate Catholics from the fear that accepting the ideas of a recent thinker like Whitehead requires rejection of essential Catholic teaching by making it clear that profound Catholic thinkers who have paid close attention to their Catholic experience have come to similar conclusions. Like so many people, I deeply admire Saint Francis. So, I am biased toward Franciscans. If we can locate Whitehead in the Franciscan tradition, wonderful. But I am in no position to say.

I was a student of Charles Hartshorne and Dan Dombrowski was a student of Hartshorne's student, Leonard Eslick. Hartshorne was a major influence on the development of process theology. Whereas Whitehead needed God to complete his cosmology, and wrote movingly on the topic, God was for Hartshorne the central question of his philosophy. His thinking was far advanced before he encountered Whitehead. He became an assistant to Whitehead and a great admirer, but his philosophy is his own. He develops a metaphysics in which God is central, whereas metaphysical ideas appear at the edges of Whitehead's cosmological discussion.

Hartshorne was a theocentric metaphysician at a time when metaphysics, at best, played a marginal role in philosophy, and when Protestant theology largely cut its ties to philosophy. His discussion partners, therefore, were largely classical theists. His work was much closer to a kind of theology that was more likely to be found in Catholic than in Protestant circles. But, as Dombrowski makes clear, he thought that the loss of credibility of theism was due to some fundamental mistakes. So, his approach to defenders of the classical tradition tended to be polemical.

His two main criticisms of classical theism were that it asserted that God is omnipotent and also immutable. This made God responsible for evil as much as for good. And it denied the God is compassionate, since that requires that he feel our feelings, which would affect his feelings. It is hard for Christians not to sympathize with Hartshorne. The simplest response is to reject the traditional doctrines.

However, Hartshorne came to call his position neoclassical. It was a correction and revision of classical theism, certainly not a rejection. And it turned out that those who found some of his emphases convincing could rethink the philosophies of Aristotle and Thomas in a way that took account of his concerns. For example, I supervised a dissertation by David Schindler that showed that "Being Itself" could be understood as the "act of being," which could then become almost indistinguishable from Whitehead's "creativity." When it is important to preserve traditional language, often that can be done while incorporating new insights.

It is my impression that Catholic teaching is now more or less successful in affirming a compassionate God who interacts with responsible human beings. Some of the credit goes to Charles Hartshorne and Catholic students in his teaching lineage such as Dan Dombrowski.

Maria-Teresa Teixeira knows both Whitehead's philosophy and Catholic thought well. She recognizes, of course, that there are differences. For one thing, Whitehead worked as a philosopher not as a theologian. What she shows, however, is that he is a philosopher who does not ignore theology. He learned a great deal from science, but he also learned more fundamental things from classical Christian theology. The issue for him is not whether an idea is grounded in Christian theology but whether it is true and illuminating.

For Catholic theologians, of course, the relation to the cumulative tradition is of central importance. However, since Catholic theology has generally been open to learning from philosophy and science and including ideas derived from them, the philosophical, and specifically cosmological, character of Whitehead's work should not be an obstacle to interaction. Teixeira makes a strong case for Catholics to pay close attention to his ideas and the reasons for them.

She notes that what has thus far been called "process theology" has been the work of Protestants. Protestant theology currently consists in whatever individual Protestants influenced by process philosophy affirm theologically. There may be ideas Catholics can use in the body of theological writings that Protestants influenced by Whitehead have written. But it is clear that a Catholic theology that shifts its metaphysical basis from substance to process will have its own distinctive character. One senses that Catholic theology has always pulled away from rigidly substantive thinking because the Bible is oriented to events rather than substantive objects. Also, systematic theology is affected by pastoral theology. The philosophical ideas of immutability and impassibility have always been qualified in Catholic theology by the understanding of God's love.

I hope that the failures and limitations of Protestant process theology will not serve as a reason for ignoring the richness and profundity of Whitehead's thought. Teixeira's chapter should help to prevent this.

Joseph Bracken has for some time proposed a shift in process metaphysics to focus on systems. Others of us have argued for a focus on ecologies. This is a shift from Whitehead's focus on individual actual occasions. But it is not a drastic shift. Whitehead's individual actual occasions are syntheses of what is derived from many occasions. The individual has no existence except as a synthesis of other occasions. He spends much of his time writing about the kinds of social order that occur among occasions. If "systems theory" had existed when he wrote, my guess is that he would have made positive use of the idea.

This is not to minimize the importance of his proposal. I think it is not only the terminology of "systems" and "ecologies" that highlight things that are not highlighted in Whitehead. I suspect that systems have a causality or agency that is different from that of the actual occasions of which they are composed. If so, there will need to be significant developments in and of his metaphysics. No one is pushing more wisely for such adjustments.

This is primarily and initially a question for philosophy. However, no one thinks purely as a philosopher. Joe Bracken is a theologian and in part his concern to emphasize systems over individual occasions arises from theological concerns. Whiteheadians in general give a much larger place to theology in their thought than do most other philosophers. The individual's relations to others are constitutive of the individual. We are members one of another. That helps us understand the family and the church. But Bracken calls our attention to the kinds of entities (systems) that are generated and their role in shaping us who are members as well as the larger society.

That it is a Catholic theologian who leads in promoting this revision and development of Whitehead's philosophy is not an accident. You experience and serve the church in its unity and wholeness far more authentically than do we Protestants. Philosophy must take account of all kinds of experience, and Catholic experience of the church is an important example. The relation between theology and philosophy should be one of mutual enrichment. In Bracken's philosophy, this is working.

Thomas Hosinski has written an excellent theological chapter on Whitehead and *creatio ex nihilo*. He appreciates the work of Whitehead in providing an alternative view of God and the world that resolves the problem of evil that has troubled Christian theology from a very early day. However, he regards *creatio ex nihilo* to be too central to Christian theology to be tossed aside in the way many Protestant theologians do. For some Protestants, it is easy to do so because it is not a biblical doctrine. For other Protestants and probably more for Catholic theologians, such rejection is not acceptable.

If a Catholic theologian, then, finds much in Whitehead's doctrine that is attractive and helpful, the theological task is to show that the best parts of his thought can be reformulated without rejecting *creatio ex nihilo*. Even if I find no need for this, I commend his work for those who do. Nevertheless, I do recognize that if I understood Whitehead to relate God and creativity in the way that Hosinski attributes to him, I might follow Hosinski's revisions. However, Hosinski finds passages in Whitehead that do not fit the position that he attributes to him, and I consider these passages to more clearly express Whitehead's position.

My understanding is that Thomas Aquinas recognized the distinction between Being Itself and the Supreme Being. He thought that God is both. My very poor knowledge of Thomism has not led me to consider this a metaphysically clear position. Meister Eckhart found it best to distinguish. Being Itself could be called "Godhead," and the "Supreme Being" God. For Whitehead, the term being in its dominant usage suggested something substantial. He replaced it with "creativity." To be actual is to be an instance of creativity, and the supreme actuality, God, is an instance of creativity, just as the Supreme Being is an instance of being.

Some of the language Whitehead uses about this relationship, such as God as an "accident" of creativity, is not helpful for theology. Hosinski thinks it implies that creativity can act independently of God. I am quite sure that Whitehead did not say so and did not think so. I will quote one passage that, I think, is compatible with everything he says on the subject, "But, of course, there is no meaning to 'creativity' apart from its 'creatures,' and no meaning to 'God' apart from the 'creativity' and the 'temporal creatures,' and no meaning to the 'temporal creatures' apart from 'creativity' and 'God.'"[1]

In my view, similarly in traditional language, there is no Being Itself if there are no beings. There is no Supreme Being unless there is Being Itself. And I incline to say also there is no God unless there are temporal beings. At least, there is no Creator God unless there are temporal beings. When the reality of something is unthinkable without the reality of something else, to think of one or the other as prior or superior in any way makes no sense to me. If theology needs a different language, I favor calling creativity the Godhead.

Palmyre Oomen displays better than I have previously encountered the vast agreement of Whitehead with Thomas Aquinas. Although I have recognized this bit by bit, I needed this overview to end a tendency, shared with many process theologians, to present them as radically different options. Instead, we should view them together as providing an alternative to the nominalism that dominated the late medieval period and modernity.

Based on her reliable formulations, one would guess that if Thomas could return today, he would be likely to be open to the changes Whitehead offers. For example, the idea that God is affected by and responsive to the failures and accomplishments, hopes and fears, of human beings brings theology much closer to basic biblical views of God as well as to popular Christian piety in every generation. My belief is that Thomas would have seen that as a gain.

I judge, and I judge that Pope Francis judges, that viewing ourselves as integral parts of the natural world is of extreme importance. Indeed, it may be a matter of life or death for the human species. In one sense, everybody knows that they live in a world that is fully actual in and of itself. But we are bombarded by epistemological theories that operate on other assumptions. Our academic disciplines are at best ambiguous. One suspects that the half-heartedness of our response to the threat of collective human suicide is at least partly due to our confusion about the status of the nonhuman world. If so, let us declare an alliance of realists and assure everyone that common sense on this matter is far more true than all the sophisticated confusion that belittles it.

Thomas Schärtl's chapter impresses me as a remarkably thorough and thoughtful summary of the theological discussion of the nature of the sacraments, especially the Mass. It notes that process theologians are by no means the first to see how the idea of substances is unhelpful in the interpretation of the Mass. I can contribute very little to the discussion as it has grown out of centuries of Catholic theology. I support movements toward processive thinking in regard to the sacraments. But rather than enter into the ongoing discussion in its terms, I will, instead, propose a different interpretation of what is going on, and, what we learn in 1 Corinthians, has been going on in the churches for two millennia.

In all the synoptic gospels and in Paul, the connections of the bread to the body and of the wine to the blood, or the new covenant, are stressed. In the synoptics, only those present were told to eat. In 1 Corinthians, the command is formulated as referring to later believers. The purpose is to remember Jesus and to proclaim his death.

The theological attention in the church has been on the meaning of Jesus's assertion that the blessed bread "is my body." Schärtl's chapter focuses on that question. It is often assumed in Catholic circles that Jesus and the later church are providing ontologically transformed bread and wine as literally salvific entities. To point out that this has little basis in the Bible is more important for Protestants like me than for Catholics. However, we, also, consider the observance of the Lord's Supper to be immensely important. And we also go beyond the text.

The text wants us to remember Jesus. We remember as we reenact. But this remembering is not, we believe, simply a cognitive recall. The reenactment makes that which is reenacted significantly present. We talk a lot about the "Real Presence" of Jesus when we observe the sacrament. This appeals to other passages. Jesus told us that when two or three are gathered in his name he is in their midst. For some of us, Jesus is present in the event as a whole rather than specifically in the physical elements.

I understand that there is some shift of Catholic interest from the bread and wine to the event as a whole. I am, as an outsider, cheering for this shift of focus. But given the dominant worldview of the West, and especially of modernity, the theoretical problem remains. In what sense can past events be present? Is what is present limited to presently created images that are intended to resemble images that were once actualized?

Whitehead's philosophy can help. In his view, every momentary occasion is a creative synthesis of past events. The past is literally present in each new moment.

To understand this, we can begin with immediately contiguous events. My experience in each moment grows out of my immediately previous experience but is also influenced by other events in the immediate context. As the process of their own subjective becoming is completed, events enter into the processes of the becoming of their successors. There is no present apart from the continuing presence of the past.

But, of course, we are formed in each moment by much more than the presence of immediately contiguous events. Consider the experience of a musical phrase. What you hear is not a succession of discontinuous sounds, each succeeding others. If the first part of the phrase is merely past, subject to being recalled, we would never hear the end of a phrase as the end of a phrase. We would not hear a phrase apart from its part in the song. At the end of the song, the whole song is present in the immediate experience.

Much past is thus present in a completely literal sense. There is a difference between two modes of presence. There is the becoming of something new in each moment. There are the past events that are present and active in this process.

Of course, most past events are present in the now becoming one only trivially. But for each of us, some are truly important for good or ill. On some occasions in childhood, one may have felt abandoned by parents. These abandoning parents are likely to play a role in many events in adulthood even if later the alienation was overcome. Their presence may be repressed or constantly thought about. Either way, it remains an element in the constitution of many experiences.

Someone may have grown up happily in a healthy church environment and then been taught in the university that believing in God is naïve and foolish. Sets of experiences in both contexts continue to live in the new occasions of her life. If she decides to live out of one of these visions, say, the atheist one, the other past events do not cease to be, but their role is likely to fade markedly over time. Our decisions about which elements in our past to accentuate are far from omnipotent, but they often make a large difference.

It is in this context that observing the Lord's Supper makes a difference in the lives of those who do so. Even if one continues to hold positive beliefs about Jesus, if one does not attend church the likelihood that Jesus will be the major presence in shaping one's life will be very slight. Even if we liberal Protestants go to church, the probabilities are not high. But if in remembrance of Jesus we participate frequently in the Lord's Supper, the chances are greatly improved.

Let me add a word. The sacrament is a public, communal event. This is very important. We join with others in remembering Jesus. He is present in our community. The reality of Christian community is determined by the presence of Jesus within it. Genuine remembering lifts up some element of the past, already present in the present, and makes its presence important.

It is my hope that whatever theory of the bread and wine best satisfies the needs of the Catholic Church, the church can also appreciate the personal presence of Jesus in the Mass as a whole, that all Christians will celebrate that presence and allow it to play a determinative role in our lives, and that we can find our deep unity in obedience to his call.

I am particularly appreciative of the chapter by John Becker. It develops what is one of the greatest contributions of Whitehead's thought, the appreciation of difference as an opportunity to grow. I am often surprised by the way most thinkers still ignore this alternative. The issue on which Becker writes is the multiplicity of ideas and insights offered in the great spiritual traditions of humankind.

Much has gone wrong with human thinking and practice in the past century, but in some areas there has been real progress. A century ago, most people viewed traditions other than their own as necessarily erroneous. Christians may have been in the lead in their assurance that the truth of their revelation implied the error of all who differed. The Protestant doctrine of *sola scriptura* may have made us the worst of all.

Today, in contrast, most people do not dismiss the positions of other communities as necessarily valueless or mistaken. Some do dismiss the spiritual traditions overall as outdated. But for those concerned with the life of the spirit, there is general recognition that this is fruitfully pursued in multiple communities and in diverse ways.

We speak of religious pluralism. Differences are not denied. But instead of seeing them as in competition over issues of truth and falsity, they are now often viewed as many paths up the same mountain. Since our goals are the same, our differences about how best to move toward them do not require mutual dismissal. We can make diverse contributions to a shared goal.

This is certainly better than endless quarrels and struggles for dominance. But process theologians have called for a more radical pluralism. There are certainly shared values and shared elements in our goals, but there are also real differences. Instead of deploring or ignoring these, we see them as opportunities. Our view is that there may be more than one path up one mountain, but when we really attend to what is sought by Zen Buddhists and by Sunni Muslims, allowing the proponents to speak freely and openly, the goals differ. We can, of course, tell them that they are mistaken about their goals, that they really are the same, but we process folk do not suppose we know what they seek better than they do. We prefer to say that there are many paths up different mountains.

Some practices are helpful on several paths. Some values are prized by almost all. We could err on the side of too much emphasis on difference. But we want to counter the dominant tendency of obscuring or devaluing it. We think that many Christians profit from practicing Zen meditation. It can benefit pianists and hunters. In Japan, the samurai found that it made them more effective soldiers. It can also benefit Christians. We think that Zen practitioners can profit from considering which improvements they really want to encourage.

It is precisely by understanding how different the goals of Jesus and of Zen are that we find we do not have to choose between them. In Japan, many Christians practice Zen. It happens elsewhere as well. We may decide that a Hindu meditation practice will help us more. That does not mean that we then oppose Zen. But rather than assuming that all meditation has the same goal, we do better to realize it affects our brain, and therefore our experience, in diverse ways.

However, making a clear distinction between the metaphysical Ultimate, Brahman, or Being Itself, or, in Whitehead's terms, "creativity," and the theistic ultimate, the Supreme Being, is disturbing to many Christians, including Becker. He sees that spiritual experience often connects with both of these. Indeed, from a process perspective, one cannot experience any being without implicitly experiencing Being Itself, and the experience of the Supreme Being is especially bound up with that of Being Itself. Rather than make distinctions, Becker gives priority to this all-inclusive experience. Limiting the role of thought seems to him better than thinking about the distinction and what it involves.

Becker, accordingly, follows a line of thought that is available only to Christians and, indeed, chiefly to Catholics. He calls this "non-dual." It is the refusal to incorporate into Catholic thought a clear distinction between the metaphysical "Ultimate," traditionally called "Being Itself," and the idea of a "Supreme Being," that is characteristic of biblical monotheism. He regards making this distinction as taking reason too far. He appeals to mysticism, but so far as I know, it is only Christian mysticism that refuses to make the distinction. The label used for the complex and mysterious doctrine that results from this refusal is said to be "non-dual," a term usually used to oppose the radical and destructive dualism of the mental and the physical. Since no one supposes that distinguishing between Being and beings is dualistic in anything like this sense, the use is confusing.

Historically, the blurring of this distinction by Christian theologians is readily understandable. The Bible presented them with a god who had become the one God who is Creator of all creatures. It offered no discussion of the metaphysical Ultimate, Being Itself. When the Bible was studied in a context in which metaphysics was considered the climactic mode of thought, it seemed best to identify the God of the Bible with what philosophical reason declared to be ultimate.

It seemed that to fail to do that implied that there was someone or some thing that was greater than God, more comprehensive, more powerful, more ultimate. How this impression can be given is made embarrassingly clear by some of Whitehead's not too careful formulations. For example, in *Process and Reality* he writes, "Every actual entity, including God, is a creature transcended by the creativity which it qualifies."[2] This can easily be read to imply that in the hierarchy of realities, God comes in second. Of course, that is not Whitehead's view. And in Whitehead's own usual formulations of "creation," God is not a creature. Like all actual entities, God is an instantiation or actualization of creativity. That is what it means to exist. But to instantiate creativity is not, in any ordinary sense, to be a creation of creativity. Also, unlike all other instantiations, God is eternal. Without God there is no creativity.

Although Whitehead's understanding of God is, in my view, remarkably congenial to the Bible, my point is that discussion that includes metaphysicians can too easily seem to belittle God. That, in response, some have identified God with the metaphysical Ultimate is certainly understandable, and that they then continue to attribute to God some of the attributes characteristic of biblical monotheism is also understandable. Also, we should recognize that this new "non-dual" view brought with it changes in religious experience. Some Protestants have carried on this tradition, but the *sola scriptura* emphasis has reduced the role of classical metaphysical thinking in favor of the Supreme Being approach.

Many Catholics prize their unique spiritual achievement and do not want to lose what they have done to overcome the distinction. Better to declare all theology mythical than to try to think through the meaning of the difference between Being Itself and the Supreme Being, what Whitehead calls "creativity" and "God." If that is their choice for themselves, so be it. I respect the choice, although I regret it. But I trust that Catholics are not asking Buddhists to view their *anatman* doctrine as myth as a condition of dialogue. It is important to distinguish between the beliefs that open the door for Catholics to engage in dialogue from an interpretation of the beliefs and attitudes toward reason and belief of their dialogue partners. Not all religious traditions are ultimately anti-intellectual.

Marc Pugliese has provided a rich account of the moral philosophy of Thomas Aquinas. He shows how, despite its rich complexity, it still has trouble with the concrete particularity of every instance that we examine. He thinks this is bound up with the substance thinking and rationality that underlie the philosophy. He then shows that a philosophy that understands the uniqueness of every event, as Whitehead does, offers a better starting point. I am, of course, easy to persuade, but so far as I know, his approach is original and has a chance of opening doors in a very fruitful way.

Protestants have tended to describe Whitehead in the context of contemporary secular thinking. Here what is striking is his strong sense of *hamartia*, missing the mark. For him, there is nothing relative about this. There is in every instance a best possible outcome and Whitehead thinks God lures us toward that. There is often resistance on our part. Given the specifics, it is possible from them to generalize as long as we know what we are doing. We are giving general advice. God's lures will generally correspond with such generalizations. Moral principles are useful. But the concrete instance in all its particularity takes precedence over what may be deduced from generalizations.

Catholic thinkers who take radical particularity seriously are speaking up and calling for revisions in procedures that privilege generalizations and what can be deduced from them. They will find support both in Whitehead's ontology and in his comments on morality. He shows us that rejecting legalism does not weaken the call to do what is best in each instance. Paul would approve.

One issue raised about process philosophy is whether it has a contribution to make. Perhaps it is inherently worthwhile, but perhaps Catholic theology has its own resources that are at least equally well-equipped to handle the issues. Leo Lefebure's paper in no way suggests that Catholic theology needs rescuing by process thought. But it does show that at least on some topics Whitehead's thought and Catholic theology are highly congenial. It goes beyond that to indicate that Whitehead's writings are well qualified to support and undergird the Pope's formulations in *Laudato Si'*.

In my view, *Laudato Si'* is a great gift to all Christians. I had been involved in a large conference subtitled: "Toward an Ecological Civilization" shortly before the appearance of the encyclical. I was immediately struck by the extreme similarity between the Pope's call for "integral ecology" and ours for "ecological civilization." Ignacio Castuera and I collected essays from some of those who had attended our conference and published them in time to greet Pope Francis when he came to the United States. We have continued to celebrate that encyclical and to do what we can to support it. We think that, as this chapter also maintains, Whitehead provides the cosmology that is implicit in the encyclical.

Is Catholic theology benefited by a supporting cosmology? Not as much as the world's floundering efforts to move forward are guided by the work of the Pope. Further, this chapter greatly helps those of us who are influenced by Whitehead to work through the implications of his thought for moving forward in alliance with Catholics, taking their lead from the Pope. But although the contribution of this chapter may be greater in other ways, it also shows that the use of Whitehead's thought to undergird the encyclical can benefit Catholic theologians as well.

Pope Francis addressed the world. He understands that the task that lies before us will require all of us. He offers the world's greatest spiritual institution, the Roman Catholic Church, to lead the world away from the precipice toward which it is headed. It is a great strength of this church that over the centuries it has been open to the contributions and cooperation of others. May it lead in that way again.

I began with a response to the chapter by David Burrell. I conclude with a response to J. J. Mueller. They express what is probably the major voice of the thoughtful Roman Catholic community. It is more positive than those of Protestants who celebrate the Reformation *sola scriptura*. They do not object in general to philosophical theology. They take process thought seriously and even agree that it makes a good many valid points. But they see the contribution as marginal and think it best to work out theology in other ways even if the results happen to agree with those of process theology on some points.

I find it interesting that Mueller's criticisms of process theology are not about errors or philosophical mistakes. On the whole, he seems to agree with many particulars. The problems are more sociological than philosophical. His often insightful discussion is more about the role of theology in the church and its proper relation to philosophy than about the accuracy of ideas. This is entirely appropriate. It might be that the ideas of process theology are accurate but largely irrelevant to the needs of the Roman Catholic Church.

In my opinion most of the chapters in this book count against his thesis. They show ways in which process ideas can play positive roles in the Catholic Church. But the question, how valuable this is, still deserves to be discussed in light of the many issues he raises.

I will comment on just one: his sense is that the church as a community has rejected process theology as an option. The evidence is certainly that process theology has not taken hold widely. This is a significant fact, but one that, in my view, Mueller deals with too simplistically. He does not pay enough attention to how ideas that are rejected in one generation may be accepted in another. Then, looking back, those who supported them when they were not popular are sometimes seen as having played a very positive role.

Another consideration is whether the rejection is primarily a popular one, showing that the ideas do not speak to the needs of the community. I am not in a position to judge definitively. But my experience as an outsider indicated that the rejection of the process option was not left to the consensus of the faithful. Churchmen in high places were sufficiently afraid that it might gain acceptance to go to some lengths to prevent it.

David Tracy was a very promising young Catholic theologian who also identified himself as a process theologian. He told me that he was asked by Cardinal Ratzinger how he could be both a process theologian and a Catholic theologian and that he sent Ratzinger a ninety-page answer and heard no more. Nevertheless, after that, he did not write explicitly as a process theologian. The possibility of process theology becoming a major topic of discussion in Catholic circles was crushed from above.

I think it should also be noted that the one period when interest and openness were growing was quite abruptly ended, not by loss of interest on the part of Catholic thinkers and schools but by hierarchical change of policy. I will speak only of my personal experience. For a decade after Vatican II, half or more of my PhD students were monks, and Catholic universities hired some of my Protestant students. That ended abruptly because of a change in the top leadership of the church. An accurate history of the relation of the Catholic Church to process theology should not speak only of what the Catholic community finds attractive.

I will make one more complaint. Mueller has read the writings of leading process theologians and he complains, probably quite justifiably, that they are often abstract and theoretical or repetitive. Of course, this is true of some Catholic theologians as well. Further, he celebrates biblical theology as well. Good theology, he rightly thinks, should be more pastoral and biblical and empirical. I will make no special claims for the quality of our more pastoral writings, but efforts in that direction have been and continue to be numerous. Also, for decades, process biblical scholars have commented each week on the scriptures assigned for preaching. He is probably not aware of our work with films, especially our annual "Common Good" film festival. Discussing film is a contemporary way of staying close to actual human experience. It is no criticism to say that he has probably not read much of our pastoral, biblical, and empirical work. He is not responsible to know about these dimensions of the process theology movement, but his apparent ignorance of them means that I cannot take his negative judgments of our efforts along these lines as decisive.

I apologize that my response is so defensive. That probably reflects the weariness and disappointment of an old man. We old-line Protestants find ourselves in decaying churches. We have not persuaded our children that these are worthy of their commitment. We experience our collective faith as collapsing and our institutions as dying. Some of us think that process theology might help new forms of faith to emerge that would be more faithful to the Bible and would be experienced by younger people as important and even salvific. We are excited about how it is catching on under the label "open and relational" among those evangelicals who have not been co-opted by Zionism or the religious right.

In contrast to our near despair, there is little hint in this chapter of any anxiety about the credibility or efficacy of Catholic teaching or about the cultural triumph of a post-Christian society. I can only envy Mueller's deep assurance that the Catholic Church is on solid ground and moving forward in a healthy way. I admire his confidence in the future of his church. If that confidence can be combined with the profound wisdom of *Laudato Si'*, Catholics can lead the world through the crises humanity faces. That is far more important than whether they make use of process thought or understand its "ins and outs."

Even so, it is my belief that process thought in its close intertwinement with ecological civilization could be of help to Catholics as well, especially to those who respect the wisdom of *Laudato Si'*. That encyclical was published shortly after our conference on "ecological civilization." The integral ecology for which Pope Francis calls is remarkably similar to the ecological civilization to which most of us process folk are committed. I hope that Catholics will welcome our efforts to support all who are guided by *Laudato Si'*. Let us at least agree to cooperate in our efforts to keep the planet habitable.

To conclude this introduction, I want to say a word about truth. Truth seems to be a casualty of modernity. We realize that truth is "relative" in the sense that no two people experience things in just the same way. However, for process thinkers, God knows or perhaps better is or includes the truth. By being aware of the diversity of perspectives and especially of the distorting elements in our own, we can come closer to the divine one. Truth is not ultimately relative although our approximations are. It is as important to recognize that all that we say falls short of the truth as that ultimately the truth is what it is and that our task as thinkers is to approximate to it more and more.

My attraction to Whitehead is at least partly my belief that he had no goal in his thinking other than truth and that no one could have been more emphatic that he was very far from his goal. To me, this should be the stance of any thinker. Perhaps all theologians intend to accept it, but much that is said about theology obscures that goal. One gathers that other norms are more important for some theologians. Perhaps they are right. Certainly, truth spoken out of season can be destructive.

But our world now suffers from the realization that, for almost everyone, other considerations trump truth routinely. We know that the leaders of our nations tell us what they want us to believe. Whether it is true or false makes little difference to them. For a while, we thought that we could trust scientists or academic "experts." For many kinds of facts, they are certainly the best source, but they are swayed by considerations of money and power and personal status and what will be good for the scientific community. They have defined their roles in ways that do not include self-criticism of their disciplines. They avoid important questions. They have abandoned the intellectual quest with which they started.

Our hope that our Christian leaders would be truthful has also been dashed. For the sake of the church and its leadership, they have engaged in massive cover-ups and deceptions. They are often more interested in influencing beliefs in ways favorable to the church than in the truth. The hunger for certainty has led to claims for the Bible or for the church that are in fact idolatrous.

Our political, scientific, educational, and religious institutions have subordinated the question of truth to their view of what benefits themselves. As this has become increasingly obvious, and the fact that the very idea of truth has been questioned, they express themselves in nihilism on the one hand and arbitrary following of misleading demagogues on the other.

My understanding of my role as a theologian is that I should be guided in all that I do by the ever-elusive goal of truth. Some charge that the result is not "Christian." I like to think that it is faithful to the best in our Christian history and especially to Jesus. I think, hopefully, that a community of people who sought to be faithful to Jesus and to truth might yet regain some confidence in a spiritually starving world.

I am deeply convinced that modernity took a wrong turn. It happened that this led to enormous advances in science and technology. Sadly, this has functioned to deepen the hold of a life-denying metaphysics. Most Protestant thinkers have juxtaposed to this a theology that claims to be directly derivative from the literature of ancient Israel. This inherently marginalizes Protestantism as an alternative to materialism. Catholicism has offered the strongest alternative because it grounds its thinking in Greece as well as Israel. But now that most people have come to see modernity as a fundamental advance beyond anything preceding it, Catholic commitment to Greek and medieval thought has marginalized it as well.

Could Christianity play a different role over against the dehumanization and nihilism in which modernity has ended? Could it, instead of calling the world back to the past, call the world forward to the implications of what science has learned? Whitehead offers us that alternative. A scattering of individual liberal Protestants is responding. But liberal Protestantism is dying.

There was a time just after the Second Vatican Council that I had great hopes that the Catholic Church would seize this opportunity to lead the world again. Sadly, it used its hierarchical organization to block that move. But in reading these chapters I sense that the possibility is returning. What if the Catholic Church showed that Christ is not just the past, but the redemptive future, that to follow Christ is to shake free from bad habits of thought and action and affirm the truth that alone can save us! Whitehead and Pope Francis together offer you that chance.

NOTES

1. Alfred North Whitehead, *Process and Reality: An Essay in Cosmology* (1929), corrected ed., ed. David Ray Griffin and Donald W. Sherburne (New York: Free Press, 1978), 225.

2. Ibid., 88.

BIBLIOGRAPHY

Whitehead, Alfred North. *Process and Reality: An Essay in Cosmology.* 1929. Corrected ed. Edited by David Ray Griffin and Donald W. Sherburne. New York: Free Press, 1978.

Chapter 1

Does Process Theology Rest on a Mistake?[1]

David B. Burrell, C. S. C.

The dynamics of proposing and assuming theological frameworks, or of questioning and rejecting them, are so labyrinthine that one can never hope to bring the entire transaction to light. The best we can try to do is to submit it to scrutiny, in the hope of becoming more conscious ourselves of the reasons for our preferences. When the issues are neatly philosophical, such scrutiny is difficult enough, as most of us find ourselves too easily moved by shorthand references to philosophical schools or movements. A chord (or discord) is struck with our own intellectual formation, firmly channeling the subsequent discussion for better or worse. When the issues are properly theological, however, an added complication renders disentanglement nearly impossible, for we must attempt to discern the mix of religious and philosophical motives which should decide the outcome, and many of us divide regarding the proper weights to be assigned, say, to a "faithful rendering of one's tradition" over against a "conceptualization adequate to one's time."

I have become convinced, however, that we do far better discriminating such issues in practice than we do in a more "principled" discussion. Hence faculty find themselves more in operative agreement in structuring a course introducing theology than in discussing questions of method. (This is not to say they agree in practice; it is only to remark that the transaction between faithful rendition and critical inquiry displays itself in such a course to be part of the very activity of doing theology, so that the penchant toward the simplistic and ideological in each of us is severely tempered.) So this chapter attempts to identify those places in the recent discussions involving "process theology" where we might exercise the powers of discernment which we do in fact employ in theological discussions more generally. In that sense, of course, it is discourse in method. That is, it does not answer the question posed but seeks to highlight the joints of the discussion in a way designed to

1

help readers answer it to their satisfaction. Not that method is a mere matter of choice; rather that we are all surer in practice than when we attempt to articulate our criteria.

The provocative title is deliberate, for I believe that the general outlines of the discussion have already been sketched, and admirably so, yet the points of divergence have not always been marked so clearly. So relying on these outlines, I intend to mark those points clearly enough to provoke the kind of inquiry which ought now to ensue. A recent article by Barry Whitney resumes the immutability discussion quite fairly, although his references to William Hill, O. P., and W. Norris Clarke, S. J., need to be amplified by a subsequent article and monograph, respectively, which have markedly advanced the discussion.[2] Each of these authors displays a command of traditional categories, theological and philosophical, as well as a scrupulous ear for dialogue. The tenor of their appreciation and critique of process thought regarding divinity shows how this debate can touch issues utterly central to both disciplines. While the majorly theological concern of Hill fills out the primarily philosophical orientation of Clarke, it is precisely at the intersection of these disciplines that the issues are joined—another sign of the force of the process critique, even if a certain theory about the relations between the disciplines renders it peculiarly vulnerable on second look.

The extensive references in Whitney's work, plus the mention of Hill's and Clarke's later contributions, spare me the need to resume the contents of the discussion and allow me to concentrate on its form. I shall delineate four situations which, if true, would display misunderstandings endemic to the enterprise we know as process theology. If I am correct in my characterization, and if all the conditions are in fact realized, the answer to the question would be an unequivocal "yes"; if my characterization can be challenged, or if some of the situations remain unclarified, the response may waver from "probably so" to "probably not"; and if the characterizations can be discredited or the situations shown not to obtain, the verdict would veer more definitely toward "no"—barring more insightful critiques to come. I am taking such an approach, be it noted, not to discredit the venture known as process theology but in an effort to disengage argument from rhetoric.[3] Moreover, it should be noted that even a firm affirmative answer could not discredit the enterprise, for in philosophical theology significant mistakes may indeed advance the discussion—significantly.

Process theology would be based on a mistake if (1) its founding polemic against "classical theism" were discovered to be quite wide of the mark; (2) its claims to offer a superior philosophical synthesis for Christian faith were seriously questioned; (3) its capacity for illuminating central elements of the Christian tradition were shown to be deficient; and (4) it were found to embody a conception of theological inquiry which, when made explicit, would diverge considerably from that accepted by practicing theologians, or at least divide them clearly into separate camps. Of these conditions, the first is more historical, the second philosophical, and the third theological—although they overlap in practice. The fourth we might call "internal": it involves unraveling the presuppositions implicit in much of the discussion, notably by making moves *not* taken into regions where dialogue has quite inexplicably failed to join the issues. In exploring each condition, I shall indicate the respects in which current discussion has clarified the situation, as well as note those complications which continue to confuse the issue.

CLASSICAL THEISM

The first thesis displays both sides with dismaying clarity. Responses to Hartshorne's caricature of classical theism have shown how a modicum of sensitivity to the earlier and later medieval contexts could have avoided his drawing the conclusions he did from Aquinas' insistence that God was not *really* related to God's world.[4] Norris Clarke's explication of the accepted distinction between "real" and "intentional" being offers a positive assist in unraveling this misunderstanding.[5] Yet Hartshorne had struck a chord, and the caricature, like a good cartoon, nosed out an imbedded theological misconception. That the "greats" might be exempted from his charge did not make it less accurate as an indictment of a widespread theological attitude. If his "Hellenization" thesis was to meet the fate of most such generic theses, yet other elements had nonetheless conspired to concoct a more or less official notion of God which bore little relation to the Jewish and Christian scriptures it was supposed to embody. One suspects these elements to be more cultural than conceptual, yet powerful they have been, leading directly to Blake's "old Nobodaddy" and to Nietszche's demand that such a god must die if humanity is to live.[6] So Hartshorne's historical misidentification—the first "mistake," if you will—only serves to sharpen our lookout for the real culprits: the first indication how significant mistakes can advance an issue dialectically.

A SUPERIOR PHILOSOPHICAL SYNTHESIS

This claim is perhaps the most vexatious, especially since it is difficult to disentangle from the third. (In fact, a particular conception of theology surfaces here, as I shall note in discussing thesis four.) For it is a surveyable fact that philosophers have simply not been as impressed with Whitehead's revisionary claims as they were supposed to be. Historically, his polemic against a "substance ontology" has been shown to fall well this side of Aristotle or

Aquinas, and most have found his alternative proposals to be quite baffling.[7] It is perhaps unfortunate that his earlier work in *Principia* seemed to carry greater philosophical consequences than his constructive philosophy, and that those consequences generally dampened enthusiasm for metaphysical proposals; yet the fact remains that a more recent renewal of metaphysical concerns has not found its way to him either. On purely philosophical grounds, therefore, any claim for the superiority of a Whiteheadian explanatory scheme will have to overcome purely philosophical skepticism. Perhaps this is the reason why theologians have tended to be more enthusiastic here than those expressly trained in philosophy.

Norris Clarke's studies display more patience with unraveling Whiteheadian categories than would most philosophers, and in his irenic way he raises one critical question after another to those who presume to have found a superior conceptualization of Christian faith or of divinity in a Whiteheadian philosophical scheme. Yet it is Hill who touches, I believe, the most serious philosophical deficiency in that scheme for theological discourse. Despite its constant reference to "relatedness," the notion of an "agent" remains underdeveloped in process thought: "the God of process theology in loving the world is not a person at all but only a principle."[8]

The best way to bring this point into relief is to ask which primary analog one returns to in one's explication of divine activity. From the time of Augustine through the medievals, and despite their fascination with Aristotle, the prime analogate has been the self, the human person. The history of the people of God from Abraham forward has ever taken the narrative form of a response to a personal call. When God chose to be revealed perspicuously, it was in the person of Jesus. On a more reflective note, when theologians proceeded to elaborate the consequences of this revelation in calling on the conceptual resources available to them to delineate the inner life of God, they fleshed out the maverick category of relation with analogical reference to "persons." And when Augustine, followed by Aquinas, offered a more developed treatment of the triune God, it was with reference to the intentional capacities of human persons to relate to their world through understanding and the love which follows upon it.

If one considers the complementary doctrines of incarnation and Trinity and notes how the history of their development acted to refine the notion of person in Christianity East and West, one wonders what might be gained by seeking illumination in a philosophical mode which takes its principal analogies from natural process, however sympathetically described, and resolves to endemically abstract notions like creativity, concretion, and even process, rather than return us to the individual agent as the prime analogate.[9] To be sure, these notions are proposed as explanatory, and so may justly remain themselves abstract, but the tortuous prose required to bring them into a position whence they can do their explanatory work leaves all but the most indefatigable believers weary—especially, I might note, those who have attained a fair mastery of metaphysical exercises.

Aquinas comes to mind at this point, as one also enamored of a philosophical system. A selective reading of his corpus might lead one to believe that he found Aristotle's analysis of change and causality more useful than the intentional schemes of Augustine. At times, no doubt, he did, and the way in which he responded to the query whether God was "really related" to the world represents one of these. Yet, however much he used such schemes for illuminating specific issues, he never *resolved* a discussion in their terms. His treatise on grace, for example, shows in its critical junctures how acutely he was aware that the "supernatural order" was through and through one of interpersonal exchange: divine initiative linked to human response. Nor was the so-called "natural order" any less gratuitous, even if its transactions tended to be impersonal—so much so that the doctrine of creation has been called the hidden element in Thomas' philosophy.[10]

If the founding polemics, then, of Whiteheadian metaphysics against a "substance ontology" have been shown to be wide of their mark by more recent analyses of classical philosophical positions, and if process theologians' predilection for Whiteheadian explanatory categories has lured them away from developing the notion of person so central to Christian theology, wherein lies the appeal? There can, no doubt, be several answers to such a question, and I shall return to it at the end. I raise it at this point by way of transition to the third point: process theology's capacity to illuminate central elements of the Christian tradition. Whitehead's program as announced is appealing: to offer an explanatory scheme for nature which includes elements of intentionality, and his language is suitably evocative. Indeed, it was this claim to have found a better way to render God's interaction with creatures, a specifically intentional exchange, which made it such an initially promising contender on the theological scene.

Yet its appeal was bound to be strongest, I suspect, with those who had either lost or deliberately renounced any other resources for relating God with the world, for those, that is, for whom the teachings of incarnation and Trinity had become little more than vestigial myths. It was only at the end of a careful critique of some philosophical confusions in process theology that I came to suspect why otherwise well-instructed individuals might be tempted to stumble into such blunders both of historical interpretation and of philosophical analysis.[11] For a classical (nineteenth-century) liberal theologian who can no longer relate God intentionally to us through the Word made flesh in Jesus, or rely on the fully intentional inner life of a triune God, a new and promising conceptuality could be very tempting, for a logical consequence of the resulting "monotheism" is bound to be a remote and solitary divinity. From such a vantage point, classical treatments of divine transcendence, shorn of their intentional side as developed in the doctrines of incarnation and of Trinity, could appear to be in need of radical revision. But in retrospect it might appear that so drastic a revision was required only because the earlier surgery had been so radical.[12] My suspicion is handily corroborated by the contention of leading proponents of this school that Christianity is indistinguishable from "monotheism." Clearly, for such a one, the doctrines of incarnation and Trinity may be part of the inherited picture but are in principle replaceable by an appropriate explanatory scheme. Such is the role claimed for process theology by its principal advocates, and these may well be the reasons why it is given so grand a task.

ILLUMINATING THE TRADITION

Both Hartshorne and Ogden have consistently represented their theological task as one which is more faithful to the biblical view than classical theologians proved able to be, notably in portraying "God as related to the world, responsive to the appeal of prayer, and involved in human history, not by coercion but by persuasion."[13] Skeptics have continued to query whether the one they present can also claim to be divine. One test case—for Jews, Christians, and Muslims, at least—is creation.

Whoever confesses to "believe in one God, Creator of heaven and earth" is not usually making a philosophical statement but a religious affirmation. In so confessing our faith, we are reminding ourselves and one another that all this is gift, and indeed the gift of one "acting out of superabundant goodness with the unselfish purpose simply to share."[14] This doctrine, Diogenes Allen has shown, anchors our conception of God and of ourselves in relation to God in an ontological context of free gift.[15] Moreover, it is this doctrine—not something so irreducibly vague as "monotheism"—which links Christians with Jews at their very roots (with Islam as well, but the linkage is less direct, so one cannot properly speak of a *doctrinal* connection). Yet on this very confession process thought wavers, and that for systemic reasons.

The reasons are philosophical and have to do with Whitehead's insistence that creativity, or creative process, reigns supreme. The role reserved to God can be described as, "giving to all actual events the initial aims that are highest and best possible in their concrete circumstances."[16] And in doing so, "His aim for it is depth of satisfaction as an intermediate step towards the fulfilment of his own being."[17] Certainly, such a one cannot be described as the "beginning and end of all things, and of reasoning creatures especially," except in a fashion so roundabout as to make one wonder why the circumlocution.[18] Interaction, then, is purchased at the price of an initiating, gratuitous actor, and the price is paid in the name of philosophical consistency.

Recent theological reflection carried out in exchange with Jewish thinkers helps one to see how profoundly the Christian teaching on grace and divine initiative is anchored in a common confession of God's creating initiative. If there be two "orders," the second is already adumbrated in the first: nature itself is gift—"Master of the universe, blessed be He!" The narratives of the scriptures manage to offer poignant examples of divine–human interaction without diluting that initial affirmation. If process theologians are unable to do so, is it that they have allowed themselves to be more constrained by systemic demands than by fidelity to the central assertion of the scriptures shared by Jews and Christians alike? This question, which arises throughout, will be met directly in considering the fourth and last hurdle.

With regard to the central doctrines of Trinity and incarnation, one should be able to formulate the question from observations already made. To what end offer a conceptuality where the notion of agent is underdeveloped, in an effort to shed new light on doctrines so instrumental in refining our very notion of person? More trenchantly still, if these refined notions of intentionality are linked with closer attention to narrative, as in Hans Frei's work, one need not fear to assert how, in Jesus, God shares our life and especially our human suffering as no other can.[19] Norris Clarke has shown how this line of reflection can be developed, as have Heribert Mühlen and Jean Galot in more explicitly theological terms.[20] What Diogenes Allen has accomplished with the doctrine of creation, these have developed with the incarnation, and Eberhard Jüngel with the Trinity.[21] By exploiting the claims in these doctrines to demand an eminently personal characterization of divinity, these authors have at once shown how powerfully the doctrines themselves elucidate the exchange between God and created persons, and done so precisely by the relational character of a person. In the wake of these developments, it is hard to know what meaning one might attribute to the recommendation that one should develop the doctrine of the Trinity along process lines.[22]

Finally, one cannot but query, as does Norris Clarke, where process theology lands one on the issue of immortality and resurrection.[23] Here again, it is not a question of the need to revise earlier explanatory schemes, but of the tendency to presume that one is now in possession of one so adequate as to allow it to replace the underlying doctrinal assertions as well. It is indeed that very tendency—to accept consistency with Whiteheadian philosophy as the principal criterion—which leads us to the fourth and final test.

CONCEPTION OF THEOLOGICAL INQUIRY

I have already noted the remarkable affinities, in tenor and in purpose, with what we now think of as "classical" liberal theology. In fact, as my suspicionary hypothesis put it: if process theology were in direct lineage with this

movement, its strategies become readily comprehensible. All that remains is
to identify a yet more decisive characteristic they share in common, to tease
out the conception of theological inquiry endemic to process thought. For
what, after all, led this loosely organized school to relinquish the doctrines of
incarnation and Trinity? A desire, certainly, to bring theological (and eventually religious) assertion within the scope of what could be intelligible to one's
intellectual contemporaries. Usually not linked with a specific philosophical
system so much as with a temper and mood of inquiry, liberal theology has
ever been inclined to seek first intelligibility in presenting the kingdom.

Our more acutely anthropological perspective may find so stark a use of
"intelligibility" quite naïve, and certainly some of the accommodations made
in the name of modernity now seem to us rather quaint, but the strategy was
clear. Yet I think one can just as clearly ask how *theological* it was, for one
of the demands of an "adequate theological conceptuality" has always been
to illuminate and recover the tradition—and where these are many, to try to
make sense of the plurality.[24] When the manner of resolution neglects this
dialectical exercise, however, in favor of the reigning "conceptuality," then
one is hard pressed to call the resulting developments theology in a more than
archeological sense.

Such a strategy, moreover, often fosters ironic consequences, as an appeal
to a philosophical idiom in the name of universal intelligibility can often
bring its own degree of insularity. Such proved to be the case with the
Thomistic project, certainly, and we have noted similar results with process
theology's adherence to Whitehead. While it was conceived in a far less
parochial climate than Thomism, the fact remains that one must overcome
one's philosophical difficulties with Whitehead to engage in fruitful conversation. A thoughtful and temperate critique of the venture in these very terms
has recently appeared in Robert Neville's *Creativity and God*, subtitled *A
Challenge to Process Theology*. Neville examines its principal proponents
to find them wanting in philosophical cogency. Yet even his critique fails to
question the theological pertinency of the basic strategy, for it is one with
which he is in sympathy.[25] My approach has been rather to concentrate on
the claims for theological superiority made on behalf of the enterprise called
"process theology"; for a more internal critique, I can best refer the reader to
Neville's work.

Do the four queries we have made offer a fair way of testing current
efforts to extend theological inquiry which accept the label of process theology? One can only judge that by testing individual efforts against them to
see whether any critical purchase results. To my mind, evidence on the first
two points is already in and decisive: the founding polemic against classical
theism exploded a caricature, and claims for a superior philosophical synthesis have floundered on philosophical grounds. Evidence against the third

claim—capacity for illuminating the tradition—is mounting and increasingly negative. The fourth remains more controversial—theological method—yet the tendency of process theology to prefer explanation to careful historical and interpretative analysis either renders it suspect as theology or (if you prefer) places it squarely in a theological school which has not fared so well in more recent times. All of which leads one to ask why erstwhile theologians should show any interest.

Two reasons might be given after all—the first innocuous and the second frightening. One of a more philosophical temper might well ask: What is wrong with exploring such a scheme with an eye to theological understanding? To such a one the only answer would be nothing, of course. Philosophers explore all sorts of things, and now and again even turn something up. So if exploration is your game, why not Whitehead? Or Quine? Or whomever? Theologians, however, are normally of a bit more practical cut, asking why rather than why not.

The other reason I hesitate to mention, but recent experience demands that I do so. Some may be driven to this new and promising field of inquiry because they have successfully negotiated an educational system, secondary, collegiate, and university, which leaves them singularly unequipped, both linguistically and conceptually, to deal with theological traditions. For them, classical theism is no caricature, for they have never encountered the original. Fortified with the GRE illusion that we must be more intelligent than whoever went before us, why not take the latest? If this observation sounds cranky, look to the ease with which slogans and trendy judgments dominate current theological writing, and ask what sort of educational standard that reflects. I have long treasured a colleague's warning that we would be reprehensible as teachers were we to hand on to our students less than was passed on to us. Cultural shifts may sometimes make us reprehensible in spite of ourselves, but one wonders whether we may have given over to them too easily. Mercifully, it just may be "student demand" which recalls us to our vocations as teachers of theology, and should that occur I have no doubt that in the process our students will wonder why all the fuss about process—and alarums like this one will have been rendered otiose.

NOTES

1. This chapter is a reprint of David B. Burrell, C. S. C., "Does Process Theology Rest on a Mistake?" *Theological Studies* 43.1 (1982): 125–35. Copyright © 1982 by SAGE Publications. Reprinted by Permission of SAGE Publications, Ltd.

2. Barry Whitney, "Divine Immutability in Process Philosophy and Contemporary Thomism," *Horizons* 7 (1980): 49–68. The further items are William Hill, O. P.,

"Two Gods of Love: Aquinas and Whitehead," *Listening* 14 (1976): 249–64—in an issue of this DePaul University periodical devoted to "Process Thought in Theology and Ecumenism" and W. Norris Clarke, S. J., *The Philosophical Approach to God* (Winston-Salem, NC: Wake Forest University, 1979).

3. The exasperation which Cathleen M. Going expresses in her review of Lewis S. Ford's *The Lure of God* (Philadelphia, PA: Fortress, 1978) must surely find an echo in every trained philosopher's response to much of this literature; see Cathleen M. Going, review of *The Lure of God: A Biblical Background for Process Theism*, by Lewis S. Ford, *Horizons* 7 (1980): 118.

4. The careful critical article of Merold Westphal, "Temporality and Finitude in Hartshorne's Theism," *Review of Metaphysics* 19 (1966): 550–64, proved as helpful to me in composing the fifth chapter of *Aquinas God and Action* (Notre Dame, IN: University of Notre Dame Press, 1979) as it did avowedly to Norris Clarke.

5. For the distinction between "real" and "intentional" as sometimes implicit but always operative in the medieval context, see Clarke (n. 2 above).

6. This is indeed the force of Langdon Gilkey's review of Schubert Ogden's *The Reality of God and Other Essays* (New York: Harper & Row, 1966) in *Interpretation* 21 (1967): 447–59.

7. My essay on "A Performative View of Substance" will appear in *Substances and Things: Aristotle's Physical Substance in Recent Essays*, ed. Mary L. O'Hara, C. S. J. (Lanham, MD: University Press of America, 1982), 224–49, yet the foundational work has been done by Wilfrid Sellars (C. F. Delaney, Michael J. Loux, Gary Gutting, and W. David Solomon, eds., *The Synoptic Vision: Essays on the Philosophy of Wilfrid Sellars* [Notre Dame, IN: University of Notre Dame Press, 1977]).

8. Hill, "Two Gods," 262–63.

9. Hence Clarke: "It should be remembered, too, that creativity for Whitehead is not an actuality in and for itself, but only a generalized abstract description of what is a matter of fact instantiated in every actual occasion in the universe" (*The Philosophical Approach*, 72).

10. Cf. Joseph Pieper, *The Silence of St. Thomas* (New York: Pantheon, 1957), 48.

11. Cf. chapter five in my *Aquinas* (n. 4 above).

12. If this suspicion be correct, it should lead us to submit to careful scrutiny ventures that describe themselves as "process Christologies." It also makes suspect ritual deferences to "process theology" as they currently appear in American theological writing: for example, if Leo O'Donovan's careful analysis of Jüngel's development of the interpersonal relations appropriate to the Christian God renders the process maneuver otiose, why ask him to take it into consideration?

13. John H. Wright, "Method of Process Theology: An Evaluation," *Communio* 6 (1979): 38.

14. Ibid., 52.

15. Cf. Diogenes Allen, *Finding Our Father* (Atlanta, GA: John Knox Press, 1974), notably the chapters on human love and on perfect love.

16. Wright, "Method" 48.

17. Alfred North Whitehead, *Process and Reality* (New York: Humanities Press, 1929), 161.

18. The quotation is Aquinas's shorthand device for introducing the God in whom Christians believe and for which he will offer a theological elucidation (*Summa theologica*, Ia.2, pr.).

19. Cf. Hans Frei, *The Identity of Jesus Christ: The Hermeneutical Bases for Dogmatic Theology* (Philadelphia, PA: Fortress Press, 1975) and John H. Wright, "Divine Knowledge and Human Freedom," *Theological Studies* 38.3 (1977): 450–77.

20. Clarke offers the references to Heribert Mühlen, *Die Veränderlichkeit Gottes als Horizont einer zukünftigen Christologie* (Münster: Aschendorff, 1969) and Jean Galot, S. J., "La réalité de la souffrance de Dieu," *Nouvelle Revue Théologique* 101.2 (1979): 224–45.

21. For a splendid exposition of Jüngel's thought, see Leo J. O'Donovan, S. J., "The Mystery of God as a History of Love: Eberhard Jüngel's Doctrine of God," *Theological Studies* 42.2 (1981): 251–71.

22. I have in mind the suggestion of David Tracy in *The Analogical Imagination* (New York: Crossroad, 1981): "that a distinctively Christian systematic theological language would, in fact, prove to be trinitarian, yet a trinitarian language that would follow from the central metaphor 'God is Love' Hence [*sic*] a trinitarian understanding of God would employ process-language" (443 n. 30).

23. Clarke puts it nicely: "For like creation, this is a nonnegotiable belief of all streams of Christianity that still remain in contact with their roots" (*The Philosophical Approach*, 103). I believe his assertion would find general agreement among the Christian faithful.

24. The phrase is Ogden's in *The Reality of God*, passim.

25. Robert C. Neville, *Creativity and God: A Challenge to Process Theology* (New York: The Seabury Press, 1980). Neville's easy adoption of David Tracy's preferred term of "public" for theological inquiry begs many questions regarding the intrinsically historical and communal character of theological inquiry. By suggesting this to have been the greatest contribution of process theology (142–46), he aligns himself with its claims more than with its achievements. It is not clear at all, however, that the university has proven to be the most favorable locus for theological inquiry, and Tracy's own modification of "public" to include the classics of distinct traditions makes this point with a certain poignancy, for it is not clear that the university will be fertile ground for future classics, any more than Tracy can offer his recent treatment as a more refined sense of "public." See my critical remarks in the Tracy symposium in *Horizons* (David Burrell, "The Analogical Imagination: Christian Theology and the Culture of Pluralism. Four Perspectives — II," *Horizons* 8.2 [1981]: 319–23).

BIBLIOGRAPHY

Allen, Diogenes. *Finding Our Father*. Atlanta, GA: John Knox Press, 1974.

Aquinas, Thomas. *Summa theologica*. 2nd and Rev. ed. Translated by Fathers of the English Dominican Province. 10 vols. London: Burns, Oates & Washbourne, 1920–22.

Burrell, David. "The Analogical Imagination: Christian Theology and the Culture of Pluralism. Four Perspectives — II." *Horizons* 8.2 (1981): 319–23.

Burrell, David. *Aquinas: God and Action*. Notre Dame, IN: University of Notre Dame Press, 1979.

Burrell, David. "Substance in Aristotle: A Performative Account." In *Substances and Things: Aristotle's Physical Substance in Recent Essays*, edited by Mary L. O'Hara, C. S. J., 224–49. Lanham, MD: University Press of America, 1982.

Clarke, W. Norris, S. J., *The Philosophical Approach to God*. Winston-Salem, NC: Wake Forest University, 1979.

Delaney, C. F., Michael J. Loux, Gary Gutting, and W. David Solomon, eds. *The Synoptic Vision: Essays on the Philosophy of Wilfrid Sellars*. Notre Dame, IN: University of Notre Dame Press, 1977.

Ford, Lewis S. *The Lure of God: A Biblical Background for Process Theism*. Philadelphia, PA: Fortress, 1978.

Frei, Hans. *The Identity of Jesus Christ: The Hermeneutical Bases for Dogmatic Theology*. Philadelphia, PA: Fortress Press, 1975.

Galot, Jean, S. J. "La réalité de la souffrance de Dieu." *Nouvelle Revue Théologique* 101.2 (1979): 224–45.

Gilkey, Langdon. Review of *The Reality of God and Other Essays*, by Schubert Ogden. *Interpretation* 21 (1967): 447–59.

Going, Cathleen M. Review of *The Lure of God: A Biblical Background for Process Theism*, by Lewis S. Ford. *Horizons* 7 (1980): 117–18.

Hill, William, O. P., "Two Gods of Love: Aquinas and Whitehead." *Listening* 14 (1976): 249–64.

Mühlen, Heribert. *Die Veränderlichkeit Gottes als Horizont einer zukünftigen Christologie*. Münster: Aschendorff, 1969.

O'Donovan, Leo J., S. J., "The Mystery of God as a History of Love: Eberhard Jüngel's Doctrine of God." *Theological Studies* 42.2 (1981): 251–71.

Ogden, Schubert M. *The Reality of God and Other Essays*. New York: Harper & Row, 1966.

Neville, Robert C. *Creativity and God: A Challenge to Process Theology*. New York: The Seabury Press, 1980.

Pieper, Joseph. *The Silence of St. Thomas*. New York: Pantheon, 1957.

Tracy, David. *The Analogical Imagination: Christian Theology and the Culture of Pluralism*. New York: Crossroad, 1981.

Westphal, Merold. "Temporality and Finitude in Hartshorne's Theism." *Review of Metaphysics* 19 (1966): 550–64.

Whitehead, Alfred North. *Process and Reality*. New York: Humanities Press, 1929.

Whitney, Barry. "Divine Immutability in Process Philosophy and Contemporary Thomism." *Horizons* 7 (1980): 49–68.

Wright, John H. "Divine Knowledge and Human Freedom." *Theological Studies* 38.3 (1977): 450–77.

Wright, John H. "Method of Process Theology: An Evaluation." *Communio* 6 (1979): 38–55.

Chapter 2

Process Theology and the Catholic Theological Community[1]

J. J. Mueller, S. J.

The eminent Catholic theologian Edward Schillebeeckx reflected on the development of Catholic and Protestant theology since 1870 and spotted two distinct patterns. On the Protestant side, represented by the Reformed tradition, theological authority arises from individual scholars whose statures form a series of outstanding mountain peaks: Barth, Bultmann, Tillich, Ebeling and Fuchs, Moltmann and Pannenberg, and so on. On the Catholic side, however, these peaks are more relative: "theology seems to be borne along by a wider stream which carries all kinds of vessels along with it, but within which a current that is somewhat faster than the stream itself can from time to time be observed."[2] For Schillebeeckx, the distinctive difference in theological development lies in the Catholic idea of church. While the radical need for interpretation is no less acknowledged in Protestant theology, Catholic theology attaches a far greater importance to the whole community of believers (*fides ecclesiae*) than to the finest syntheses of theologians. Moreover, the catholicity of faith seems spontaneously to resist the authority of one personal synthesis, however successful this may be at a given period, whether a Thomas Aquinas or a Karl Rahner. Every Catholic theologian knows from the beginning that he or she remains subject to the criticism of a community of faith. The Catholic theological principle *lex orandi est lex credendi* (the law of praying is the law of believing) expresses well this inextricable unity of life and doctrine, worship and understanding, prayer and belief. Thus, while the theologian takes a formative part in the direction of theology, he or she remains always in a subordinate relationship to a larger undertaking.[3]

Of course, Schillebeeckx had the development of European theology in mind, but in fact his insight applies to the American theological scene as well. Perhaps, on the one hand, American theology might even be interpreted by some as a backwash of European theology and thereby even more dependent upon the strong current of the stream to carry it along and refresh its still waters.[4] On the other hand, others might interpret theology in America as no less a part of the driving current in the middle of the fast-moving stream but without calling attention to itself. While the former interpretation describes our past history, the latter sets the stage for the future. Theology in America benefits from the insights of the most technologically advanced country, where new models of science, forms of interpretation, and futuristic possibilities come together today to present the challenges for tomorrow's theology. Whatever American scenario eventuates, the manner will remain the same: theology will be interrelated with the faith life of a believing community and be responsible to its interpretation.

Process theology and its parent, process philosophy, are part of this American Catholic scenario. The vital, searching, and honest question is not an explanation of process theology or process philosophy, nor even how they relate together. Although these are extremely important academic questions, they avoid the painfully personal faith question: How does the American Catholic theological community understand and evaluate process theology and philosophy in the light of its own fidelity to the God of Jesus Christ? In other words, process philosophy and theology provide potential meaning to a community of interpretation, in this case the Catholic Church, that applies principles of interpretation, namely, fidelity to the faith (*fides ecclesiae*), and that instinctively resists the authority of a one-person synthesis.

The purpose of this chapter is a critical appraisal of process theology. Such an appraisal, I submit, can best take place within a community of interpretation. My point of reference throughout is the American Catholic theological community, and my point of focus is the relationship of process theology to that community. Because they are beyond the scope of this discussion and not because I regard them as unimportant, I will neither explain how the Catholic community interprets new theologies nor justify the rationale for its hermeneutical principles. I accept a magisterium, or teaching authority, and a *sensus fidei* as givens in Catholic theology. I will develop the chapter in three steps: (1) the anatomy of the problem, (2) the history of the problem revisited, and (3) the challenge to process theology for the future.

ANATOMY OF THE PROBLEM

My thesis is that process theology has not made significant inroads into the American Catholic theological community. I would consider a significant inroad to include, but not be limited to, a Catholic faculty identifiably in the process camp, a Catholic publishing house using process material, an identifiable journal, a major Catholic theologian of national prominence providing leadership in process thought, or a popular groundswell calling for process insights.

On all the evidence, process theology would seem to be a fortunate find in the Catholic community when the search for the inculturation of theology has arisen. It boasts American roots stemming from an identifiable American philosophy, offers Catholic theology in a time of growing pluralism a possible alternative to the historically dominant Thomistic and scholastic frameworks, draws on modern science as a vehicle of common worldwide discourse, supplies a philosophical support to speculative theology, and in general is in tune with a world that must live with constant and unavoidable change. To someone who wants to know whether or not there exists a future for process theology especially in the United States, the prediction would be a resounding yes. This prediction, however, would be like weighing the pros and cons of one's favorite football game: for all our figuring, what occurs on paper does not necessarily occur on the field. And so it has been with process theology. For all its attractive features, process theology has not caught on in the American Catholic theological community. No Catholic faculty in the United States can be identified with process theology; no Catholic publishing houses of books or Catholic journals are identifiable process in orientation; no outstanding Catholic theologian of national prominence exists who can be clearly identified as a process theologian; and the popular groundswell seems content to examine development in favor of process insights. In fact—and what seems to be an emotional conviction rather than an intellectual position—when process theology is mentioned among the Catholic faithful, it is regularly greeted with strong negative feelings and even hostility. One conclusion from the contemporary Catholic situation is that, with relatively few exceptions, the Catholic tradition has never tapped the roots of American intellectual life. Another conclusion is that the American Catholic community is facing a new and basic option in direction.

It is also interesting that Catholic theologians have been varied and frequent opponents of process theology. If I may use the outstanding Catholic journal *Theological Studies* as an indicator, David Burrell, who represents one extreme, has suggested that process theology rests upon a mistake; John Wright, less extreme, has criticized process' misunderstanding of knowledge and human freedom and Thomas's adequacy to explain it; Leo O'Donovan, a less combative opponent, has indicated through his analysis of Jüngel's interpersonal relations the indifference to process categories.[5] My own work, favorable to its insights, has argued for its contribution to theology but also its critical limits.[6] Why, when so many indicators point in favor of process theology, has it been thus resisted and not taken root in the American Catholic theological community?

HISTORY OF THE PROBLEM REVISITED

While a complete cause-and-effect explanation of the problem between process theology and the Catholic theological community cannot be given, seven
dynamics can be discerned which indicate the history of the problem and set
the agenda for the future.

(1) *The Catholic context of authority.* In the Catholic view of church, theology is done within an authority structure between the polarities of *sensus fidei*
and magisterium. For some, authority is a pejorative word which conjures up
repressive measures like the Galileo affair, the Index of Forbidden Books,
doctrinal anathemas against heresies, or the censure of writers such as Hans
Küng or Leonardo Boff. However, while authority possesses its continual
tensions, the overall picture is not one of repression so much as one of preserving and proclaiming the faith of the people in both the past and the present. In some areas the magisterium leads (e.g., social encyclicals), in other
areas it trails behind (e.g., women's issues). Today, even in secular newspa-
pers and journals, authority and how it is used are increasingly discussed, too
openly for some. In the final analysis, the authority of the church is subject to
the authority of Jesus Christ, is judged by it, and answers to it. In this sense,
the authority of the church is itself always under continual judgment to search
for the truth of faith. By being answerable to God, authority in the church is
not constitutively negative or repressive, even if instances show the contrary.
By accepting an authority beyond itself, theology is not like other disciplines,
whose principles of truth and accuracy reside within the canons of the discipline. Actually, a salutary wholeness to theology exists when it is done in this
way: it remains at the service of the worshiping faithful and is not locked up
in academic correctness.[7]

(2) *The formation of a Catholic theologian.* It is impossible to separate
Catholic theology from the type of theological formation that prevailed until
recent times. Catholic theologians before Vatican II were almost universally
clergy. Without question, since the time of the Reformation when seminaries
began, the clergy were the theologians and theologians came from the clergy.
Until recently, lay theologians were few and far between. One example of this
domination, from the latter part of the nineteenth century, is the great English
convert Cardinal John Henry Newman, who, desiring to start a university
in Dublin, refused Orestes Brownson, one of the most creative American
theological minds of the time, a position as a teacher of theology because he
was a layman. Instead, he offered Brownson the chair of geography; angered,
Brownson refused.

Given that Catholic theologians were drawn from the clergy, what kind of
training was prescribed for them? The *Code of Canon Law* in 1917 prescribed
for ordination to priesthood two years of philosophy followed by four years

of theology.[8] After ordination, scholars specializing in theology might take additional formal training. Hence, in the Catholic Church and especially in its theological community, a close, even intrinsic connection has existed between philosophy and theology. From a Catholic viewpoint, one cannot do theology without at the same time philosophizing.

(3) *The historical development of theology and philosophy in the Catholic community.* In 1870, with the dogmatic constitution *Dei Filius* and then in 1879 with the encyclical *Aeterni Patris*, the Catholic Church officially adopted Thomas and scholasticism as the *optimum modum philosophandi.* The modernist crisis at the end of the last century and the condemnation of modernism in the first decade of this century intensified the need for sound thinking in a world exploding with "modern" thoughts. However retrogressive this decision might sound to those who wanted openness to the new developments, the strategic decision to remain solidly aligned with the tested durability of Thomism as a philosophical basis provided a strong support for theology. In fact, Thomism proved not to be as bogged down in the past as many progressives expected, because many varieties of Thomism blossomed: the neo-Thomism of Kleutgen and Rousselot, and the three irreducibly distinct emphases developed between the First and Second World Wars which gathered schools of followers around the formative thinkers—Maritain and his use of tradition, Gilson and his use of the historical texts of Thomas, and Maréchal and his use of the transcendental method.[9]

The choice of Thomas and scholasticism as "the best way to philosophize" had far-reaching ramifications which continue to the present day. The principal one for our purposes is that until Vatican II the philosophical training for theology was Thomistic. By the trickle-down theory, this meant that Catholic universities throughout the United States shared this theological and philosophical basis with their students in theology and philosophy courses and generally throughout the curriculum. The enormity of this unified theological enterprise and its continued influence can be measured by simply taking the number of existing Catholic schools that bear this tradition and present the educational leverage that still exists. We are speaking about 319 seminaries and 239 Catholic colleges and universities in the United States.[10] This represents a potentially formidable alignment of thought by any standard. From top to bottom, the theological community in the Catholic community accepted its relationship with philosophy as a working partner. Such an affiliation would present both special concerns and advantages to process thought.

When process philosophy (and now I am speaking of Whitehead as the central proponent and classical presentation of process philosophy, which he called "a philosophy of organism") burst on the scene in the 1920s and 1930s,[11] Catholic philosophy was still forming theologians, clergy, and students with Thomistic thought. Process philosophy did not dent Catholic thought during this period and would not be recognized as a serious option until the late 1960s and 1970s. On the theological side, the critical power of neoorthodoxy with the Niebuhrs and Tillich in the United States reigned before the Second World War[12] but spent itself with the changes that came after the Second World War. A theological vacuum developed, and the beginnings of process theology emerged with Wieman's *The Source of Human Good* (1946),[13] Meland's *Faith and Culture* (1953),[14] Williams's *The Spirit and Forms of Love* (1968),[15] and although the late Bernard Loomer did not publish much, as dean and teacher at the University of Chicago and later at the GTU in Berkeley he made a strong impact. A second generation emerged in John Cobb Jr. and Schubert Ogden, who began their impact in the early to mid-1960s. Norman Pittenger remained the foremost popularizer of process thought and an important figure. The philosophy of Charles Hartshorne was also significant—for example, *The Divine Relativity* (1948)[16] and *Reality as Social Process* (1953).[17] These two generations were nurtured by Liberal Protestantism.[18]

The demise of much of the existing theology continued with the death-of-God theology which exploded on the scene in the early and mid-1960s, signaling to many the corruption of theology and its dubious relationship to new philosophies. At the same time many diverse movements, both liberal and fundamental, vied for credibility in what was an unraveling situation bordering on panic and calling for new directions. Born from the devastation of the Second World War, existentialism began to undercut classical metaphysics. Many more Protestant theologians began to study process philosophy as a possible direction. Meanwhile, riding the momentum built up from the previous decades, Catholic theologians continued to delve into the new and growing discoveries of Thomas and his perennial contribution to thought. And in a chaotic intellectual climate, his philosophical underpinnings seemed even more helpful and true. Stability, vigor, and optimism represented the benchmark for Catholic thought throughout these halcyon years of the 1950s. It culminated in a new Catholic consciousness when John F. Kennedy, who symbolized much of the Catholic community, became president of the United States. Catholics had come of age. The golden age of Catholic life seemed to have arrived and the appropriateness of the Thomistic choice was vindicated.[19]

(4) *Emerging pluralism in Catholic theology.* Emerging from a century of consolidation, Vatican II (1962–1965) recognized new responsibilities occurring in the world and opened its windows to new challenges for proclaiming the gospel. With the recognition of diverse cultural dynamics at work, a pluralism of philosophical systems also emerged. Existentialism, phenomenology, empiricism, language analysis, structural analysis, and semantics were only a few of the philosophies that claimed attention. In addition to

individual systems, the whole history of philosophy was opened to new interpretations. In the midst of this turmoil, dialogue partners and what they stood for changed. At this time, when process philosophy was marshaling its greatest arguments against the so-called classical tradition (perhaps against Descartes rather than the tradition), the classical tradition as appropriated by the Catholic community continued to develop, became interested in all kinds of philosophies, and by its own choice dissolved its monolithic façade. Thus the classical philosophical position which so readily was identified with the Catholic community gradually ceased to apply. In fact, by not remaining uniformly Thomistic, Vatican II changed three relationships: it left process theology without a clear adversary; it welcomed process insights, thereby relativizing process thought to one philosophical voice among many; and it remained an advocate, along with process thought, for strong philosophical relationships to theology.

Meanwhile, theology was finding its roots less dependent upon philosophy, especially metaphysics, which was under considerable attack by the academic community, and more dependent upon the growing discoveries in scriptural studies. In the 1943 document *Divino afflante Spiritu*, the Catholic Church officially subscribed to historical-critical methods as part of its interpretation of scripture and began to train a generation of scholars who emerged in the late 1950s. By the 1960s new doors had opened and scriptural scholarship became an exciting and thrilling addition that was disseminating throughout the Catholic community. Moreover, Vatican II insisted that all theological formations return to scripture as its source. Without doubt, the advance in scripture is the most important contribution to theology in this century. Historical dynamics again worked against each other: while process theology championed the underpinnings of a new philosophy, Catholic theology moved away from its previous relationship to philosophy to include scripture. An emancipation from what had been a dependent relationship to philosophy in the last century had been accomplished. Catholic theology matured to a more independent identity that would relate to all disciplines in its own responsible ways.

In summary, although the prognosis indicated that pluralism in Catholic theology would aid process' entrance into the Catholic theological community, the opposite occurred. Pluralism opened up thought extensively beyond American borders to a smorgasbord of ideas where process was only one small voice among many.

(5) *The Catholic concern with the relationship of process theology to process philosophy*. Process theology depends directly upon process philosophy as expounded by Whitehead. In his introduction to *Process and Reality*, Whitehead stated that he was trying to rescue the larger empirical tradition of Bergson, James, and Dewey from the charges of "anti-intellectualism."[20] He

called his new thought "a philosophy of organism." Hartshorne attributes the coining of the word "process" to Loomer. Process philosophy, then, though emerging from the empirical tradition in the United States, has come to be associated exclusively with Whitehead. His seminal treatment of God occurs from the short part five, chapter two, of *Process and Reality* and seems more like an afterthought than his main concern. Whitehead did not think that God should be an exception to metaphysical categories. The universe as disclosed in modern scientific observation does provide some knowledge of the way God is which will be complemented by the documents of the religions of the world.[21] It is from this chapter that the process philosophy of God is elaborated and becomes the cornerstone for process theology. From its conception—and this is an important genetic point—process theology is the intellectual child of process philosophy. The relationship is not a philosophy which underpins theology so much as a philosophy which generates a theology. Even the name "process" indicates a familial, dependent relationship upon process philosophy. So then, if one does not accept the philosophical presuppositions of process philosophy, does one reject the theology? If one accepts the theological insights, is one really doing a philosophy of religion? Does process theology require a twofold acceptance of both its theological insights and its philosophical basis? Whether one argues for an organic intellectual unity between philosophy and theology or only the theological use of the philosophical insights, a close connection does exist and the acceptance of one does imply the acceptance of the other. In any case, the question arises whether process theology has sufficiently understood and explained its own starting point in philosophy.

(6) *The Catholic concern of theological philosophy.* Process philosophy is decidedly metaphysical in concern, and with Whitehead really cosmological. It is necessarily abstract and theoretical. Anyone who has read Whitehead's *Process and Reality* can testify to the many new terms and expressions such as prehensions, concrescences, and eternal objects. Because the vocabulary and related mental constructs are abstracted from their experiential grounding, process philosophy is predominantly knowledge-oriented as opposed to life-oriented. During this same time, the Catholic theological community found a voice in Teilhard de Chardin, who provided an alternative vision, also tied to new concepts but spoken with the poetic description of a mystic rather than a logician. In what became a search for an appropriate language that empowered and enhanced people's experience, process vocabulary seemed restricted to the classrooms of university professors and graduate students. When the mood was ready for a hearing, process thought seemed encased in a foreign language that first had to be learned before people could apply it. The effort alone made it impractical for the ordinary language of experiences.

Another turn occurred. Process theology took on a combative temperament against classical theology and proceeded with a dogmatic righteousness to cut human experience to fit the Procrustean bed of Whitehead's cosmology, a movement that Whitehead himself, if alive, would have resisted. Rather than the pursuit of his inductive approach, which was a return to experience, a deductive explanation removed from experience resulted. An important non-Whiteheadian switch had come about whereby people repeated Whitehead's answers instead of repeating his method. Just as the return to Thomism by the Catholic intellectual community actually served to free Thomas from what people thought Thomas said (Thomism), so process theology would do well to liberate Whitehead from Whiteheadianism. Simply repeating answers, whether of Thomas or Whitehead or anyone else, becomes a tiring explanation that circumvents the process of thinking.

Because of strong and definite underpinnings by process philosophy, process theology is open to the criticism that it is really a philosophy of religion whose cornerstone is not faith but the clarification and extension of a cosmology into the religious realm. Instead of regarding philosophy as a system unto itself, the Catholic community asks the question of philosophy's relationship to the life of faith. In this relationship, theology, defined as faith seeking understanding, *fides quaerens intellectum*, calls upon philosophy to help clarify understanding. Theology is the queen of the sciences and philosophy is its handmaid, *ancilla theologiae*. Process theology seems to operate in the reverse direction, as a theology serving a philosophy: understanding seeking faith. Hence any tendency to baptize process philosophy or canonize Whitehead would be resisted quite spontaneously and emotionally within the Catholic community. While Catholic theology does not take away the need for epistemology, metaphysics, and cosmology—in fact, has championed such thinking—process theology would have to be rethought from the perspective of faith experience.

This is a very serious statement to the twentieth-century theological community, because it is too akin to the unfortunate Bultmannian choice of this century—a kind of intellectual sin against the Holy Spirit, if you will, which is unforgivable. Bultmann remains continually scolded for the decision he made as a theologian to find a philosophy which would underpin his work. As he looked around, he saw Heidegger's philosophy as the most reasonable, well-argued, and influential philosophy. Therefore, he adopted it. In a sense, he baptized a philosophy into his theological work. If the adage "once bit, twice shy" teaches any lesson, then his decision indicates that theology will not tolerate a full-scale, mass conversion of philosophy into theology. Theology has matured and taken a more critical stance toward philosophy. Any protestations of "I'm for Thomas" or "I'm for Whitehead" or "I'm for Heidegger" will meet the same fate, no matter who proclaims it.

(7) *The Catholic return to experience.* When the pluralism of philosophical systems was admitted into the Catholic theological community after Vatican II, simultaneously several emphases emerged which dealt with inculturating theology. Liberation theology in Latin America, contextual theology in Africa, indigenous theology in Southeast Asia, and political theology in Europe began raising strident cries about the nature and purpose of theology. Liberation theology continued to develop under many forms, for example, black and feminist theologies in this country. In general, theology shifted its emphasis to life-oriented theologies, which were characterized as moving from the bottom up, that is, from experience to reflection, and resisted any appearance of slicing experience into already determined, aprioristic categories which came from the top down. Reflection, they all insisted, must spring from action (praxis) and is tested by its effects, which for some were measured against the cries of the poor and oppressed; for others, social justice; for still others, the renunciation of oppression.

This method was foreign neither to the American intellectual tradition, especially pragmatism, nor to the generalized U.S. preference for practicality. Although U.S. Catholics did not consciously bring their American roots into relation with their theology, and allowed European categories to dominate, the reality pervaded American Catholic behavior. When these new theological developments emerged from around the world, they provided a context by which our own distinctive American identity could be compared, contrasted, and recognized. The resulting changes of awareness among U.S. Catholic theologians indicate that, unexpectedly, liberation theology and not process theology has tapped into the American character, even though process theology is "homegrown." The result is that liberation theology has made the most significant inroads into the U.S. Catholic theological community in the last twenty years.[22]

At the same time, Vatican II encouraged the laity to assume greater responsibility for their role in the church. This emergence of the laity also signaled changes in theology. Since theology would no longer be so totally dominated by the clergy, the way theological formation was performed in the United States was altered. For example, because the preparation of the lay theologian was not controlled by canon law, the two-year preparation in philosophy was not required. In addition, whereas theological doctorates had normally been taken in Europe, for many reasons now the number of Catholic doctorates in theology from American universities increased dramatically.

The rift between philosophy and theology continued to widen and deepen. Theology went its own way, due primarily to scripture scholarship and the "return to the sources" mandated by Vatican II's directives for theological formation. A significant rearrangement of the way theology was done took place. Scripture replaced philosophy as the practical preparation for theology.

At the same time, the practical importance of theology continued as believers insisted that theology speak to them in a relevant and pastoral way. Hence theology established a pastoral connection to life such as it had not enjoyed for centuries. Experience thus became far more integrated with theology both as a starting point and ending point. In sum, by incorporating scripture and experience as sources for theology, every area of theology underwent a transition from the ground up. By the call for a practical theology, theology became more concrete and less abstract.[23]

Two ships were passing in the night. One ship, the Catholic community, sailed into more pastoral and practical waters with more diverse dialogue partners in philosophy than ever before, while slowly divesting itself from what appeared to be constitutive or derivative relationships to philosophy. The other ship process theology remained anchored in abstract and theoretical constructs separated from the experience of the faithful and tied closely to philosophy. It seems that the dynamic of process theology was anchored in harbor as far as Catholic theology was concerned. What process theology offered, Catholic theology was not interested in purchasing, because the wares were yesterday's frigates and unsuitable for the needs of today.

CHALLENGE TO PROCESS THEOLOGY TODAY

From the previous paragraph, it would seem that process theology and the Catholic theological community have sailed in different directions due to external historical developments, differences in perspective, and internal evolutions. Personally, I do not see the prospects for process theology growing greater within the Catholic theological ranks. I believe they are diminishing. Does this mean that, like the grass in the field that is here today and gone tomorrow, so has been the fate of process theology? The answer will depend upon the following challenge.

Taking a lead from the communication style of Jesus of Nazareth, who found that mental pictures told more than words, let me begin with a parable. There was a giant and beautiful flower that bloomed taller and taller and finally was out of proportion to the rest of the plant. Its quick growth sapped the life from the main stem. While growing, it drew the attention of everyone who saw it. People began to consider it as potentially a whole new plant itself, taking over every inch of space. Imaginations ran wild with new possibilities and new uses for this plant. Popular magazines wrote about it. Finally, in size and beauty, the flower eclipsed the plant from which it drew its life. Indeed, to all it seemed that the flower was the plant. And then it happened. People noticed that the flower had grown so large that it could not sustain itself and was quickly growing itself to death. The flower so dominated that it seemed to be a different plant, but it was not. In its prominence, it continued even more to depend upon its trunk and roots. Moreover, serious considerations needed attention. The flower might have to be cut off and its stem pruned. Yet, precious and precarious life remained in the dwarfed main plant, which, though obscured, continually fed the real life to the flower. Hope remained: if it could be saved, the life of the main plant might continue and offer new blooms and give life to other flowers.

The point of the parable? The fast-blooming flower is process philosophy, which came along at a time and place in American thought that brought together many dynamics from science, critical theory, and new models of thinking about the world in terms of change and processes. Drawing nourishment from its main plant, process philosophy had a quick growth spurt in popularity and appeal which suggested great potential for the future. But the danger was that it grew beyond and at the expense of the main plant, as if it had the ability to live alone. The point is, if process thought tries to live as if it were the plant, it will die either by its own self-contained growth or by being pruned as expendable.

What is this main plant which today continues to live and give nourishment to other flowers? It is the empirical tradition, which takes experience seriously. In philosophy, the empirical tradition has given rise to many flowers such as pragmatism, which remains a truly American contribution to philosophy. Pragmatism itself resides within the wider blossom of the American classical tradition of Peirce, James, Royce, Santayana, and Dewey to whom, not incidentally, Whitehead was indebted and whom he consciously tried to defend against charges of anti-intellectualism. Whitehead himself suggested this connection to the main plant and the constant return to it as a source: "the transitions to new fruitfulness of understanding are achieved by recurrence to the utmost depths of intuition for the refreshment of imagination."[24] The larger category of experience still remains deep in the American soul as part of our preferred personality and is called upon to nourish our intuitions, dreams, and theoretical constructs.

In theology, the empirical tradition in the United States also contains an experiential tradition of longstanding that found its first American voice in Jonathan Edwards. It is the experiential dimension that captivated American theology in its beginnings and continues to do so today. Liberation theology, praxis theology, pastoral theology, theology of hope, and even spirituality emphasize a beginning point in experience itself and fascinate American theology today. While theology is chary of philosophy dictating its terms— the Bultmannian sin clearly typifying the fruit that will be avoided in this garden—nevertheless, the empirical tradition in philosophy still provides a viable root for collaboration with theology. Process philosophy can help interpret one facet of experience but remains too narrow or limiting as a philosophical system for wholesale use in theology. But there is hope: while, on the one hand, process philosophical theology is not catching on and, on the other, the empirical dimension of theology is taking root, process philosophy can serve theology by challenging it to return to its understanding of experience, especially in the area of experience as social and relational.

Process philosophical theology might be growing itself to a rapid death. It cannot become the plant itself. It must become one of many flowers for the life of the whole. Insights gained from process philosophical theology will continue to come forth, particularly in the arena of relationships. Loomer, to whom Hartshorne attributes the label "process," later said that the word is too narrow by itself to adequately convey the real insights; he preferred the clumsy but more adequate description of "process/relational" theology. While process thought has its critics, few deny the contributions it has made to understanding the human person as socially related, what Whitehead called the "individual-in-community." But, for all its good points, process theology has remained too much of a proponent and defendant of Whitehead's philosophy to the neglect of the empirical tradition from which his philosophy emerges and to which it needs to remain connected. Even within the process tradition itself, the call to rethink Whitehead in light of the empirical tradition has been made by no less a person than Meland[25] and is a challenge that process theology faces.[26]

A second challenge is interpreting the community's religious experience. Theology cannot remain content to explain itself in abstract and theoretical ways, leaving itself to speculative theology only.[27] No theology can nourish life when it is separated from the people it serves. For example, the God that inspires worship in song, that we pray to when our child is sick, that we preach about with loving passion, that we celebrate in sacrament cannot be described to people as "abstract and consequent poles." It is very difficult to pray with any affection to a "dipolar God." While the construct is intellectually stimulating, no popular groundswell clamors for a dipolar God. Thus some mediation from people to theology and theology to people needs to be done whereby a theological vocabulary responsive and understandable to people's experiences develops. The community remains an indispensable interpreter of theology. When the *lex orandi* and *lex credendi* enhance each other, theology serves its community well.

A corollary to this second challenge requests that process theology not remain selective in its arguments. If it wishes to claim an entire metaphysical underpinning for theology—which I believe it does and must argue for—then it must also provide, as Whitehead himself demands of any system, an adequate and coherent explanation of the entire faith life. Except for some initial inroads into faith by Meland, love by Daniel Day Williams, Christology by Cobb, to mention only a few topics, process theology has not dealt with the foundational, systematic, and practical experiences of the faithed life. Until and unless it does, it will remain a promise and not fulfillment. Because theology holds a fundamental unity between thought and action, or between doctrine and life, I see this challenge a very telling one to process theology today and little prospects on the horizon. My fear is that process theology has so exclusively bogged down in metaphysical arguments like the omnipotence of God that it cannot extricate itself and return to its empirical basis. If so, then it will suffer a quicker and more certain death than I have imagined.

The road ahead for process theology is a difficult one. Whether this road is a dead end or a through road will depend, in my judgment, upon a return to the empirical basis in which its roots were sunk and from which it drew nourishment. The Catholic theological community will remain critical of process theology and its relationship to a cosmology that seems to dictate the theology. This community will require a clearer delineation of the relationship between philosophy and theology. At the same time, it will admit no usurpation of its tradition of 2,000 years nor take theology away from the worshiping faithful. One can expect a theology that dialogues in the future with many philosophies and will subject them to the critical function of its interpreting community. This community will continue to issue demands that doctrine and life be combined and mingled together in an integrated whole, thus providing nourishment for faith on the practical and theoretical levels. Further, this community will require a complete explanation of faith as it relates both to its traditional doctrines and to its legacy from past communities who also sought and found the God of Jesus Christ. If these dimensions of the challenge are met, process theology will enter a new phase in its own life of thought whose identity may be transformed into one flower among many and with a new and more lasting life.

NOTES

1. This chapter is a reprint of J. J. Mueller, S. J., "Process Theology and the Catholic Theological Community?" *Theological Studies* 47.3 (1986): 412–27. Copyright © 1986 by SAGE Publications. Permission of SAGE Publications, Ltd.

2. Edward Schillebeeckx, O. P., Introduction to *A Survey of Catholic Theology 1800–1970*, by T. Mark Schoof, O. P. (Toronto: Paulist Press, 1970), 1.

3. Ibid., 2.

4. The pre-Vatican II dependence in theological formation upon European scholarship in the form of Thomism, and even the use of Latin manuals from Europe, seem to confirm this view. Since Vatican II, Latin American liberation theology, which attempts to develop a theology responsible to its cultural context, also serves to disclose the lack of any truly North American theology.

5. David B. Burrell, C. S. C., "Does Process Theology Rest on a Mistake?" *Theological Studies* 43.1 (1982): 125–35, and the appraisal by Burrell of O'Donovan, ibid., 130n11; John Wright, S. J., "Divine Knowledge and Human Freedom," *Theological Studies* 38.3 (1977): 450–77; Leo O'Donovan, S. J., "The Mystery of God as a History of Love: Eberhard Jüngel's Doctrine of God," *Theological Studies* 42.2 (1981): 251–71.

6. J. J. Mueller, S. J., "Appreciative Awareness: The Feeling-Dimension in Religious Experience," *Theological Studies* 45.1 (1984): 57–79. As the third part of that paper argues, I see my work within the larger empirical process tradition (ibid., 73–79).

7. While I do not disagree with David Tracy's three centers of responsibility—church, academy, society—I do not find the interrelationships among them sufficiently delineated, especially the role of the church as the central interpreting community which this chapter examines. Cf. David Tracy, *The Analogical Imagination: Christian Theology and the Culture of Pluralism* (New York: Crossroad, 1981), 3–46.

8. Cf. the 1917 *Code of Canon Law* (*Codex Iuris Canonici* [New York: P. J. Kenedy & Sons, 1918]), canons 1364–66. For an extensively documented history of seminaries, see *Seminaria ecclesiae catholicae* (Vatican City: Librería Editrice Vaticana, 1963).

9. Gerald A. McCool, *Catholic Theology in the Nineteenth Century* (New York: Seabury, 1977), 241–67.

10. *The Official Catholic Directory* 1985 (*The Official Catholic Directory* [Wilmette, IL: P. J. Kenedy & Sons, 1985]). My use of 1984 statistics emphasizes the continued influence. If one returns to 1965 statistics to understand the potential at the end of the pre-Vatican II period, the comparable statistics are 596 seminaries and 304 Catholic colleges and universities. If one examines the longer historical influence, some of the comparable statistics are in 1950, 388 seminaries and 225 Catholic colleges and universities; in 1940, 202 seminaries and 143 Catholic colleges for men 683 Catholic "colleges and academies for girls"; in 1920, 113 seminaries and 215 colleges for men and 710 colleges and academies for girls (ibid.).

11. For a moving account of how this new philosophy captured the imagination of the faculty at the University of Chicago in 1924, see Bernard E. Meland, "The Empirical Tradition in Theology at Chicago," in *The Future of Empirical Theology*, ed. Bernard E. Meland (Chicago: University of Chicago Press, 1969), 283–306.

12. Sidney Ahlstrom, *Theology in America* (New York: Bobbs-Merrill, 1967), 76–91.

13. Henry Nelson Wieman, *The Source of Human Good* (Chicago: University of Chicago Press, 1946).

14. Bernard E. Meland, *Faith and Culture* (Carbondale, IL: Southern Illinois University Press, 1953).

15. Daniel Day Williams, *The Spirit and the Forms of Love* (New York: Harper & Row, 1968).

16. Charles Hartshorne, *The Divine Relativity: A Social Conception of God* (New Haven, CT: Yale University Press, 1948).

17. Charles Hartshorne, *Reality as Social Process: Studies in Metaphysics and Religion* (Boston, MA: Beacon Press, 1953).

18. Dean Fowler, "A Process Theology of Interdependence," *Theological Studies* 40.1 (1979): 44–45. He sees the Catholic theologians David Tracy and Bernard Lee as a part of the third generation, a statement that I believe needs the nuancing this chapter provides.

19. The 1950s in U.S. Catholicism is a decade whose story needs telling both in itself and in its relationship to the continuing movements of history. For example, explosive dynamics were unleashed in the 1950s with which we are coming to grips today: the expansion of all Catholic educational institutions, the swelling of religious vocations, and the general upward mobility of immigrants come-of-age in the socio-economic arena.

20. Alfred North Whitehead, *Process and Reality: An Essay in Cosmology* (1929), corrected ed., ed. David Ray Griffin and Donald W. Sherburne (New York: Free Press, 1978), xii.

21. Laurence F. Wilmot, *Whitehead and God: Prolegomena to Theological Reconstruction* (Ontario: Wilfred Laurier University Press, 1979).

22. "Inroads" that indicate liberation theology's influence are the publishing house of Orbis, the social justice emphasis on the intellectual and popular levels, and major Catholic theologians identified with it (e.g., Gutiérrez, Boff, Segundo, Sobrino).

23. For a current explanation of theological education and how it has changed, especially with respect to the pastoral dimension of theological formation, see T. Howland Sanks, S. J., "Education for Ministry since Vatican II," *Theological Studies* 45.3 (1984): 481–500.

24. Alfred North Whitehead, *Adventures of Ideas* (New York: Macmillan, 1933), 203–4. Wilmot makes the observation that rethinking of Whitehead could be undertaken if empirical evidences found in religious experience required it—the point I am suggesting. Cf. Wilmot, *Whitehead and God*, 83.

25. Cf. Meland's review of Craig Eisendrath's work on William James and Whitehead (Bernard E. Meland, review of *The Unifying Moment: The Psychological Philosophy of William James and Alfred North Whitehead*, by Craig Eisendrath, *Process Studies* 3 [1973]: 285–90).

26. I have argued for the empirical dimension of process thinking in "Appreciative Awareness," 57–79.

27. This statement does not undermine the recognized contributions of process theology to speculative theology; cf. Robert C. Neville, *Creativity and God: A Challenge to Process Theology* (New York: Seabury, 1980), 137–46.

BIBLIOGRAPHY

Ahlstrom, Sidney. *Theology in America*. New York: Bobbs-Merrill, 1967.

Burrell, David, C. S. C. "Does Process Theology Rest on a Mistake?" *Theological Studies* 43.1 (1982): 125–35.

Codex Iuris Canonici. New York: P. J. Kenedy, 1918.

Eisendrath, Craig R. *The Unifying Moment: The Psychological Philosophy of William James and Alfred North Whitehead*. Cambridge, MA: Harvard University Press, 1971.

Fowler, Dean. "A Process Theology of Interdependence." *Theological Studies* 40.1 (1979): 44–45.

Hartshorne, Charles. *The Divine Relativity: A Social Conception of God*. New Haven, CT: Yale University Press, 1948.

Hartshorne, Charles. *Reality as Social Process: Studies in Metaphysics and Religion*. Boston, MA: Beacon Press, 1953.

McCool, Gerald A. *Catholic Theology in the Nineteenth Century*. New York: Seabury, 1977.

Meland, Bernard E. "The Empirical Tradition in Theology at Chicago." In *The Future of Empirical Theology*, edited by Bernard E. Meland, 283–306. Chicago: University of Chicago, 1969.

Meland, Bernard E. *Faith and Culture*. Carbondale, IL: Southern Illinois University Press, 1953.

Meland, Bernard E. "Review of *The Unifying Moment: The Psychological Philosophy of William James and Alfred North Whitehead*, by Craig Eisendrath." *Process Studies* 3 (1973): 285–90.

Mueller, J. J., S. J. "Appreciative Awareness: The Feeling-Dimension in Religious Experience." *Theological Studies* 45.1 (1984): 57–79.

Neville, Robert C. *Creativity and God: A Challenge to Process Theology*. New York: Seabury, 1980.

O'Donovan, Leo, S. J. "The Mystery of God as a History of Love: Eberhard Jüngel's Doctrine of God." *Theological Studies* 42.2 (1981): 251–71.

The Official Catholic Directory. Wilmette, IL: P. J. Kenedy & Sons, 1985.

Sanks, T. Howland, S. J. "Education for Ministry since Vatican II." *Theological Studies* 45.3 (1984): 481–500.

Schillebeeckx, Edward, O. P. Introduction to *A Survey of Catholic Theology 1800–1970*, by T. Mark Schoof, O. P., 1–5. Toronto: Paulist Press, 1970.

Seminaria ecclesiae catholicae. Vatican City: Librería Editrice Vaticana, 1963.

Tracy, David. *The Analogical Imagination: Christian Theology and the Culture of Pluralism*. New York: Crossroad, 1981.

Whitehead, Alfred North. *Adventures of Ideas*. New York: Macmillan, 1933.

Whitehead, Alfred North. *Process and Reality: An Essay in Cosmology*. 1929. Corrected ed. Edited by David Ray Griffin and Donald W. Sherburne. New York: Free Press, 1978.

Wieman, Henry Nelson. *The Source of Human Good*. Chicago: University of Chicago Press, 1946.

Williams, Daniel Day. *The Spirit and the Forms of Love*. New York: Harper & Row, 1968.

Wilmot, Laurence F. *Whitehead and God: Prolegomena to Theological Reconstruction*. Ontario: Wilfred Laurier University Press, 1979.

Wright, John, S. J. "Divine Knowledge and Human Freedom." *Theological Studies* 38.3 (1977): 450–77.

Chapter 3

Duns Scotus, Catholicity, and the Roots of Process Thought

Ilia Delio, O. S. F.

The word "catholic" originated with the Greeks and is related to the word *kosmos* which was first used in Homer's *Iliad* to mean "in good order" or the order that gives rise to beauty.[1] The Greek word *katholikos* is based on the preposition *kata* and the noun *holos*, when coupled become *kath' holou*, an adverb meaning "wholly" or *katholikos*, a substantive that is best rendered "catholicity" in English.[2] The word "catholic" describes a movement toward or consciousness of wholeness. Catholicity is not a physical order or a spiritual one; rather, catholicity belongs to the noumenal and ontological plane and describes a dynamic principle of wholemaking.[3] In this respect, catholicity marks the insights of Franciscan medieval theologian John Duns Scotus and the philosopher Alfred North Whitehead both of whom described a deep relationality of existence, oriented toward beauty and communion. While Whitehead's process thought emerged in a world of modern science, Scotus's Franciscan theology emerged in a world shaped by scholasticism, a world growing suspicious of Aristotle and natural philosophy. Scotus's thought is complex, subtle, and technical; yet, like Whitehead, he probes the capacity of the human mind to know God in a world of concrete reality. The results are stunning and exclude the need for platonic nostalgia. Concrete reality holds eternal value. Scotus's vision of cosmic beauty and Whitehead's world as organism are "catholic" paradigms of ultimate meaning, grounded in an incarnational vision of reality. In this chapter, I will explore how the roots of process theology began with the medieval Franciscan and blossomed in Whitehead's post-Einsteinian universe, in which Whitehead reconceived the God–world relationship and a new vision of science and religion.

DUNS SCOTUS AND FRANCISCAN THEOLOGY

It is not unusual to see scholars oppose Duns Scotus to the Dominican Thomas Aquinas, as if the Franciscan wrote to counter the Dominican. But this description is inaccurate or, rather, contrived. Although the Islamic philosophers who influenced Aquinas, Avicenna, and Averroës also shaped Scotus, his primary influence was the religious experience of Francis of Assisi, a poor itinerant follower of Christ who saw material reality as the mirror of God's goodness. Some regard him as "the first materialist" in the best sense of the word because of the way he looked on the material world—not for *what* it is but for *how* it is—God's creation.[4]

John Duns Scotus was born in 1266 and educated at Oxford University. He was a careful thinker whose insights reflect an understanding of reality as dynamic and interconnected in relation to God. Jeremiah Hackett writes, "He knew some works by Aquinas, and in some respects, both Aquinas and Scotus shared a common concern: the interpretation for the Christian world of the philosophy of Aristotle."[5] However, Scotus belonged to a generation of scholars that emerged after the condemnations of Aristotelian philosophy in 1270 and 1277, a fallout that brought even the work of Thomas Aquinas under suspicion.[6]

A theologian with a scientific mind, the originality of Scotus was his turn to the contingent as a valid domain of scientific and philosophical reflection. He viewed contingency and relationality as coterminous, indicating that the contingency of creation is not arbitrary but depends on the freedom of a personal God. It is not a necessary world but a contingent one based on the generosity of God's love, "in the same way that a work of art has no intrinsic reason to exist, other than the desire of the artist to express herself in this particular way."[7]

While Scotus did not write against Thomas Aquinas, he did aim his remarks at Henry of Ghent (d. 1293), a French scholastic relational philosopher who was an adversary of Thomas Aquinas. Ghent was an eclectic thinker, neither Aristotelian nor Augustinian, who taught among other things that matter could be created by God to exist independent of form, and that there was no real distinction between essence and existence, or between the soul and its faculties.[8] Scotus responded to Ghent's arguments by appealing to a wider interpretation of Aristotle's philosophy, describing a world of relationality, creativity, and love. He was, in a sense, a "proto-process" thinker. His analytical insights on being and relationality planted the seeds of process thought in the late thirteenth century, although such ideas blossomed in the scientific world of the twentieth century. Like Whitehead, Scotus thought in terms of relationships.[9] Both thinkers describe a living world of interrelatedness where God plays a vital role in the communion of being, a world grounded in the creativity of divine love, an interconnected whole that represents the best of catholicity.

METAPHYSICS AND EPISTEMOLOGY

To map out Scotus's system of thought is not easy, as the complexity of his ideas must be teased out in their subtle distinctions (hence the title given to him *Doctor Subtilis*). His chief concern was the relationship between epistemology and metaphysics. How can we know God? For Scotus, it is not God but rather being which is the proper object of human knowledge. The Subtle Doctor was concerned to show how the human mind is present to all that exists and the intricate way in which all that exists is present to the human mind. He elaborates upon the Aristotelian approach in two ways. First, he expands the cognitional act from abstraction to include intuition, a higher, more direct act of intellection within the power of the human mind in the present state (*pro statu isto*). Second, he shifts the focus from the mental species or *quidditas* to the concept of being (*ens*) as the primary object of intellection. Mary Beth Ingham and Mechtild Dreyer write:

> Scotus uses the categories of revelation to approach the question of cognition and the use of language. It is the beatific vision, along with its natural conditions, that inform the development of the double cognitive capacity of abstractive and intuitive intellection. Human nature, rather than the human condition, serves as the point of departure for a reflection that argues for the possibility of certain knowledge, the immediate experience of extra-mental reality, and the subjective awareness of internal states.[10]

In his discussion of cognition, Scotus balances the objective and subjective, favoring the subjective realm. The act of intuitive cognition turns the attention of the philosopher from knowing as a representational act to knowing as an act both immediate and certain.[11] His moderate realism means that concepts exist in a relationship to reality. The object of cognition (*ens*) cannot be understood independently of the sorts of cognitive acts of which the human intellect is capable (both abstractive and intuitive). Rather, reality and mind exist in a dynamic relationship of mutual presence that gives rise to concepts and to the language within which such concepts are expressed.

Epistemology is integral to metaphysics for the Subtle Doctor. His novel approach to metaphysics began by taking the minor element of metaphysics, the transcendentals, and making them the primary object of metaphysics: metaphysics is the study of the transcendentals.[12] Transcendental attributes, such as unity, truth, and goodness, are coextensive with being. Thus, he opened up categories of thought that transcend and ground contingent, physical experience. From a theory of transcendentals, Scotus argued that we should be able to *infer the existence of* God. In this respect, metaphysics is *natural theology*, a means by which the minds of those not committed to a dogmatic assertion about God can nevertheless arrive at Necessary Being. While Anselm described God as a being greater than which nothing greater can be conceived, Scotus described God as the highest Being without contradiction.[13]

The ability to "know" God, even in a limited sense, is dependent upon God being knowable or intelligible. Since "being" is fundamental, there must be a sense in which substances, accidents, and God all exist in reality. To make this claim, Scotus invoked the concept of univocity. Univocity is conceptual and semantic, not metaphysical. It is an utterly abstract and indeterminable concept applicable to everything that exists. Being is the only *quidditive* concept we all share; thus being is univocal and applies to God as well as to creatures. Ingham and Dreyer write:

> The univocal concept, *ens in quantum ens* (a being insofar as it is), presents metaphysics as ontology, or the science of what exists understood insofar as it exists and is present to the knower. As such, this object of metaphysical reflection is encountered as a concept within consciousness. Thus the domain of metaphysical reflection is truly located, not in extra-mental reality, but in reality as it is known by the mind. Metaphysics, logic, and epistemology are thus intimately connected.[14]

Being can be either finite or infinite (that which exceeds the finite). In designating God as an *infinite Being*, Scotus includes among God's attributes, infinite goodness, infinite truth, and pure perfections. However, to get this far, Scotus must demonstrate that in the realm of beings, *one* infinite being can actually exist and then identify this Supreme Being as God without appeal to a priori judgments. The doctrine of univocity rests in part on the claim that: "[t]he difference between God and creatures, at least with regard to God's possession of the pure perfections, is ultimately one of degree."[15] If we ascribe to God every pure perfection, then we have to affirm that we are ascribing to God *the very same thing* that we ascribe to creatures: God has it infinitely, creatures in a limited way. Thus, Scotus maintains a unity between God and world. One sees in his doctrine a harmonious cooperation between ontology (what God is) and semantics (how we can think and talk about God).[16]

The univocity of being for Scotus did not preclude the use of analogy as well, although analogy would be impossible without some more basic, common concept that is univocal. Without univocity of being, analogy would be merely equivocation, and no language or understanding of God would be possible.[17] In short, human cognition must have some natural basis from which to reflect on the divine. If the human mind has a foundational access to reality, and if that reality provides an adequate basis for natural knowledge of God, then theology can be understood as a science whose content does not exhaust the truth about God. Being, as a univocal concept, makes possible the use of language to express the experience of what transcends sense knowledge. The univocity of being along with its transcendent attributes (one, true, good) frames the horizon of language and cognition and thus offers the unity required of a science. Ingham writes, "It is the science of the trans-physical that grounds the physical. It frames both the possibility of metaphysics as a science and, more importantly, theology as meaningful discourse about God."[18] Univocity and intuitive cognition can be understood as two aspects of a single theory in which mind and matter are reciprocally related: the human mind is present to all that exists and all that exists is present to the human mind.[19] Both object and knower contribute actively to the act of intellection. The cognitive act, involving mutual presence and engagement of the knower with reality, underpins Scotus's theory of knowledge. The activity of knowing cannot occur abstractly from what is known. Attention to the act of cognitive awareness reveals the conditions required for such an act to take place. One must focus both on what presents itself to the mind at the most basic level (*ens*) and on how the mind moves out toward its primary object (via abstractive and intuitive acts). The act of knowing, therefore, moves from what is most obvious and external to what is most hidden and obscure.[20] Such knowledge is the foundation for any scientific knowledge of reality from the perspective of the knower and from the perspective of what is known.

A VISION OF THE WHOLE: INDIVIDUATION

Scotus's philosophy undergirds a rich theological vision of contingent relations. In his view every created thing has a potential to be unified with all other created things, to constitute jointly the one, singular universe. This potentiality is dependent upon the relation of parts to whole. Beauty is the harmony of the whole in its interrelated parts such that every particular being contributes to the beauty of reality. He developed this idea by reconceiving the relationship between matter and form. He argued that any individual entity (including a composite substance) can be analyzed into two really identical "components": essence and individuating feature. There is something unique and individual about what the intellect perceives as otherwise common. His account of the union of matter and form to constitute composite substance is strongly anti-reductionistic: substance is not identical with its parts or merely the aggregate of its parts.[21] Following Avicenna, there is a *natura communis* ("common nature") in a way allowing a real sense of the universal so that, on one hand, something universal can be predicated of multiple individuals; yet, there is a particularity to each existent. Dan Horan states, "He believed that *natura communis* is universal only if there are individuals to which such a 'nature' could be applied. Universality of this common nature presupposes particularity."[22] Scotus conceives of substances in terms of particulars. Instead of individuating a thing by existence, quantity, or material, he posits that, "a material substance becomes individual through a principle that contracts this common nature to singularity. . . . Scotus calls this principle the individuating entity (*entitas individualis*)."[23] In his description of individuation Scotus writes:

> This [individuating] entity, therefore, is not the matter or the form or the composite insofar as each of these is a "nature"; rather, it is the ultimate reality of the being that is the matter or that is the form or that is the composite; so that whatever is common and nevertheless determinable, no matter how much it is only one real thing, we can still distinguish further several formally distinct realities, of which this formally is not that and this is formally the entity of singularity, and that is formally the entity of a nature.[24]

This individuating entity forms his doctrine of *haecceitas*, an individuating principle or positive entity to which is ascribed singularity and which is formally other than the entity constituting the specific nature. Alan Wolter notes that this individuating entity, though formally distinct from the common nature, forms a unity with that nature so that singularity is intrinsic and not accidental to any individual.[25] Hence what makes an individual an individual, a "this" and "not that," including both material and nonmaterial things, is absolutely intrinsic and identical to that thing's very existence or being.[26] Jeremiah Hackett writes:

> For Duns Scotus, the individual is more perfect because it is a unique thing which is defined by its own uniqueness . . . something is included in the very nature of the individual which is lacking in the shared nature.[27]

Scotus speaks about the unity of the world as a whole and the contingency of its parts vis-à-vis a unified whole. The contingent relation of parts to whole stands in contrast to the lack of contingency in God. God is not a part of the universe because God is not contingent. The contingency of creation, therefore, is a contrast between the production of created things in potency to form part of a whole and God as Necessary Being without limit. Relations are potential parts of the universe and accordingly they are contingent. What is interesting is that relations are just as contingent as their created *relata*, a view compatible with contemporary systems thinking. That is, relationships are formative of existence.[28] Scotus analyzed created things in their relation to one another, as contingent at an ultimate level, while recognizing there can be orderings or patterns of imposed necessary-and-sufficient conditions between things. Every limited and bounded thing that is a part of the whole has a real relation to the whole. God cannot enter into any such relation, because God is unbounded, unlimited, and not properly speaking a part of the universe.[29]

CONCURRENCE

Whereas Thomas Aquinas held that natural causes require the cooperation of God as a primary cause, Scotus maintained a principle of concurrence. Since everything has its own unique being, the activity of each being is concurrent with divine presence as both source of each unique being and the freedom of each being to be itself, in its own creative activity. Concurrence is the simultaneous operation of primary and secondary causes, an acting-along-with rather than an acting-in.[30] As a result, Peter Leithart writes:

> the less perfect cause can add something, inasmuch as the cumulative effect of the more perfect cause and the less perfect cause is more perfect than the effect of the more perfect cause alone. The created world can thus add some perfection and nobility to what comes from the uncreated cause, which therefore is no longer necessarily more perfect or nobler than what it causes.[31]

In short, the "being of the effect does not depend any longer on [God's] gift of being."[32] Everything has its own unique being-ness, its *haecceitas*, and the activity of its being is the divine presence which is both the source of its unique being and the freedom of being to be itself, in its own creative activity. Hence there is a mutual relationship between God and created being. Scotus's natural cause principle, in light of contingent creation and the generation of possibilities, means that causes are only relatively natural and necessitated: relative to a contingently caused divine act of adopting a given set of laws (stabilizing some choice as an order of nature). Strictly speaking, there are no natural causes because there are no absolutely necessitated created states of affairs. Rather, the natural order of being is constituted in being by the absolute love and presence of God.

THE PRIMACY OF LOVE

For Scotus, God is like an artist and creation is the work of divine art. Every single aspect of the created universe exists because of God's absolute freedom and unlimited love.[33] Each being is uniquely created by the divine will of God and nothing exists necessarily except God.[34] The present moment expresses eternal perfection, in so far as creation is endowed with creative potential for fulfillment.[35]

Love is the heart of Scotus's theological vision. Since everything has its origins in God, everything has its origins in love. Scotus's emphasis on divine love as the essence of being is manifested in his doctrine of incarnation, which is the supreme act of divine initiative, liberality, self-revelation, and intimate presence to the created order. The reason for the incarnation is divine love and generosity. Whether or not original sin took place, Christ would have come. Scotus regarded the incarnation as revelatory of divine freedom, without regard to human sinfulness.[36] The incarnation reveals another dimension of God's rational intentionality: the freedom to initiate and sustain relational presence regardless of the human response.[37] Divine presence in the created order is salvific not because of any particular actions but by virtue of divine presence alone. Ingham notes that Scotus, "is pre-occupied with the act of presence." She writes:

> God's presence to the world, the presence of the mind to reality and to itself, the presence of being to cognition, the presence of the moral agent to a given set of circumstances. The act of presence is an act that unites intellect and will. Presence is ultimately an act of love, for in the act of love, the lover is united to the beloved.[38]

God is present to each moment in an act of loving immediacy and is known in the present moment by attention to the contingent order. Human reason imitates divine activity by attention to the present moment, engagement with the real, so that the act of knowing is an act of love. While love is at the heart of his doctrine, it is an ordered and rational loving. How we choose and what we choose makes a difference. For Scotus, rationality is ordered loving; right action is based on ordered love. In this respect, he sees the human person as the artisan of beauty in the world and speaks of two orientations within the will: an affection for justice (*affectio justitiae*), that is, an orientation toward right loving and right action; to act as God acts and to see as God sees is to be just. The second type of affection is for well-being and happiness (*affectio commodi*) in order to focus on a healthy life. These two desires or affections exist in us because they exist in God. These two affections working together and complementing each other are what make us rational in our choices.[39] The goal of the human moral life is the perfection of love, not only in regard to God but to all persons and creations as having God-given value. It is not the intellect but the will, the seat of love, that holds the key to rational perfection.

DID SCOTUS ANTICIPATE PROCESS REALITY?

The complexities of Scotus's ideas illuminate a brilliant mind attuned to natural philosophy and informed by faith. Would Scotus have recognized his world of mutual harmony and beauty in the writings of Alfred North Whitehead? I think so, for one can see a deep resonance between the Franciscan and the mathematician-philosopher, who gave new meaning to the whole by bringing religion and science into a unified framework. Both were complex thinkers for whom the term "God" represented Necessary Being without contradiction (Scotus), a principle of concretion (Whitehead) which provides a consistent way to reduce potentiality to actuality.[40] Univocity of being is common to Scotus and Whitehead who posit a common foundation between the mind and reality; knowledge of God is truly possible through all that exists.[41] God creates by bringing that which does not yet exist (potentiality) into being (actuality). Both thinkers held that divine being and created being exist in mutual relationship, each according to its nature. God is not Perfect Being and creation imperfect being. Rather there is a common relation between Creator and creature in regard to each other. The activity of each being is concurrent with divine presence as both source of being and the freedom of each being to be itself, in its own creative activity. Joseph Bracken has described a metaphysics of creativity that is consonant with Scotus's notion of absolute creative Being. Infinite Being is dynamic not fixed, a processive reality that is a never-ending conversion from potency to actuality. Since Being Itself is eternal movement, creativity is the ultimate reality of the universe, a ubiquitous reality embodied by every actuality.[42]

This notion of being as creativity is consonant with Whitehead's God of creative love. God's eternal purpose is to evoke creatures with the richest possible form of experience into being. Scotus would agree, although he would not see the relationship of God and finite being in the same way as Whitehead. For Scotus, the divine creative act is the ground of contingent finite being and creativity; the relationship of God to finite being is the contingency of Being Itself. Although God does not exist outside the relational ordering, as if only the effects were ordered and the cause lay outside the relationship, God is not affected by the relationship. Whitehead emphasized mutuality between God and world; God's life can be affected by created reality. He wrote, "God not only affects the world but is also affected by the world with an experience that is constantly developing and changing as the world itself develops and changes."[43] He describes a dipolar nature of God in which one pole, the primordial nature, is that dimension of God that corresponds to the absolute Being of God as eternal, transcendent, and unchanging, the "unconditioned conceptual valuation of the entire multiplicity of eternal objects" or possibilities.[44] Because of this primordial nature, God is objectified in each occasion as the ground of potentiality and novelty, a primordial subject of the never-ending act of existence, a determinate reality here and now but with unlimited capacity to acquire further determinates in later moments of divine existence. The other pole Whitehead calls the consequent nature of God, that dimension of the divine that is affected and changed by its interaction with the world.[45] The divine consequent nature is temporal, relative, immanent, and changing being, "consequent upon the creative advance of the world."[46]

The consequent nature of God means that God "shares with every new creation its actual world; and the concrescent creature (or occasion) is objecti-fied in God as a novel element in God's objectification of that actual world."[47] God can change insofar as God can be affected by events in the universe, although such change does not affect the primordial pole or unoriginated goodness of God. Marjorie Suchocki called Whitehead's God the "Supremely Related One" who works persuasively "with the world as it is in order to bring it to where it can be."[48] For Scotus, God is unchanging but absolutely free, while for Whitehead, God's freedom to grow in love involves change. Both would agree that where there is freedom, there is fidelity in love amid ever-deepening relationships.

Whitehead's God is a volitional God, driven by the eternal urge of desire; so too is Scotus's God, whose creative freedom grounded in love is expressed by divine intention and desire. Both Whitehead and Scotus per-ceive a dynamic God of intimate relationship who is deeply related to each actual occasion of being, as Roland Faber states, "more intimate to the event than is the event to itself."[49] Scotus notes that creativity and freedom define existence. For Whitehead, God influences the exercise of universal free will by offering possibilities. Like Scotus, he claimed that divine perfection rests on power and freedom; hence, God allows beings the power to resist divine persuasion. God is not omnipotent, therefore, in terms of being coercive but persuasive; God is the eternal lure who invites being into a richer world of mutual relationships. Scotus said that divine *acceptatio* shows the generous freedom of God's eternal purpose.[50] Even if creatures reject God's offer of love, God remains ever-present in love. So too, Whitehead said God's fidelity in love seeks to evoke creatures with the richest possible forms of experience.

For Whitehead, the cosmic process is an evolving reality, a mega-organism that is an ongoing unity of interconnected parts; every physical entity exists in its own subjectively constituted world, a notion that could be viewed through the lens of Scotus's *haecceitas*. Each living existent or creative society is its own world of subjective experiences, a distinct being-ness, which, for Whitehead, includes a notion of consciousness. The dynamic interrelation of beings constitutes the world at large as an ever-changing organic real-ity.[51] Scotus's doctrine of concurrence is valuable here because it is the simultaneous operation of primary and secondary causes, an acting-along-with rather than an acting-in. As a result,

> the less perfect cause can add something, inasmuch as the cumulative effect of the more perfect cause and the less perfect cause is more perfect than the effect of the more perfect cause alone. The created world can thus add some perfection and nobility to what comes from the uncreated cause, which therefore is no longer necessarily more perfect or nobler than what it causes.[52]

Everything that exists has its own unique being-ness, its *haecceittas*, and the activity of its being is the divine presence which is both the source of its unique being and the freedom of being to be itself in its own creative activity. Hence the mutual relationship between God and created being is common to Scotus and Whitehead. Existence is a dynamic mutuality between God and world oriented toward a communion of being-in-love.

CATHOLICITY IS GROUNDED IN LOVE

What we see bursting forth in these thinkers is a deep catholicity grounded in divine-created mutual relationship. That Whitehead would develop a univocal God–world relationship based on mutual relationships, creativity, and freedom reflects a deep religious dimension of reality, similar to Scotus. It is not unreasonable to suggest that the philosophical and theological ideas developed by Scotus emerged in Whitehead's process reality, although there is no direct link between them. The nineteenth-century American philosopher Charles S. Peirce studied Scotus's views on individuality and universality and developed a theory of meaning and signs, which argues for a form of realism.[53] In 1916, Martin Heidegger wrote his *Habilitationsschrift* on Duns Scotus. However, only the first part of the thesis was based on texts of Scotus concerning unity and truth.[54] In a contemporary study on relations in the Middle Ages, Mark Henninger devotes a chapter to Scotus's ideas on relations. He concludes that Duns Scotus's realist doctrine of relations set the context for future debate on the issue.[55]

It is precisely on this note that the influence of the Radical Orthodoxy movement has undermined the valuable contributions of Duns Scotus to a renewed catholicity. According to John Milbank and proponents of the "Scotus Story," the univocity of being annihilates the differences between God and the world, leading to a "flattened" relationship. The result is, "ontotheological idolatry regarding God, and the placing of God within a predefined arena of being."[56] Dan Horan, in his book *Postmodernity and*

Univocity, illumines the distortions of the "Scotus Story" constructed by
Milbank and the Radical Orthodoxy movement. He examines their arguments
based on Étienne Gilson's study of Scotus, in which the doctrine of univocity
is conflated with metaphysics.[57] Gilson made the unfortunate error of confusing God and creatures in the same genus of being. This misinterpretation led
to the claim by adherents of Radical Orthodoxy that Scotus collapsed divinity
into materiality, creating the conditions for secular modernity. According to
Horan, the Scotus Story lacks a foundation in the writings of Scotus himself.
He examines univocity through the primary texts of Scotus and shows how
univocity functioned as a semantic and conceptual idea, not a metaphysical
one.[58] While Scotus sought to dispel Neoplatonic notions of being, indicating that concrete reality holds religious meaning, Whitehead focused on the
way modern science was renewing a sense of deep relationality at the heart
of physical reality. Reality is not devoid of purpose; matter is not inert and
cannot be reduced to parts. Both Scotus and Whitehead show that the world
of experience is relational wholeness. One can know reality in a way open to
beauty, communion, and love.

CONCLUSION

Scotus and Whitehead illuminate a philosophical and theological breadth
of catholicity. Scotus developed a metaphysics of being and Whitehead
described dynamic relationships of creative societies. For both, matter bears
the weight of love, that is, a deep interrelated divine presence that cannot
be reduced to either matter or mind alone. Being is dynamic and creative;
it is relational and contingent and thus open to unity, truth, and goodness
in an absolute way. For Scotus and Whitehead, being is eternally creative
because divine freedom lies at the heart of all that exists. Love is the principal form of beauty and the harmony of all that exists. We are created for
love.

If the Catholic Church seeks to understand catholicity in a world of modern
science, then it is time to retrieve Scotus from exile and embrace the ideas
of Whitehead and process thinkers. A metaphysics of relationships and an
ontology of love can allow the church to engage modern science amid the
pluralities of a complex world, a world of change. Science, like religion,
bears witness to a living God who is dynamically present and engaged in
reality, a never-ending being-in-love, present in a world oriented toward the
harmony of beauty. In the words of Teilhard de Chardin, "Only love can
bring individual beings to their perfect completion . . . by uniting them one
with another, because only loves takes possession of them and unites them by
what lies deepest within them."[59]

NOTES

1. Rémi Brague, *The Wisdom of the World: The Human Experience of the Universe in Western Thought* (Chicago: University of Chicago Press, 2004), 19–20.

2. John C. Haughey, S. J., *Where is Knowing Going? The Horizons of the Knowing Subject* (Washington, DC: Georgetown University Press, 2010), 40.

3. Ibid., 42.

4. Paul M. Allen and Joan de Ris Allen, *Francis of Assisi's Canticle of the Creatures: A Modern Spiritual Path* (New York: Continuum, 1996), 45.

5. Jeremiah Hackett, "Duns Scotus: A Brief Introduction to his Life and Thought," *Studies in Scottish Literature* 261 (1991): 442.

6. For a good introduction to Scotus's life and works, see Mary Beth Ingham, *Scotus for Dunces: An Introduction to the Subtle Doctor* (St. Bonaventure, NY: Franciscan Institute, 2003), 13–35.

7. Mary Beth Ingham and Mechtild Dreyer, *The Philosophical Vision of John Duns Scotus: An Introduction* (Washington, DC: The Catholic University of America Press, 2004), 202.

8. See Dan P. Horan, O. F. M., *Postmodernity and Univocity: A Critical Account of Radical Orthodoxy and John Duns Scotus* (Minneapolis, MN: Fortress Press, 2014), 163–68. According to Horan, Henry of Ghent was the main interlocutor for Duns Scotus. See also, *Encyclopedia Britannica*, s. v. "Henry of Ghent," accessed June 25, 2020. https://www.britannica.com/biography/Henry-of-Ghent.

9. Richard Cross writes, "The medievals were far more sensitive than Aristotle was to the idea that physical reality should ultimately admit of mathematical description." He continues by saying that some features of material substance for Scotus would probably classify as part of mathematics. See Richard Cross, *The Physics of Duns Scotus: The Scientific Context of a Theological Vision* (Oxford: Oxford University Press, 1999), 3.

10. Ingham and Dreyer, *Philosophical Vision of John Duns Scotus,* 205.

11. Ibid.

12. Ibid., 206.

13. John K. Ryan and Bernardine M. Bonasea, eds., *John Duns Scotus: 1265–1965* (Washington, DC: The Catholic University Press, 1965); John Duns Scotus, *The De Primo Principio of John Duns Scotus: A Revised Text and Translation*, ed. Evan Roche (New York: Franciscan Institute, 1949), 687–88.

14. Ingham and Dreyer, *Philosophical Vision of John Duns Scotus,* 206.

15. Richard Cross, *Duns Scotus,* 39.

16. Thomas Williams, "John Duns Scotus," in *The Stanford Encyclopedia of Philosophy*, Winter 2019 ed., ed. Edward N. Zalta (Stanford University Center for the Study of Language and Information, 2019). https://plato.stanford.edu/archives/win2019/entries/duns-scotus/.

17. Richard Cross, "Duns Scotus, Univocity, and 'Participatory Metaphysics': Horan and the Metaphysical Consequences of Univocity," *Syndicate* (online symposium), December 11, 2017, https://syndicate.network/symposia/theology/postmodernity-and-univocity/.

18. Ingham and Dreyer, *Philosophical Vision of John Duns Scotus*, 211.

19. Ibid., 23.

20. Ibid., 24.

21. Richard Cross, "Duns Scotus's Anti-Reductionistic Account of Material Substances," *Vivarium* 332 (1995): 137–70.

22. Daniel P. Horan, O. F. M., "Beyond Essentialism and Complementarity: Toward a Theological Anthropology Rooted in *Haecceitas*," *Theological Studies* 75.1 (2014): 109. For an in-depth discussion on the development and use of the term *haecceitas*, see Robert Andrews, "Haecceity in the Metaphysics of John Duns Scotus," in *Johannes Duns Scotus 1308–2008: Die philosophischen Perspektiven seines Werkes*, ed. Ludger Honnefelder, Theo Kobusch, Hannes Möhle, and Andreas Speer (Münster: Aschendorff, 2010), 151–62.

23. Ingham and Dreyer, *Philosophical Vision of John Duns Scotus*, 113; Timothy Noone, "Universals and Individuation," in *The Cambridge Companion to Duns Scotus*, ed. Thomas Williams (New York: Cambridge University, 2003), 100–28.

24. Allan B. Wolter, "John Duns Scotus (b. ca. 1265; d. 1308)," in *Individuation in Scholasticism: The Later Middle Ages and the Counter-Reformation 1150–1650*, ed. Jorge J. E. Garcia (New York: SUNY Press, 1994), 290; Ingham, *Scotus for Dunces,* 163.

25. Allan B. Wolter, O. F. M., "Scotus's Individuation Theory," in *The Philosophical Theology of John Duns Scotus*, ed. Marilyn McCord Adams (Ithaca, NY: Cornell University Press, 1990), 110.

26. Horan, "Beyond Essentialism and Complementarity," 112.

27. Hackett, "Duns Scotus: A Brief Introduction to his Life and Thought," 439.

28. Karen Barad, "Posthuman Performativity: Toward an Understanding of How Matter Comes to Matter," *Journal of Women in Culture and Society* 283 (2003): 815.

29. John Duns Scotus, *Lectura* 1 30. 1–2, §72, cited in Cal Ledsham, "Love, Power and Consistency: Scotus's Doctrines of God's Power, Contingent Creation, Induction and Natural Law," *Sophia* 494 (2010): 562.

30. Peter Leithart, "Causality and Pure Nature," *Patheos* (blog), October 16, 2010, https://www.patheos.com/blogs/leithart/2010/10/causality-and-pure-nature/.

31. Ibid.

32. Ibid.

33. Mary Beth Ingham, "John Duns Scotus: Retrieving a Medieval Thinker for Contemporary Theology," in *Custodians of the Tradition: Reclaiming the Franciscan Intellectual Tradition,* ed. Kathleen Moffatt (Aston, PA: Valley Press, 2016), 1–4.

34. John Duns Scotus, *De primo principio* 3.21, in *John Duns Scotus: A Treatise on God as First Principle*, ed. and trans. Allan B. Wolter, O. F. M. (Chicago: Franciscan Herald Press, 1966), 52.

35. Kenan B. Osborne, "Incarnation, Individuality and Diversity," *The Cord* 45.3 (1995): 22; John Duns Scotus, *A Treatise on God as First Principle*, xvii.

36. Mary Beth Ingham, *The Harmony of Goodness: Mutuality and Moral Living According to John Duns Scotus* (Quincy, IL: Franciscan Press, 1996), 19; Cross, *Duns Scotus*, 113–32.

37. Mary Beth Ingham, "Duns Scotus, Divine Delight and Franciscan Evangelical Life," *Franciscan Studies* 64 (2006): 344.

38. Ingham and Dreyer, *Philosophical Vision of Duns Scotus,* 208.

39. Ingham, *Harmony of Goodness*, 25–40; idem, *Scotus for Dunces,* 88.

40. Alfred North Whitehead, *Science and the Modern World* (1926; repr., New York: Free Press, 1967), 174 (hereafter "*SMW*").

41. Ingham, *Scotus for Dunces*, 57–58.

42. Joseph A. Bracken, "Creativity and the Extensive Continuum as the Ultimate Ground in Alfred North Whitehead's Philosophy of Becoming," *Ultimate Reality and Meaning* 16.1–2 (1993): 110–19.

43. Andrew Davis, "God Was in Christ: Whitehead and Process Christology," *Academia.edu*, January 3, 2021, https://www.academia.edu/31885334/God_Was_in_Christ_Whitehead_and_Process_Christology.

44. Alfred North Whitehead, *Process and Reality: An Essay in Cosmology* (1929), corrected ed., ed. David Ray Griffin and Donald W. Sherburne (New York: Free Press, 1978), 343.

45. Ibid., 345.

46. Ibid.

47. Ibid.

48. Marjorie Hewitt Suchocki, *In God's Presence: Theological Reflections on Prayer* (St. Louis: Chalice Press, 1996), 18–19; Alfred North Whitehead, *Adventures of Ideas* (1933; repr., New York: Free Press, 1967), 170.

49. Ibid.

50. Ingham, *Scotus for Dunces,* 116, 118.

51. *SMW* 70.

52. Peter Leithart, "Causality and Pure Nature."

53. John F. Boler, *Charles Peirce and Scholastic Realism: A Study of Peirce's Relation to John Duns Scotus* (Seattle, WA: University of Washington Press, 1963).

54. Martin Heidegger's *Habilitationsschrift* on Duns Scotus was entitled *The Doctrine of the Categories and the Teaching of Meaning in Duns Scotus*. See Martin Heidegger, "*Die Kategorien-und Bedeutungslehre des Duns Scotus*," in *Frühe Schriften*, ed. Friedrich-Wilhelm von Herrmann (Frankfurt am Main: Vittorio Klostermann, 1978), 189–412.

55. Mark Henninger, *Relations: Medieval Theories 1250–1325* (London: Oxford University Press, 1989).

56. John Milbank, *Theology and Social Theory: Beyond Secular Reason* (Oxford: Blackwell, 2006), 4.

57. Étienne Gilson, *John Duns Scotus: Introduction to His Fundamental Positions*, trans. James Colbert (Edinburgh: T & T Clark, 2020).

58. This is the principal thesis of Horan's book *Postmodernity and Univocity* in which Horan shows that Scotus did not collapse God and creatures into the same genus, as Radical Orthodoxy theologians claim, but invoked the principle of univocity to support linguistic and conceptual knowledge of God. See Horan, *Postmodernity and Univocity*, 157–88. For an interesting and lively discussion on Horan's critique of the "Scotus Story," see the online symposium led by Justin Coyle, including an apologetic by John Milbank, Dan Horan, "Postmodernity and Univocity," *Syndicate*

(online symposium), December 4, 2017, https://syndicate.network/symposia/theology/postmodernity-and-univocity/.

59. Pierre Teilhard de Chardin, *Hymn of the Universe,* trans. Simon Bartholomew (New York: Harper & Row, 1965), 145.

BIBLIOGRAPHY

Allen, Paul M., and Joan deRis Allen. *Francis of Assisi's Canticle of the Creatures: A Modern Spiritual Path.* New York: Continuum, 1996.

Andrews, Robert. "Haecceity in the Metaphysics of John Duns Scotus." In *Johannes Duns Scotus 1308–2008: Die philosophischen Perspektiven seines Werkes,* edited by Ludger Honnefelder, Theo Kobusch, Hannes Möhle, and Andreas Speer, 151–62. Münster: Aschendorff, 2010.

Bonasea, Bernardine M., and John K. Ryan, eds. *John Duns Scotus: 1265–1965.* Washington, DC: The Catholic University Press, 1965.

Brague, Rémi. *The Wisdom of the World: The Human Experience of the Universe in Western Thought.* Chicago: University of Chicago Press, 2004.

Barad, Karen. "Posthuman Performativity: Toward an Understanding of How Matter Comes to Matter." *Journal of Women in Culture and Society* 28.3 (2003): 801–31.

Boler, John F. *Charles Peirce and Scholastic Realism: A Study of Peirce's Relation to John Duns Scotus.* Seattle, WA: University of Washington Press, 1963.

Bracken, Joseph A. "Creativity and the Extensive Continuum as the Ultimate Ground in Alfred North Whitehead's Philosophy of Becoming." *Ultimate Reality and Meaning* 16.1–2 (1993): 110–19.

Britannica, T. Editors of Encyclopaedia. "Henry of Ghent." In *Encyclopedia Britannica.* https://www.britannica.com/biography/Henry-of-Ghent.

Cross, Richard. "Duns Scotus's Anti-Reductionistic Account of Material Substances." *Vivarium* 332 (1995): 137–70.

Cross, Richard. "Duns Scotus, Univocity, and 'Participatory Metaphysics': Horan and the Metaphysical Consequences of Univocity." *Syndicate* (online symposium). December 11, 2017. https://syndicate.network/symposia/theology/postmodernity-and-univocity/.

Cross, Richard. *The Physics of Duns Scotus: The Scientific Context of a Theological Vision.* Oxford: Oxford University Press, 1999.

Davis, Andrew. "God Was in Christ: Whitehead and Process Christology." Academia.edu. January 3, 2021. https://www.academia.edu/31885334/God_Was_in_Christ_Whitehead_and_Process_Christology.

Dreyer, Mechtild, and Mary Beth Ingham. *The Philosophical Vision of John Duns Scotus: An Introduction.* Washington, DC: The Catholic University of America Press, 2004.

Duns Scotus, John. *The De Primo Principio of John Duns Scotus: A Revised Text and Translation,* edited by Evan Roche. New York: Franciscan Institute, 1949.

Gilson, Étienne. *John Duns Scotus: Introduction to his Fundamental Positions.* Translated by James Colbert. Edinburgh: T & T Clark, 2020.

Hackett, Jeremiah. "Duns Scotus: A Brief Introduction to his Life and Thought." *Studies in Scottish Literature* 261 (1991): 438–47.

Haughey, John C., S. J. *Where is Knowing Going? The Horizons of the Knowing Subject.* Washington, DC: Georgetown University Press, 2010.

Heidegger, Martin. *"Die Kategorien-und Bedeutungslehre des Duns Scotus."* In *Frühe Schriften*, edited by Friedrich-Wilhelm von Herrmann, 189–412. Frankfurt am Main: Vittorio Klostermann, 1978.

Henninger, Mark. *Relations: Medieval Theories 1250–1325*. London: Oxford University Press, 1989.

Horan, Daniel P., O. F. M. "Beyond Essentialism and Complementarity: Toward a Theological Anthropology Rooted in *Haecceitas.*" *Theological Studies* 75.1 (2014): 94–177.

Horan, Daniel P., O. F. M. "Postmodernity and Univocity." *Syndicate* (online symposium). December 4, 2017. https://syndicate.network/symposia/theology/postmodernity-and-univocity/.

Horan, Daniel P., O. F. M. *Postmodernity and Univocity: A Critical Account of Radical Orthodoxy and John Duns Scotus.* Minneapolis, MN: Fortress Press, 2014.

Ingham, Mary Beth. "Duns Scotus, Divine Delight and Franciscan Evangelical Life." *Franciscan Studies* 64 (2006): 337–62.

Ingham, Mary Beth. *The Harmony of Goodness: Mutuality and Moral Living According to John Duns Scotus.* Quincy, IL: Franciscan Press, 1996.

Ingham, Mary Beth. "John Duns Scotus: Retrieving a Medieval Thinker for Contemporary Theology." In *Custodians of the Tradition: Reclaiming the Franciscan Intellectual Tradition,* edited by Kathleen Moffatt, 1–4. Aston, PA: Valley Press, 2016.

Ingham, Mary Beth. *Scotus for Dunces: An Introduction to the Subtle Doctor.* St. Bonaventure, NY: Franciscan Institute, 2003.

Ledsham, Cal. "Love, Power and Consistency: Scotus's Doctrines of God's Power, Contingent Creation, Induction and Natural Law." *Sophia* 494 (2010): 552–75.

Leithart, Peter. "Causality and Pure Nature." *Patheos* (blog), October 16, 2010. https://www.patheos.com/blogs/leithart/2010/10/causality-and-pure-nature/.

Milbank, John. *Theology and Social Theory: Beyond Secular Reason.* Oxford: Blackwell, 2006.

Noone, Timothy. "Universals and Individuation." In *The Cambridge Companion to Duns Scotus*, edited by Thomas Williams, 100–28. New York: Cambridge University, 2003.

Osborne, Kenan B. "Incarnation, Individuality and Diversity." *The Cord* 45.3 (1995): 19–26.

Scotus, John Duns. *A Treatise on God as First Principle.* Edited and Translated by Allan B. Wolter, O. F. M. Chicago: Franciscan Herald Press, 1966.

Suchocki, Marjorie Hewitt. *In God's Presence: Theological Reflections on Prayer.* St. Louis: Chalice Press, 1996.

Teilhard de Chardin, Pierre. *Hymn of the Universe.* Translated by Simon Bartholomew. New York: Harper & Row, 1965.

Whitehead, Alfred North. *Adventures of Ideas*. 1933. Reprint, New York: The Free Press, 1967.

Whitehead, Alfred North. *Process and Reality: An Essay in Cosmology*. 1929. Corrected ed. Edited by David Ray Griffin and Donald W. Sherburne. New York: Free Press, 1978.

Whitehead, Alfred North. *Science and the Modern World*. 1926. Reprint, New York: Free Press, 1967.

Williams, Thomas. "John Duns Scotus." *The Stanford Encyclopedia of Philosophy*, Winter 2019. Editor Edward N. Zalta. https://plato.stanford.edu/archives/win2019/entries/duns-scotus/.

Wolter, Allan B., O. F. M. "John Duns Scotus (b. ca. 1265; d. 1308)." In *Individuation in Scholasticism: The Later Middle Ages and the Counter-Reformation 1150–1650*, edited by Jorge J. E. Garcia, 271–98. New York: SUNY Press, 1994.

Wolter, Allan B., O. F. M. "Scotus's Individuation Theory." In *The Philosophical Theology of John Duns Scotus*, edited by Marilyn McCord Adams, 68–97. Ithaca, NY: Cornell University Press, 1990.

Chapter 4

Charles Hartshorne and the Catholic Intellectual Tradition

Daniel A. Dombrowski

In the present chapter, I will be examining the relationship between one of the greatest process thinkers, Charles Hartshorne (1897–2000), and the Catholic intellectual tradition. In section I, I will deal with this relationship in general terms so as to set the stage for the core of the chapter in section II, where I will argue in favor of Hartshorne's dipolar, neoclassical concept of God, in contrast to the monopolar, classical concept of God found in many or most Catholic philosophers and theologians. In section III, I will very briefly treat a possible future avenue for interaction between process thinkers and Catholicism.

I

In some of his earlier publications, Hartshorne exhibited an antipathy to Roman Catholicism that is reminiscent of the tensions between Protestants and Roman Catholics that go back to the early modern period. Despite the fact that he grew up in a very liberal religious household, with his father an Episcopal minister and with Quaker ancestors, he absorbed some negative stereotypes about Catholicism that were unfortunately somewhat correct regarding Catholicism in the early decades of the twentieth century. He complained about the "gigantic hoax of priestcraft"[1] and the difficulty Catholics have in avoiding papal decrees, which cultivate a sort of obeisance to authority.[2] However, he detected in Catholics something that he would later come to admire, the veneration (Hartshorne says "worship") of Mary, which, although problematic, nonetheless points toward a genuinely social concept of God in contrast to the Thomistic Unmoved Mover.[3]

Hartshorne also notes the negative political implications of Thomistic belief in a God who is Pure Act and immune from all creaturely influence. This encourages imperious tyrants, he thinks, such that Hitler's Catholic origins are not accidental. Ontolatry is conducive to state-olatry. However, Hartshorne also notes that neither Protestants nor Catholics did a good job of saving Germany from Hitler's devastation.[4] Despite enormous differences between Protestant fundamentalists and Catholics in other areas, the latter are like the former regarding the supposed infallibility of revelation, in contrast to Hartshorne's own belief that religious experience, real as it is, should always be treated as fallible and as open to criticism.[5]

Early in his career, Hartshorne doubted if any Roman Catholics would be persuaded by his ideas and this because, although there was disagreement among Protestants between "conservatives" and "liberals," he could find no such disagreement among Catholics.[6] However and herein lies a point of transition to Hartshorne's later, more favorable view of Roman Catholicism, *both* Roman Catholics and Protestants were firmly in the grip of a dangerous version of classical theism.[7] The important thing moving forward is that, despite Hartshorne's theocentrism, which is reminiscent of the God-centered approach of medieval philosophers, there can be no simple return to medieval assumptions about the concept of God.[8]

Hartshorne came to see that his neoclassical theism *did* have a positive effect on certain Catholic thinkers, even if they were officially opposed by the church.[9] He continued to think that what is amazing is not the breakdown of the medieval synthesis, but that this synthesis lasted as long as it did. The problem is that Augustine and other medieval thinkers in many ways combined the worst in the ancient and biblical traditions in the development of what Hartshorne calls classical theism. He found solace in the realization that some Catholic thinkers (e.g., a French monk named Lucien Laberthonnière) saw things in a similar way.[10]

Some crucial passages for the topic of the present chapter are to be found in Hartshorne's 1948 classic *The Divine Relativity*. Here he acknowledges that, despite his sometimes polemical tone regarding classical theism, he is indebted to Thomas Aquinas almost as much as he is to Alfred North Whitehead! This remarkable claim is perhaps made more intelligible when it is realized that gratitude is not to be measured by complete agreement. In memorable imagery, Hartshorne tells us that, although Aquinas developed a concept of God that was shipwrecked on the rocks of contradiction, he left us with an admirable, indeed an unparalleled, chart of where the rocks are. That is, it is not obvious that numerous analytic philosophers who today are classical theists really help us to navigate our way through philosophical problems like theodicy, divine omniscience and human freedom, and so on, better than Aquinas.[11] The problem is that the magnificent technical virtues found in the justification of Aquinas's theorems were not in play regarding his fundamental axioms, which are simply assumed, as in the idea that change is inferior to permanence.[12]

Although Hartshorne criticizes Thomas's doctrine that God has no internal relations with creatures, he is quite favorable regarding Thomas's doctrine of analogy.[13] Hartshorne's concern is that Thomas's own concept of God violates his doctrine of analogy such that Hartshorne's neoclassical theism can be seen as an attempt to think through more carefully than Thomas himself did the Thomistic doctrine of analogy regarding discourse about God. This makes Hartshorne something of an anti-Thomistic Thomist.[14]

The Protestant Reformation was, according to Hartshorne, a colossal failure regarding the effort to develop a more defensible concept of God. Leibniz's effort, for example, to reconcile Protestants and Catholics was hampered by the classical theism that hobbled both traditions. Although most Catholic thinkers, along with most Protestant thinkers, are classical theists, the former have the advantage, Hartshorne thinks, of a tradition that preserves the *aesthetic* appeal of worship, an appeal that provides a lure toward a better concept of the greatest being.[15] Hartshorne also admires Catholic thinkers who are very often well-trained in the history of philosophy and theology and who are, as a result of Pope John XXIII, freed up to relax their classical theistic assumptions. In fact, Hartshorne wished that Protestants and religious skeptics would do the same by abandoning the assumption that classical theism just *is* theism.[16] Further, he thought that Catholics, Protestants, and Muslim thinkers would all be well served if they took more seriously the attitude toward death typically found in Jewish thinkers.[17]

We will see that Hartshorne is more like Thomas Aquinas than he is like an analytic philosopher like William Alston in believing that divine attributes like potentiality, contingency, change, and temporality go together such that if one of these is attributed to God, they all must be attributed.[18] Further, belief in a deity who changes, say in response to creaturely suffering, fosters a more humane politics than that found historically among classical theists, in general. In this regard, Hartshorne commends the American Catholic bishops for their stand taken against the buildup of nuclear weapons in the 1980s.[19]

An example of the sort of theism Hartshorne defends can be found in the Jesuit thinker Pierre Teilhard de Chardin, whose conclusions are close to Hartshorne's own, even if their methods are quite different. The attempt to resist the historical hegemony of being over becoming is one of the things about Teilhard's thought that appeals to Hartshorne, along with the emphasis on creaturely freedom instead of divine fiat, the realization that chance plays a crucial role in evolutionary history, and the critique of unqualified divine immutability.[20] However, Hartshorne is not convinced by Teilhard's concept of what amounts to a group mind.[21] James Ross is another Catholic thinker who took process thought seriously, even if he was not as process oriented as Teilhard.[22] Hartshorne welcomed the various positive approaches to the concept of God in contemporary Catholic philosophy and theology and regretted that he was not able to make a speaking engagement to which he was invited at a Trappist monastery.[23]

Early in life, Hartshorne came into contact with very few Catholics; an exception was a pious nurse named Lillie.[24] But later in life he met and frequently communicated with several Catholic thinkers—for example, Fr. Meehan, Ferdinand Bergenthal, Albert Menne, and James Devlin—and engaged in book review exchanges with several other great scholars—for example, James Collins, Joseph Rickaby, and Étienne Gilson.[25] Hartshorne himself reviewed Karol Wojtyla's book *The Acting Person*.[26] In this review, Hartshorne commends Wojtyla's attempt to appropriate Aristotle for the purposes of contemporary philosophy, but he is not convinced that Scheler-like phenomenology is the only or best way to do this. Further, Hartshorne is not convinced by Wojtyla's claim that nature apart from the human person is completely determined.

James Felt and W. Norris Clarke, both Jesuits, show us how paying careful processual attention to Aristotelian concepts like *dynamis* and *kinesis* can be most fruitful.[27] Because of frequent criticisms by process thinkers of the subject–predicate logic of Aristotle, based as it is on a metaphysics centered on the substance–accident distinction, some might conclude that process metaphysics is completely removed from Aristotle and from those Catholics Aristotle influenced from the time of Thomas Aquinas until the present. But the situation is more complicated than it might seem initially.[28] Process-enriched Thomists like Felt and Clarke try to rescue Aristotle and Thomas from the charge that there is insufficient dynamism in metaphysics, with process thought providing the inspiration for their efforts. In the Aristotelian-Thomistic tradition, on their interpretation, matter is not the vacuous actuality, it is in Descartes in that it is always informed. Or again, the whole point to Aristotelian-Thomistic hylomorphism is to suggest that matter without form and form without matter are the results of abstraction in that concrete reality is populated by "formbodies" or "mindbodies" or "soulbodies," to coin terms that try to capture the non-dualistic character of hylomorphs. The Aristotelian idea that mind is, in a manner, all things is a protest against the view that mind is what is left over when one abstracts away from either behavior or matter; rather, matter in motion just *is* mind in some fashion.[29]

Process thought is "medieval" in the sense that Scholastic thinkers often distinguished (albeit inconsistently) between the categories, which were concepts that were applicable to all creatures but not to God, and the transcendentals, which were concepts that were applicable to all beings, including God. It is often noticed that among the transcendentals were oneness, goodness, truth, and beauty. In addition, there was *power*, the ability to influence others, and, in process thinking, the ability to be influenced. The dynamic power to receive influence from others, as well as the dynamic power to creatively advance beyond such influence (in that there are never sufficient causal conditions from the past to determine completely concrete actuality in the present, although there are necessary conditions of some sort), is a transcendental.[30]

In short, Hartshorne thinks of himself as part of a general move on the part of Abrahamic (and some Eastern) thinkers to extricate themselves from theoretical follies.[31] The fact that members of every religious denomination, including Roman Catholicism, have found encouragement in his work ironically both pleases and troubles him. Hartshorne's worry is the same as Whitehead's that, because religion for so long has been a synonym for hatred, it is not clear that a significant number of dedicated thinkers will continue to take the concept of God seriously enough to try to improve it.[32]

II

The purpose of this section is both to examine the classical theism that informs most Catholic philosophers and theologians and to argue for the advantages of Hartshorne's process or neoclassical concept of God that might appeal to many more Catholic thinkers once they become familiar with it. I would like to make it clear that by "classical theism" Hartshorne refers to a view of God in philosophy and theology, not to scriptural theism. (It is an interesting question, and an open one, whether classical theism or neoclassical theism does a better job of preserving the best insights regarding the concept of God in the Bible.) The classical theistic view that characterizes many or most Catholic thinkers (most thinkers in Christianity, in general, as well as most Jewish and Muslim thinkers) involves at least the following five features:

1. Omnipotence (including the related claim that God created the world out of absolute nothingness).
2. Omniscience (in the sense of God knowing, with absolute assurance and in minute detail, everything that will happen in the future).
3. Omnibenevolence.
4. Eternity (in the sense not of God existing everlastingly throughout all of time, but rather of God existing outside of time altogether).
5. Monopolarity (to be described momentarily).

It will be to our advantage to be as clear as we can on what we mean by the term "God."[33] In this effort, we will be able to see more clearly the strengths and weaknesses of the classical theistic view. I will use the term "God" to refer to the supremely excellent or all-worshipful being. A debt to Anselm is evident in this preliminary definition. It closely resembles Anselm's "that than which no greater can be conceived." In this regard, it should be noted that Hartshorne was responsible for the revitalization of Anselm's ontological argument in the mid-decades of the twentieth century by discovering the modal version of the argument in *Proslogion*, chapter 3, and by offering a formal version of the argument that influenced many other theists, including Norman Malcolm and Alvin Plantinga.[34]

However, the ontological argument is not what is at stake here. Even if the argument fails (which I doubt), the preliminary definition of God as the supremely excellent being, the all-worshipful being, or the greatest conceivable being seems unobjectionable. To say that God can be defined in these ways still leaves open the possibility that God is even more excellent or worshipful than our ability to conceive. This allows us to avoid objections from those in mystical theology who might fear that by defining God we might be limiting God to "merely" human language. I am simply suggesting that when we think of God we must be thinking of a being who surpasses all others or else we are not thinking of God. Even the atheist or agnostic would admit this much. When the atheist says, "There is no God," there is a denial that a supremely excellent, all-worshipful, greatest conceivable being exists.

The excellent–inferior contrast is the truly invidious contrast when applied to God. If to be invidious is to be injurious, then this contrast is the most invidious one of all when both terms are applied to God, because God is only excellent. God is inferior in no way. Period. To suggest that God is in some small way inferior to some other being is no longer to speak about God, but about some being that is not supremely excellent, all-worshipful, or the greatest conceivable. The neoclassical or process theist's major criticism of classical theism is that it assumes that all contrasts, or most of them, when applied to God are at least somewhat invidious.

Let us assume that God exists. What attributes does God possess? Consider the following two columns of attributes in polar contrast to each other:

One	Many
being	becoming
activity	passivity
permanence	change
necessity	contingency
self-sufficient	dependent
actual	potential
absolute	relative
abstract	concrete

Classical theism tends toward oversimplification. It is comparatively easy to say "God is strong rather than weak, so in all relations God is active, not passive." In each case, the classical theist decides which member of the contrasting pair is good (on the left), then attributes it to God, while wholly denying the contrasting term (on the right). Hence, God is one but not many, permanent but not changing, and so on. This leads to what can be called the monopolar prejudice. Monopolarity is common to both classical theism and pantheism, with the major difference between the two being the fact that classical theism admits the reality of plurality, potentiality, and becoming as a secondary form of existence "outside" God (on the right), whereas in pantheism God includes all reality within itself. Common to both classical theism and pantheism is the belief that the categorical contrasts listed previously are invidious. The dilemma these two positions face is that either deity is only one constituent of the whole (classical theism) or else that the alleged inferior pole in each contrast (on the right) is illusory (pantheism).

However, this dilemma is artificial. It is produced by the assumption that excellence is found by separating and purifying one pole (on the left) and denigrating the other (on the right). That this is not the case can be seen by analyzing some of the attributes in the right-hand column. Classical theists have been convinced that God's eternity means not that God endures through all time everlastingly, but that God is outside of time altogether, and is not, cannot, be receptive to temporal change and creaturely feelings. Thomas Aquinas (following Aristotle, who was the greatest predecessor to classical theism) identified God as unmoved. Yet both activity and passivity can be either good or bad. Good passivity is likely to be called sensitivity, responsiveness, adaptability, sympathy, and the like. Insufficiently subtle or defective passivity is called wooden inflexibility, mulish stubbornness, inadaptability, unresponsiveness, and the like. Passivity per se refers to the way in which an individual's activity takes account of, and renders itself appropriate to, the activities of others. To deny God passivity altogether is to deny God those aspects of passivity that are excellences. Or, put another way, to altogether deny God the ability to change does avoid fickleness, but at the expense of the ability to lovingly react to the sufferings of others, a reaction that is central to the testimony of the great theistic mystics.

The terms on the left side also have both good and bad aspects. Oneness can mean wholeness, but it also can mean monotony or triviality. Actuality can mean definiteness, or it can mean non-relatedness to others. What happens to divine love when God is claimed by Thomas to be *pure* actuality? God ends up loving the world, but is not intrinsically related to it, whatever sort of love that may be. Self-sufficiency can, at times, be selfishness.

The task when thinking of God is to attribute to God all excellences (left and right sides together) and not to attribute to God any inferiorities (right and left sides). In short, excellent–inferior, knowledge–ignorance, or good–evil are invidious contrasts, but One–Many, being–becoming, and the like are non-invidious contrasts. Evil is not a category and hence it cannot be attributed to God. It is not a category because it is not universal, and it is not universal because animals cannot commit it, even if they can be its victims. That is, both animals and God can feel evil, but they cannot commit it, God because of the supreme goodness in the divine nature and animals because of their ignorance of moral principles.

Within each pole of a non-invidious contrast (e.g., permanence–change), there are invidious or injurious elements (inferior permanence or inferior change) but also non-invidious, good elements (excellent permanence or excellent change). The dipolar, process theist does not believe in two gods, one unified and the other plural. Rather, there is a belief that what are often thought to be contradictories or contraries are really mutually interdependent correlatives. The good is unity-in-variety or variety-in-unity. Too much variety leads to chaos or discord, whereas too much unity leads to monotony or triviality.

Supreme excellence, to be truly so, must somehow be able to integrate all the complexity there is in the world into itself as one spiritual whole. The word "must" indicates divine necessity, along with God's essence, which is to necessarily exist. The word "complexity" refers to the diverse influences that affect God through creaturely decisions. In the classical theistic view, however, God is identified solely with the stony immobility of the absolute, implying non-relatedness to the world. God's abstract nature, God's Being, may in a way escape from the temporal flux, but a living God is related to the world of becoming, which entails a divine becoming as well, if the world in some way is internally related to God.

The classical theist's alternative to this view suggests that all relationships to God are external to divinity, once again threatening not only God's love but also God's nobility. A dog's being behind a particular rock affects the dog in certain ways, and thus this relation is an internal relation to the dog, but it does not affect the rock, whose relationship with the dog is external to the rock's nature. Does this not show the superiority of canine consciousness, which is aware of the rock, to rock-like existence, which is unaware of the dog? Is it not therefore peculiar that God has been described by many Catholic thinkers influenced by Thomas solely in rock-like terms: pure actuality, permanence, having only external relations, unmoved, being and not becoming?

One may wonder at this point why classical theism has been so popular among Catholic and other Abrahamic thinkers when it has so many defects. One can imagine at least four reasons, none of which establish the case for classical, monopolar theism:

(1) It is easier to accept monopolarity than dipolarity. That is, it is simpler to accept one and reject the other of contrasting (or better, correlative, non-invidious) categories than to show how each, in its own appropriate fashion, applies to an aspect of the divine nature. Yet the simplicity of calling God "the absolute" can come back to haunt the classical theist if absoluteness precludes relativity in the sense of internal relatedness to the world, including relations with those who enter into mystical union with God.

(2) If the decision to accept monopolarity has been made, it is simpler to identify God as the absolute than to identify God as the most relative. Yet this does not deny divine relatedness, nor that God, who loves all, would therefore have to be related to all, or to use a roughly synonymous term, be "relative" to all. God may well be the most relative of all as well as the most absolute of all, in the senses that, and to the extent that, both of these are excellences. Of course, God is absolute and relative in different aspects of the divine nature.

(3) There are emotional considerations favoring divine permanence, as found in the longing to escape the risks and uncertainties of life. Yet even if these considerations obtain, they should not blind us to other emotional considerations, like those that give us the solace that comes from knowing that the outcome of our sufferings and volitions makes a difference in the divine life, which, if it is all-loving, will certainly not be unmoved by the suffering of creatures.

(4) Monopolarity is seen as more easily made compatible with monotheism. Yet the innocent monotheistic contrast between the One and the Many deals with God as an individual, not with the dogmatic claim that the divine individual cannot have parts or aspects of relatedness with the world.

In short, the Divine Being becomes or the divine becoming is. God's being and becoming form a single reality and there is no reason to leave the two poles in a paradoxical state: God *always changes* and both words are crucial. There is no logical contradiction in attributing contrasting predicates to the same individual provided they apply to different aspects of this individual. Hence, the remedy for "ontolatry," the classical theistic worship of being, is not the contrary pole, "gignolatry," the worship of becoming. God's *existence* is everlastingly permanent, but God's *actuality* (how God exists concretely from moment to moment) is constantly changing.

The Hartshornian theism I am defending and which I am recommending to other Catholic thinkers is (1) *dipolar* because excellences can be found on both sides of contrasting categories (i.e., they are correlative and non-invidious); (2) a *neoclassical* theism because it relies on the belief that classical theists (especially Anselm) were on the correct track when they described God as the supremely excellent, all-worshipful, greatest conceivable being, but classical theists (including Anselm) do an insufficient job of thinking through the logic of perfection; (3) a *process* theism because it sees the need for God to become in order for God to be called perfect, but not at the expense of God's always (i.e., permanently) being greater than all others; and (4) a theism that can be called *panentheism*, which literally means "all in God." God is neither completely removed from the world—that is, unmoved by it—as in classical theism, nor completely identified with the world, as in pantheism. Rather, God is (1) world-inclusive, in the sense that God cares for all the world and knows everything in the world that is knowable, and all feelings in the world—especially suffering feelings—are felt by God, and (2) transcendent, in the sense that God is greater than any other being, especially because of God's everlasting existence and preeminent relational love. Thus, we should reject the concept of God as an Unmoved Mover not knowing the moving world (Aristotle); as the Unmoved Mover inconsistently knowing the moving world (classical theism); and as the Unmoved Mover knowing an ultimately unmoving, or at least noncontingent, world (Stoics, Spinoza, pantheism).

Two objections may be raised by classical theists who are Catholic that ought to be considered. To the objection that if God changed God would not be perfect, for if God were perfect there would be no need to change, there is this reply: in order to be supremely excellent God must be at any particular time the greatest conceivable being, the all-worshipful being. At a later time, however, or in a situation where some creature who previously did not suffer now suffers, God has new opportunities to exhibit divine, supreme excellence. That is, God's perfection does not merely allow God to change, but requires God to change.

The other objection might be that God is neither One nor Many, neither actual nor potential, and so forth, because no human concept whatsoever applies to God literally or univocally, but at most analogically. The classical theist would say, perhaps, that God is more unitary than unity, more actual than actuality, as these are humanly known. Yet one wonders how classical theists, once they have admitted the insufficiency of human concepts, can legitimately give a favored status to one side (the left side) of conceptual contrasts at the expense of the other. Why, if God is simpler than the One, is God not also more complex, in terms of relatedness to diverse actual occasions, than the Many? Analogical predication and negative theology can just as easily fall victim to the monopolar prejudice as univocal predication. To be agent and patient together is much better than being either alone. This is preeminently the case with God, and a human being is more of an agent and patient than is an ape, who is more of both than a stone. Stones can neither talk nor listen, nor can they decide or appreciate others' decisions. The problem is not with analogical discourse regarding God per se but rather with analogical discourse when distorted in a monopolar way. That is, the Hartshornian process theism that I am defending can intelligibly be called a version of *dual transcendence*, in partial contrast to the less impressive monopolar transcendence of classical theism.

David Tracy[35] sees two major contributions made by Hartshorne. (1) The logical rigor of Hartshorne's concept of God results in the conclusion that theistic metaphysics deals not with contingent facts (Anselm's discovery), but with meanings. The key question is not so much whether God exists, but whether we can reach a coherent concept of God. If we can, then (via the ontological argument) God exists necessarily; if not, then God is impossible. (2) A coherent concept of God, however, demands a critique of monopolar classical theism. Dipolar neoclassical theism rests on the distinction between existence and actuality (Hartshorne's greatest discovery). Although Hartshorne accepts Thomas Aquinas's doctrine of analogy, he thinks that Thomas did an insufficient job of thinking through this doctrine in the case of God. Tracy nonetheless thinks that, despite Hartshorne's significant contributions to the concept of God, there is still work to be done in thinking through even better than Hartshorne did the proper application of analogical (and metaphorical) language regarding God.

It probably does not even occur to Catholic thinkers who are classical theists to question seriously the idea that God is wholly immutable and nontemporal in that it is simply assumed that mutability and temporality constitute the order of the created. Or again, Catholic thinkers who are classical theists do not see as problematic the seemingly obvious contradiction between a concept of God as not compassionate (because immutable) and the evidence of mystical experience wherein God is eminently compassionate. Somehow or other God helps those in misery without sympathizing with them. It is simply assumed that not to suffer is better than to suffer, rather than to think through carefully the dipolar (rather than monopolar) logic of perfection.

III

It is well known that the Catholic intellectual tradition has an incredibly rich past. My hope is that it will have a rich future as well. But this future richness is by no means guaranteed. My suspicion is that the greatest impediment to the continued flourishing of this tradition is an attitude toward sex and gender issues that is incredibly at odds with the beliefs of most intelligent, reflective people (e.g., regarding contraception, abortion, female priests, married priests, divorce, homosexuality, masturbation, premarital sex, and pedophilia and its cover-up). Perhaps the most controversial of these issues— abortion—could be illuminated by a processual, rather than a substantialist, view of fetal development.[36]

In addition to divisive issues regarding sex and gender, the Catholic intellectual tradition, in order to remain vital, must continue to concern itself with the most abstract issues concerning the concept of God. The present chapter is an attempt to make a small contribution to the clarification of this important concept, indeed the *most* important concept. Neoclassical theism, it should be emphasized, is as much *classical* as it is *neo*. Whereas classical theists are perhaps fearful of the "neo" part of neoclassical theism, religious skeptics are perhaps skittish regarding the "classical" part. Although the present chapter is not intended to engage with religious skeptics, it *is* an attempt to continue dialogue with classical theists, specifically with classical theists who are Roman Catholics.

An analogy with science will be helpful. Isaac Newton is universally honored as one of the greatest scientists in history, despite the fact that his great discoveries now have to be placed within a more comprehensive view wherein his insights are qualified and modified by discoveries in relativity and quantum theories. It is to be hoped that religious thinkers will develop a similar spirit of adventure regarding gradual progress in the concept of God. If Thomas Aquinas and other classical theists are half right in the concept of God, there is a sense in which we should praise Aquinas for getting things 50 percent accurate by the thirteenth century, which is, as I see things, a very high percentage. But there is still work to be done. The present chapter has tried to do some of this additional work through analysis of monopolarity and dipolarity. Similar work needs to be done regarding the concepts of classical theistic omnipotence (in contrast to the neoclassical concept of ideal, persuasive power) and classical theistic omniscience, which leads or should lead to determinism (in contrast to the neoclassical view of God knowing everything that is logically knowable, which does not include the outcome of future contingencies in that these are not here yet to be known).

In this chapter, we have seen that Tracy's fundamentally positive assessment of Hartshorne's work, when supplemented by a more careful analysis of some of the classic texts in traditional theism and more careful attention paid to analogical and metaphorical language used in discourse about God, can lead to genuine progress regarding some of the key issues in the Catholic intellectual tradition. Among these is a better philosophical understanding of the claim that God is love and a firmer philosophical grasp of what the great mystics in the tradition say about the God they have experienced.

NOTES

1. Charles Hartshorne, *The Divine Relativity: A Social Conception of God* (New Haven, CT: Yale University Press, 1948), 26.

2. Ibid., 50, 52.

3. Ibid., 57.

4. Charles Hartshorne, *Beyond Humanism* (Chicago: Willett, Clark & Company, 1937), 34; idem, *Whitehead's View of Reality* (New York: Pilgrim Press, 1981), 83; idem, "Democracy and Religion," in *The Zero Fallacy and Other Essays in Neoclassical Philosophy*, ed. Mohammed Valady (La Salle, IL: Open Court, 1997), 76.

5. Charles Hartshorne, *Reality as Social Process: Studies in Metaphysics and Religion* (Boston, MA: Beacon Press, 1953), 132.

6. Ibid., 145.

7. Ibid., 167.

8. Charles Hartshorne, *The Philosophy and Psychology of Sensation* (Chicago: University of Chicago Press, 1934), 271.

9. Charles Hartshorne, *Man's Vision of God and the Logic of Theism* (New York: Harper and Brothers, 1941), 2.

10. Charles Hartshorne, *Insights and Oversights of Great Thinkers* (Albany, NY: SUNY Press, 1983), 69, 74, 76.

11. Hartshorne, *The Divine Relativity*, xii.

12. Charles Hartshorne, *Aquinas to Whitehead: Seven Centuries of Metaphysics of Religion* (Milwaukee: Marquette University Press, 1976), 4; also see, Hartshorne, *Man's Vision of God*, 69.

13. Hartshorne, *The Divine Relativity*, 15, 32, 77.

14. Hartshorne *Aquinas to Whitehead*, 2.

15. Hartshorne, *Whitehead's View of Reality*, 83; idem, "Democracy and Religion," in *The Zero Fallacy and Other Essays in Neoclassical Philosophy*, ed. Mohammed Valady (La Salle, IL: Open Court, 1997), 71; idem, "Why Classical Theism has been Believed by so Many for so Long," in *The Zero Fallacy and Other Essays in Neoclassical Philosophy*, ed. Mohammed Valady (La Salle, IL: Open Court, 1997), 79; idem, "The Zero Fallacy in Philosophy: Accentuate the Positive," in *The Zero Fallacy and Other Essays in Neoclassical Philosophy*, ed. Mohammed Valady (La Salle, IL: Open Court, 1997), 163.

16. Charles Hartshorne, "A Reply to My Critics," in *The Philosophy of Charles Hartshorne*, ed. Lewis Edwin Hahn (La Salle, IL: Open Court, 1991), 633.

17. Hartshorne, "Democracy and Religion," 75.

18. Charles Hartshorne, "Response by Charles Hartshorne," in *Existence and Actuality: Conversations with Charles Hartshorne*, ed. John B. Cobb Jr., and Franklin I. Gamwell (Chicago: University of Chicago Press, 1984), 67, 75.

19. Charles Hartshorne, *Creativity and American Philosophy* (Albany, NY: SUNY Press, 1984), 263.

20. Charles Hartshorne, *Creative Synthesis and Philosophic Method* (La Salle, IL: Open Court, 1970), xv; Donald Wayne Viney, "Teilhard de Chardin and Process Philosophy Redux," *Process Studies* 35.1 (2006): 1–42.

21. Charles Hartshorne, "The Intelligibility of Sensations," *Monist* 44.2 (1934): 177.

22. Hartshorne, *Creative Synthesis and Philosophic Method*, 242. Also see James F. Ross, "An Impasse on Competing Descriptions of God," *International Journal for Philosophy of Religion* 8.4 (1977): 233–49.

23. Charles Hartshorne, "Points of View: A Brisk Dialogue," in *The Zero Fallacy and Other Essays in Neoclassical Philosophy*, ed. Mohammed Valady (La Salle, IL: Open Court, 1997), 39.

24. Charles Hartshorne, *The Darkness and the Light* (Albany, NY: SUNY Press, 1990), 101.

25. Charles Hartshorne, "The Divine Relativity and Absoluteness," *Review of Metaphysics* 4.1 (1950): 47.

26. Karol Wojtyla, *The Acting Person*, trans., Andrzej Potocki (Dordrecht: D. Reidel, 1979).

27. W. Norris Clarke, S. J., *The Philosophical Approach to God*, rev. ed. (New York: Fordham University Press, 2007); James W. Felt, *Coming to Be: Toward a Thomistic-Whiteheadian Metaphysics of Becoming* (Albany, NY: SUNY Press, 2001).

28. See William Christian's *An Interpretation of Whitehead's Metaphysics* (New Haven, CT: Yale University Press, 1959), especially chapter five.

29. See Charles Hartshorne, "The Case for Metaphysical Idealism," in *Creative Experiencing: A Philosophy of Freedom*, ed. Donald Wayne Viney and Jincheol O (Albany, NY: SUNY Press, 2011), 58. Also see Daniel A. Dombrowski, "Coming to Be: On Process-Enriched Thomism," *Philosophy and Theology* 24.2 (2012): 255–73.

30. Charles Hartshorne, "Categories, Transcendentals, and Creative Experiencing," in *Creative Experiencing*, ed. Donald Wayne Viney and Jincheol O. (Albany, NY: SUNY Press, 2011), 113–19.

31. Charles Hartshorne, "The Intelligibility of Sensations," 184.

32. Charles Hartshorne, "God and Nature," *Anticipation* 25 (1979): 62.

33. Especially Hartshorne's introduction in *Philosophers Speak of God*, by Charles Hartshorne and William L. Reese (Chicago: University of Chicago Press, 1953).

34. See Hartshorne's *The Logic of Perfection (and Other Essays in Neoclassical Metaphysics)* (La Salle, IL: Open Court, 1962) and idem, *Anselm's Discovery* (La Salle, IL: Open Court, 1965).

35. See, David Tracy, *Blessed Rage for Order: The New Pluralism in Theology* (New York: Seabury, 1975), also, idem, "Analogy, Metaphor, and God-Language: Charles Hartshorne," *Modern Schoolman* 62 (1985): 249–64.

36. Daniel A. Dombrowski, *A Brief, Liberal, Catholic Defense of Abortion* (Chicago: University of Illinois Press, 2000).

BIBLIOGRAPHY

Christian, William. *An Interpretation of Whitehead's Metaphysics*. New Haven, CT: Yale University Press, 1959.

Clarke, W. Norris, S. J. *The Philosophical Approach to God.* Rev. ed. New York: Fordham University Press, 2007.

Dombrowski, Daniel, A. *A Brief, Liberal, Catholic Defense of Abortion.* Chicago: University of Illinois Press, 2000.

Dombrowski, Daniel, A. "Coming to Be: On Process-Enriched Thomism." *Philosophy and Theology* 24.2 (2012): 255–73.

Felt, James W. *Coming to Be: Toward a Thomistic-Whiteheadian Metaphysics of Becoming.* Albany: SUNY Press, 2001.

Hartshorne, Charles. *Anselm's Discovery.* La Salle, IL: Open Court, 1965.

Hartshorne, Charles. *Aquinas to Whitehead: Seven Centuries of Metaphysics of Religion.* Milwaukee: Marquette University Press, 1976.

Hartshorne, Charles. *Beyond Humanism.* Chicago: Willett, Clark & Company, 1937.

Hartshorne, Charles. "The Case for Metaphysical Idealism." In *Creative Experiencing: A Philosophy of Freedom,* edited by Donald Wayne Viney and Jincheol O, 55–70. Albany, NY: SUNY Press, 2011.

Hartshorne, Charles. "Categories, Transcendentals, and Creative Experiencing." In *Creative Experiencing: A Philosophy of Freedom,* edited by Donald Wayne Viney and Jincheol O, 113–28. Albany, NY: SUNY Press, 2011.

Hartshorne, Charles. *Creative Synthesis and Philosophic Method.* La Salle, IL: Open Court, 1970.

Hartshorne, Charles. *Creativity and American Philosophy.* Albany, NY: SUNY Press, 1984.

Hartshorne, Charles. *The Darkness and the Light.* Albany, NY: SUNY Press, 1990.

Hartshorne, Charles. "Democracy and Religion." In *The Zero Fallacy and Other Essays in Neoclassical Philosophy,* edited by Mohammad Valady, 67–77. La Salle, IL: Open Court, 1997.

Hartshorne, Charles. *The Divine Relativity: A Social Conception of God.* New Haven, CT: Yale University Press, 1948.

Hartshorne, Charles. "The Divine Relativity and Absoluteness." *Review of Metaphysics* 4.1 (1950): 31–60.

Hartshorne, Charles. "God and Nature." *Anticipation* 25 (1979): 58–64.

Hartshorne, Charles. *Insights and Oversights of Great Thinkers.* Albany, NY: SUNY Press, 1983.

Hartshorne, Charles. "The Intelligibility of Sensations." *Monist* 44.2 (1934): 161–85.

Hartshorne, Charles. *The Logic of Perfection (and Other Essays in Neoclassical Metaphysics).* La Salle, IL: Open Court, 1962.

Hartshorne, Charles. *Man's Vision of God and the Logic of Theism.* New York: Harper and Brothers, 1941.

Hartshorne, Charles. *The Philosophy and Psychology of Sensation.* Chicago: University of Chicago Press, 1934.

Hartshorne, Charles. "Points of View: A Brisk Dialogue." In *The Zero Fallacy and Other Essays in Neoclassical Philosophy,* edited by Mohammad Valady, 1–42. La Salle, IL: Open Court, 1997.

Hartshorne, Charles. *Reality as Social Process: Studies in Metaphysics and Religion.* Boston, MA: Beacon Press, 1953.

Hartshorne, Charles. "Reply to My Critics." In *The Philosophy of Charles Hartshorne*, edited by Lewis Edwin Hahn, 569–731. La Salle, IL: Open Court, 1991.

Hartshorne, Charles. "Response by Charles Hartshorne." In *Existence and Actuality: Conversations with Charles Hartshorne*, edited by John B. Cobb Jr. and Franklin I. Gamwell, 66–77. Chicago: University of Chicago Press, 1984.

Hartshorne, Charles. *Whitehead's View of Reality*. New York: Pilgrim Press, 1981.

Hartshorne, Charles. "Why Classical Theism has been Believed by so Many for so Long." In *The Zero Fallacy and Other Essays in Neoclassical Philosophy*, edited by Mohammed Valady, 79–94. La Salle, IL: Open Court, 1997.

Hartshorne, Charles. "The Zero Fallacy in Philosophy: Accentuate the Positive." In *The Zero Fallacy and Other Essays in Neoclassical Philosophy*, edited by Mohammad Valady, 161–72. La Salle, IL: Open Court, 1997.

Hartshorne, Charles, and William L. Reese. *Philosophers Speak of God*. Chicago: University of Chicago Press, 1953.

Ross, James F. "An Impasse on Competing Descriptions of God." *International Journal for Philosophy of Religion* 8.4 (1977): 233–49.

Tracy, David. "Analogy, Metaphor, and God-Language: Charles Hartshorne." *Modern Schoolman* 62 (1985): 249–64.

Tracy, David. *Blessed Rage for Order: The New Pluralism in Theology*. New York: Seabury, 1975.

Viney, Donald Wayne. "Teilhard de Chardin and Process Philosophy Redux." *Process Studies* 35.1 (2006): 1–42.

Wojtyla, Karol. *The Acting Person*. Translated by Andrzej Potocki. Dordrecht: D. Reidel, 1979.

Chapter 5

A Catholic Approach to Process Philosophy

Maria-Teresa Teixeira

Process philosophy is currently associated with Protestant theology. For that reason, it is sometimes thought that it is difficult to reconcile it with a Catholic worldview. Protestant theologies tend to focus on intellectual and sometimes almost literal interpretations of the scriptures. The Catholic doctrine tends to distance itself from the texts and rely more on tradition and living experience.

In this chapter, we will hold that Catholic worldviews tend to be easily harmonized with process thought. We will examine the philosophy of Alfred North Whitehead in the context of Catholic doctrine. He was greatly influenced by Cardinal Newman, who was himself a convert to the Roman Catholic Church. Whitehead, however, stopped short of converting to Catholicism; he mainly rejected the infallibility and authority of the Roman Church, although he was very sympathetic to many of its teachings.

Some Whiteheadian categories that are fundamental to process philosophy like potentiality, immanence, and transcendence, process, relationship, interconnectedness, wholeness, self-determination, and creativity are easily integrated into a Catholic worldview.

In a first approach to Whitehead's philosophy, one is always struck by his concept of God. Whitehead's God is above all an element in his metaphysical system. God is, in some way, a necessary element for the coherence and viability of his philosophical system. But Whitehead's God is not a foundational element like Aristotle's Prime Mover. He is, however, essential in the whole metaphysical construct. God is intrinsic to Whitehead's metaphysical and cosmological system from the very beginning and cannot be separated from it. God is primarily a "God of the philosophers," not the God of Christianity. In spite of many affinities and even a strong empathy in many cases, Whitehead's approach to Christian religions was indeed very cautious.

Whitehead actually rejected or reinterpreted many elements of Christian doctrine.

Whitehead's God is both temporal and eternal, infinite and finite, immanent and transcendent, omniscient and limited in his knowledge, "a creature of creativity and a condition for creativity."[1] God has two natures: a primordial nature and a consequent nature. In his primordial nature, he is the "primordial created fact," "the all-inclusive unfettered valuation," and "the timeless source of all order."[2] In his primordial nature, God has no actuality—"It is God in abstraction, alone with himself."[3] The actual world presupposes God in his primordial, conceptual facet. But God has also a consequent nature: "He is the beginning and the end."[4]

In his consequent nature, God relates to the temporal world. God is actual and keeps growing by incorporating everything in the world that can be saved. God's consequent nature results from the reciprocal action between God and the world. The world influences God and is objectified in God. God, who is always in concrescence, shares the world with every actual entity.

THE SUBJECTIVE AIM,
SELF-DETERMINATION, AND CREATION

In his primordial nature God envisages all potentiality, thus allowing for actualities to happen. The ontological principle determines that "there is nothing which floats into the world from nowhere."[5] Every actual entity in the world is connected to some other actual entity. There is always some relationship between actual entities. God is the principle of concretion from which every actual entity gets its initial, subjective aim that makes its autonomous process of coming into being real. Every actual entity in the process of becoming aims at its self-constitution but it needs to get its initial, subjective aim from somewhere; every subject in the process of becoming forcefully inherits from the ordering of things, which ordering is conceptually present in the primordial nature of God.[6] Every actual occasion gets its initial aim from God, who is also an actual entity, so that it can initiate its process of self-determination, which is also a process of self-causation.

In this sense, God is indeed the beginning of everything, for every actual entity proceeds from God because it gets its initial aim from him. As every actual entity self-constitutes itself, it gets its purpose and sense of orientation from its subjective aim originating from God. This initial aim does not jeopardize self-determination. Actual entities constitute themselves in freedom but in accordance with their own nature, which is established through the initial subjective aim. Self-causation can be near to human freedom or be a mere rough self-constitution with hardly any associated process of choice.

As Henri Bergson, the French philosopher who is also considered a process philosopher, reminds us frequently, in every coming into existence there is always some trace of choice. But real freedom is rare, even in human lives.

Some degree of self-determination is a requisite for self-creation. Each actual entity is *causa sui* and, as such, is not conditioned by external factors. However, it draws on antecedent actualities for its formation and also on its subjective aim. The subjective aim is its purpose inherited from God; antecedent actualities form the background environment from which new actual entities can emerge creatively and freely. Actual entities always relate to antecedent actual occasions. A novel actual entity finds its foundations on previous actualities and its self-purpose in the subjective aim. It abides by the ontological principle which says that things cannot emerge from nothing. However, actual entities are also an issue of creativity because self-determination is the only relevant factor in their development.

God as the principle of concretion gives each actual entity its initial subjective aim from which it can initiate the process of constituting its own being. Causality becomes causative of itself.

Therefore, God in his primordial nature envisages all possibilities; he contemplates all possibilities that can become actualities. Some of those will never become actual. Those that become themselves do so in a process of self-constitution, which ultimately is the unravelling of freedom. Every actual entity is *causa sui*. God is the provider of the subjective aim so that actual entities can become in accordance with their own nature, and the ordering of things.

OMNISCIENCE, CREATIVITY, AND FREEDOM

[T]he transition of the creativity from an actual world to the correlate novel concrescence is conditioned by the relevance of God's all-embracing conceptual valuations . . . we can say that God and the actual world jointly constitute the character of the creativity for the initial phase of the novel concrescence.[7]

"God's all-embracing conceptual valuations" can be said to be God's omniscience. God holds all the concepts in his primordial nature. This all-comprehensive inclusion of every concept is what enables the allocation of the initial aim to every will-be actual occasion. Conceiving God's omniscience as such solves the classical problems resulting from this divine attribute and its relation to freedom. God does not know about the concrete future facts that will happen, relating to each actual entity that is given an initial subjective aim. But he holds within his divine nature all the possibilities that can come into existence.

Whitehead referred to the omniscience of God as having to be disentangled from immanence, which he considered a positive element in the Christian tradition.[8] But he did not discard omniscience:

> God, who is the ground antecedent to transition, must include all possibilities of physical value conceptually, thereby holding the ideal forms apart in equal, conceptual realization of knowledge. Thus, as concepts, they are grasped together in the synthesis of omniscience.[9]

This divine omniscience taken as a synthesis of concepts is merely ideal. It does not and cannot preclude freedom.

In fact, the whole process of self-constitution, which is itself an act of self-determination, roots itself in God. And freedom develops side by side with creativity. The self-constitution of actual entities is a creative act that is necessarily an act of choice; it can ultimately be a free act. There is no freedom without creativity.

Henri Bergson also linked freedom to ontological constitution and creativity. In *Time and Free Will*,[10] he compares the free act to the growing and coming into being of a work of art, and the empathy existing between the artist and her work. It is a kind of ontological symbiosis between freedom and our emerging constitution and between the artist and her piece of art. He writes, "We are free when our acts spring from our whole personality, when they express it, when they have that indefinable resemblance to it which one sometimes finds between the artist and his work."[11] Freedom is thus of an ontological nature. It emerges from our very "self-onto-constitution." We can determine ourselves in freedom because our acts express our personality and are the outcome of our very nature.

Likewise, freedom and creativity are also essential ontological elements in Whitehead's system. Creativity is the basis of everything that comes into being. And it is also the essence of freedom. For Whitehead, creativity is inherent in reality and cannot be taken apart from God or creatures. Subjective aims originate from God and are meant to enable the free constitution of every creature. God is thus the final cause of every creature. Every actual entity is similar to God because it derives itself from its mental pole, like God. It also gets its conceptual aim from God. The actual entity is yet undetermined although its initial aim was provided by God. It will make its choices and take its decisions. In this process, it will finally determine itself including all the novelties in its constitution. In order to sustain the coherence of their concrescence, actual entities have this subjective aim, initially provided by God, as the unifying element that governs the phases of their concrescence.[12] They preserve their wholeness from the very beginning of their process, which is itself indivisible.

In this way, God is the ontological source of everything. The subjective aim provided by God leaves all the decisions to the novel entity that will emerge in its wholeness from its very concrescence. God is thus the Creator of every entity because he provides every entity with its aim. However, the word "Creator" should not be taken in its usual sense. Whitehead's God is not a Creator *ex nihilo* as he is understood in the traditional Catholic doctrine. But Whitehead's God is certainly a God who favors the self-constitution and freedom of his creatures, letting them come into existence in pure self-determination. The Catholic doctrine places a very similar emphasis on human freedom. God's love for his children is so great that he endows them with freedom.

In Whitehead's philosophy, there is no separation between creativity, God, and creatures. In providing the initial aim God is Creator, but he is not separated from his creatures. In his primordial facet, he provides them with an aim. God offers his creatures novelty, which is ultimately freedom. God, creativity, and creatures merge together into novelty. And God is also an issue of creativity:

> In this sense, God can be termed the Creator of each temporal actual entity. But the phrase is apt to be misleading by its suggestion that the ultimate creativity of the universe is to be ascribed to God's volition. The true metaphysical position is that God is the aboriginal instance of this creativity, and is therefore the aboriginal condition which qualifies its action . . . there is no meaning to "creativity" apart from its "creatures," and no meaning to "God" apart from the "creativity" and the "temporal creatures," and no meaning to the "temporal creatures" apart from "creativity" and "God."[13]

Although God is the first instance of creativity, he is also the first condition of creativity. In this sense, God participates in the initiation of each and every actual entity, but they are not the result of his volition. They simply derive their conceptual aim from God, but this aim is full of indetermination. They will make their own decisions creatively and freely. God introduces order into reality. Without this order, the world would be void of novelty. It is in this sense that God is the Creator.

With no intervention from God, there would be no novelty and no order in the world.[14] The order and novelty introduced in the world by God justify the statement that God is an issue of creativity. The subjective aim enhances and intensifies experience because order is not enough. There is much more complexity to reality. Order must "mix" with novelty. Otherwise, order would be nothing else than repetition, and novelty would not have the much-needed system framework.[15] God and the emerging entity share the subjective aim. Its origin comes from God, but its concretion belongs to the new subject that constitutes itself. In so doing, it forms its own individuality. This is solely due to the fact that actual entities are able to make their own decisions as their process of self-constitution develops, "To be *causa sui* means that the process of concrescence is its own reason. . . . The freedom inherent in the universe is constituted by this element of self-causation."[16] Creation emerges with every actual entity that is itself a result of creativity. Every entity is creator of itself, and every actual entity including God concurs with the "cosmic conspiracy."[17]

Whitehead's doctrine of creation is amazingly divergent from Christian traditional teaching and yet it resonates with the importance and emphasis Roman Catholicism places on freedom and co-creation. Saying that God is a creature, even if he is a creature of creativity, is almost certainly a heresy, but deriving every actual entity's determination from God's incentive is in line with the idea that true will can only result from freedom and freedom ultimately coincides with God's will. It is a soundly formed will that is a characteristic of novelty rightly introducing itself into process, although novelty is not always good. In Catholicism, the image of a God as a loving father, whose love is so great that he bestows freedom on each and every one of his children, is certainly very close to Whitehead's theory of the initial subjective aim together with the idea that every actual entity is *causa sui*.

It should be noted that a sound self-determination is not the same as an advanced autonomous determination. Only human freedom instantiates, in a supreme form, the self-determination shared by all actual occasions. It is the ultimate and complete instance of freedom hardly comparable to the determination of a much less significant actual occasion, such as an electronic occasion.

EVIL AND NOVELTY

When actual entities realize their subjective aim, they attain completion. This completion is what Whitehead calls satisfaction, and it implies full determination and individualization. It also implies that some potentiality has been realized and some has remained undetermined in the conceptual, abstract, divine nature. It should be noted that the actualization of potentiality is not necessarily good. Evil can emerge from novelty:

> The novelty may promote or destroy order; it may be good or bad. But it is new, a new type of individual, and not merely a new intensity of individual feeling. That member of the locus has introduced a new form into the actual world; or, at least, an old form in a new function.[18]

Novelty may upset order. It may have a new role although it is an old arrangement. It may be a bad positioning. But still, it introduces something new into the world. What is new is not necessarily good. It may have its flaws.

Whitehead is quite optimistic in considering the problem of evil. He sees evil as an obstacle in the way of process. He implicitly refuses the idea of evil as a substance or as an entity. Evil is a hindrance or a kind of stumbling block that presents itself in the way of emerging actual entities. The reason for evil is that novelty is not necessarily good, because it may emerge at the wrong time:

> A new actuality may appear in the wrong society, amid which its claims to efficacy act mainly as inhibitions. Then a weary task is set for creative function, by an epoch of new creations to remove the inhibition. Insistence on birth at the wrong season is the trick of evil. In other words, the novel fact may throw back, inhibit, and delay. But the advance, when it does arrive, will be richer in content, more fully conditioned, and more stable.[19]

Evil resulting from novelty refers to self-determination. The very fact that an actual entity is *causa sui* may lead to a "wrong" outcome. Ultimately, this "naughty" nature of evil conceived as a delay or an inhibitor does not hamper the movement of progress. The creative advance will arrive in due course and establish the conditions for a better efficacious outcome.

Thus, Whitehead seems to ignore important facets of the problem of evil, like the suffering of the innocent. However, it should be noted that in *Religion in the Making*, while referring to the book of Job, Whitehead had already highlighted moral evil and suffering: "No religion which faces facts can minimize the evil in the world, not merely the moral evil, but the pain and the suffering. The book of Job is the revolt against the facile solution, so esteemed by fortunate people, that the sufferer is the evil person."[20] If evil is considered to be only a result of human choice then many facets of suffering will be distorted.

Roman Catholicism sometimes tends to consider suffering as always the consequence of sin, and sin is in some way a consequence of human freedom. In a Catholic worldview, the suffering of the innocent also remains a mystery.

The book of Job is quite relevant to this matter. Whitehead considers Job as introducing rationality into religion. The order that underlies reality is also a kind of moral order, and order is almost synonymous with rationality for Whitehead. In considering evil as the appearance of obstacles, Whitehead affirms it as an element in reality. He also sees it as unstable and as something that will end up destroying itself or end up in degradation. He argues that degradation by itself cannot be seen as evil. Evil emerges from the comparison of a state of degradation with what might have come into existence:

A hog is not an evil beast, but when a man is degraded to the level of a hog, with the accompanying atrophy of finer elements, he is no more evil than a hog. The evil of the final degradation lies in the comparison of what is with what might have been. During the process of degradation the comparison is an evil for the man himself, and at its final stage it remains an evil for others.[21]

Evil emerges from the opposition of different objectives; it is unstable, but it can end up being removed. However, the temporal nature of evil, that is, the fact that evil consists mainly in an actual entity being born at the wrong time, may raise another question, namely, that of the irrevocability of evil.

God integrates in himself all that can be preserved from the actual world. He saves all that can be saved. In this way, actual entities are able to acquire objective immortality. This is God's consequent nature. God only saves what can be saved, what can be used; it would be absurd if God integrated in himself what is dubious, unsafe, or evil. What should we say then about irrevocability? Evil is integrated into the world although it is unstable, and it will eventually be overcome. That integration of evil is an element in the constitution of the world. Its instability and its transiency will not erase it from the world. Whitehead, however, minimizes the importance of evil. He considers how evil can always be transformed and included in a harmonious whole: "The revolts of destructive evil . . . are dismissed into their triviality of merely individual facts; and yet the good they did achieve . . . is yet saved by its relation to the completed whole."[22] It seems that the completion of wholeness excludes by its very nature evil, which cannot be an element of wholeness. What is important is the outcome of process in its integrity. The wholeness of process and the inextricability of the elements in the concrescence dilute evil and make it irrelevant. Evil is always an individual fact that can be dismissed because of its very triviality.

This can be clarified because God does not prehend actual entities as they are in this world. He salvages whatever is worth salvaging. What he incorporates in his nature has a different configuration from its worldly formation. God's judgment on the world is a judgement of tenderness and infinite patience. Evil is trivial and can be dismissed as an individual fact. We can thus hold that Whitehead rejects any form of ontological evil[23]

The consequent nature of God is his judgement on the world. He saves the world as it passes into the immediacy of his own life. It is the judgement of a tenderness which loses nothing that can be saved. It is also the judgement of a wisdom which uses what in the temporal world is mere wreckage.[24]

The Catholic view of suffering also sees God as saving the world, as salvaging what can be used from sin and suffering. God can "transform" evil into good. Also, God can force suffering on humans so that they can conquer evil and grow out of evil and suffering. Through suffering God draws people to him. But evil still remains evil, although God brings about the good that flows from evil, thus attaining greatness. From God's perspective, everything is ultimately good because God saves everything, and his nature can only be good. Like Whitehead, Catholics do not recognize ontological evil. Every sin is open to pardon and can be removed through repentance and God's grace.

IMMANENCE AND OBJECTIVE IMMORTALITY

God's consequent nature comes from his physical prehension of actual entities.[25] God, in his consequent nature, is an entity in process, always in concrescence, and deriving his consequent nature from the world.[26] His consequent nature leads to determination, actualization, and consciousness. His prehension includes every element that can be taken into harmony. He thus prehends the sufferings, sorrows, failures, triumphs, and joys of every actuality.[27]

Wisdom enables what is a mere ruin in this world to be carried into harmony. God does not fight force with force, or destruction with destruction. He fosters congruity, kindness, and peacefulness, "He does not create the world, he saves it . . . he is the poet of the world, with tender patience leading it by his vision of truth, beauty, and goodness."[28] This is so because actual entities are self-determining, getting their subjective aim from God, but becoming toward completion in a process that is unique to each one of them.

By prehending every actual entity, God "preserves" it through its objective immortality, "The consequent nature of God is the fluent world become 'everlasting' by its objective immortality in God."[29] Each actual entity is incorporated in God, thus overcoming self-perishing. God's consequent nature results from the completion of finite facts; actual occasions, on the other hand, come to completion through an everlasting union with the eternal order, that is, with God.

The world is thus immanent in God and God is immanent in the world. Likewise, the world transcends God as God transcends the world.[30] God and every actual entity are transcendent and immanent entities, "The notion of God . . . is that of an actual entity immanent in the actual world, but transcending any finite cosmic epoch—a being at once actual, eternal, immanent, and transcendent."[31] It is not only God who is transcendent. Novelty makes every actual entity transcend the world and even God. Transcendence is an outcome of process and novelty, and it applies to all reality.

But God is also immanent. The immanence of God justifies his omnipresence and omniscience in Christian doctrine. Immanence is important in

Roman Catholicism not only for the previous reasons but because it justifies creation by God and also by his creatures. We are co-creators because we are part of God and God is part of the world. God is everywhere. God is in our most intimate thoughts and in the most insignificant bit of matter: "The Semitic God is omniscient; but, in addition to that, the Christian God is a factor in the universe."[32] Whitehead goes on to cite *The Sayings of Christ*, "an early Christian compilation," "found in an Egyptian tomb," "Cleave the wood, and I am there. . . . This is merely one example of an emphatic assertion of immanence, and shows a serious divergence from the Semitic concept."[33]

In our process of becoming, we are the authors of our self-creation, which is enabled by God who provides our initial subjective aim, welcoming us finally into his very being in a synthesis that is called by Whitehead "objective immortality." God is thus the end of everything.

Our dignity is rooted in this creative function, in our condition of being God's adjuncts:

> God is *in* the world, or nowhere, creating continually in us and around us. This creative principle is everywhere, in animate and so-called inanimate matter, in the ether, water, earth, human hearts. But this creation is a continuing process, and "the process is itself the actuality," since no sooner do you arrive than you start on a fresh journey. In so far as man partakes of this creative process does he partake of the divine, of God, and that participation is his immortality, reducing the question of whether his individuality survives death of the body to the estate of an irrelevancy. His true destiny as co-creator in the universe is his dignity and his grandeur.[34]

The category of the *adjutores Dei* (1 Cor. 3:9) elevates human beings from their human condition, raising them to a divine status.

This condition of co-creator together with one's integration into God through his consequent nature, when the concrescence is complete, brushes aside the importance of individual salvation and underlines the relevance of the "ontological contribution" of each and every actual entity to the world.

Whitehead's objective immortality is thus quite divergent from the Catholic immortal salvation, which is individual and establishes a direct, personal relationship with God. However, co-creation, for Whitehead, is beyond individual salvation. It is a kind of human ennoblement, a human destiny that may or may not be fulfilled by elevation to the divine. The Catholic doctrine, on the other hand, emphasizes co-creation without precluding individual salvation.

In Roman Catholicism, the immanence of God is related to God's essence and activity permeating all creation, that is, all created beings. But the immanence of God does not preclude transcendence, nor does God coincide with the universe. Pantheism is rejected both by Roman Catholicism and Whitehead. Whitehead's panentheism goes beyond simplistic, pantheist interpretations. Both immanence and transcendence belong in Catholic and Whiteheadian doctrines.

CONCLUSION

Whitehead's metaphysical system enhances the idea of God as a God of the philosophers. Catholicism, however, is not based on such philosophical assertions. But, on a closer look, one may spot some influence of Catholicism on Whitehead's philosophy. One may also find that Whitehead gets much inspiration from some facets of the Catholic doctrine, and he is even able to develop and deepen many Catholic insights.

The envisagement of all potentiality by God is one such instance. Every actual entity gets its subjective aim from God. Notwithstanding, its process of constitution is pure self-determination. God's respect for the freedom of his creatures is an act of love and grace in Roman Catholicism.

God's conceptual valuations can be seen as God's omniscience. His all-comprehensiveness leads to an all-knowing synthesis that cannot be taken as the knowledge God might have of future facts but only as an all-encompassing conceptual principle.

Whitehead states that God is a creature of creativity. This is not compatible with the Catholic doctrine. However, the initial subjective aim enables creativity and freedom, which are inextricably interwoven. Process is whole and indivisible. God thus emerges as the Creator in Whitehead's philosophy. This Creator bears many resemblances to the Catholic Creator who cherishes freedom and integrity.

The problem of evil seen by Whitehead has some notable similarities with the Catholic doctrine. According to Whitehead, evil can emerge from novelty and upset order, but it will always be overcome by the creative advance. Evil is always an obstacle that emerges in the way of creativity, closely mirroring the Catholic absence of good. Evil is never substantial, neither does it have an ontological effect. God saves all that can be saved. The Catholic version of this salvaging of the world's wreckage is pardon and salvation. Whitehead's objective immortality, however, excludes individual salvation, a cornerstone of the Catholic doctrine.

In short, Roman Catholicism and Whitehead's philosophy may exhibit substantial differences. On a second approach, however, a deep kinship emerges. Ontological self-emergence, creative creation, and the redemption of the world are among these affinities.

NOTES

1. Alfred North Whitehead, *Process and Reality: An Essay in Cosmology* (1929), corrected ed., ed. David Ray Griffin and Donald W. Sherburne (New York: Free Press, 1978), 31 (hereafter *"PR"*).

2. Ibid., 31, 32.

3. Ibid., 34.

4. Ibid., 345.

5. Ibid., 244.

6. Ibid.

7. Ibid., 244–45.

8. Alfred North Whitehead, *Religion in the Making* (1926; repr., New York: Fordham University Press, 1996), 75 (hereafter *"RM"*).

9. Ibid., 153.

10. Henri Bergson, *Time and Free Will: An Essay on the Immediate Data of Consciousness*, trans. Frank Lubecki Pogson (New York: Macmillan, 1910). This is the English translation of his 1889 doctoral thesis.

11. "Nous sommes libres quand nos actes émanent de notre personnalité entière, quand ils l'expriment, quand ils ont avec elle cette indéfinissable ressemblance qu'on trouve parfois entre l'œuvre et l'artiste" (Henri Bergson, *Essai sur les donneées immédiates de la conscience* [Paris: Presses universitaires de France, 2011], 129).

12. *PR* 224.

13. Ibid., 225.

14. Ibid., 247.

15. Ibid., 339.

16. Ibid., 88.

17. Plotinus, II *Ennead*, 3, §7.

18. *PR* 187.

19. Ibid., 223.

20. *RM* 49.

21. Ibid., 97.

22. *PR* 346.

23. Other process philosophers like Vladimir Jankélévitch have highlighted the importance of ontological evil. See Vladimir Jankélévitch, *L' imprescriptible* (Paris: Éditions du Seuil, 1986) and Hannah Arendt, *The Origins of Totalitarianism* (San Diego, CA: Harcourt Brace, 1985). *Process and Reality* was published in 1929. One could say Whitehead was still living in a bygone era, one that was not yet fully acquainted with the horrors of wars, genocide, and ecocide that pervaded the remainder of the twentieth century and the beginning of the twenty-first century.

24. *PR* 346.

25. Ibid., 31.

26. Ibid., 31, 347.

27. Ibid., 346.

28. Ibid.

29. Ibid., 347.

30. Ibid., 348.
31. Ibid., 93.
32. *RM* 73.
33. Ibid., 74.
34. Alfred North Whitehead, *Dialogues of Alfred North Whitehead*, ed. Lucien Price (1954; repr., Boston, MA: David R. Godine, 2001), 366.

BIBLIOGRAPHY

Arendt, Hannah. *The Origins of Totalitarianism*. San Diego, CA: Harcourt Brace, 1985.

Bergson, Henri. *Essai sur les données immédiates de la conscience*. Paris: Presses universitaires de France, 2011.

Bergson, Henri. *Time and Free Will: An Essay on the Immediate Data of Consciousness*. Translated by Frank Lubecki Pogson. New York: Macmillan, 1910.

Jankélévitch, Vladimir. *L' imprescriptible*. Paris: Éditions du Seuil, 1986.

Plotinus. *The Enneads*. Edited by Lloyd P. Gerson. Translated by George Boys-Stones, John M. Dillon, Lloyd P. Gerson, R. A. H. King, Andrew Smith, and James Wilberding. Cambridge: Cambridge University Press, 2018.

Whitehead, Alfred North. *Dialogues of Alfred North Whitehead*. Edited by Lucien Price. 1954. Reprint, Boston, MA: David R. Godine, 2001.

Whitehead, Alfred North. *Process and Reality: An Essay in Cosmology*. 1929. Corrected ed. Edited by David Ray Griffin and Donald W. Sherburne. New York: Free Press, 1978.

Whitehead, Alfred North. *Religion in the Making*. 1926. Reprint, New York: Fordham University Press, 1996.

Chapter 6

Balancing Permanence and Change in a Systems-Oriented Metaphysics

Joseph A. Bracken, S. J.

In Part Five of *Process and Reality*, Alfred North Whitehead notes that a philosophical cosmology necessarily deals with "the final opposites, joy and sorrow, good and evil, disjunction and conjunction—that is to say, the Many-in-One—flux and permanence, greatness and triviality, freedom and necessity, God and the world."[1] Something always survives in "the inescapable flux"; something always eludes "the overwhelming permanence."[2] Hence, every philosophical cosmology is constrained by these limitations. In concentrating on either permanence or flux, the metaphysical scheme will have trouble explaining the reality and significance of the other alternative. Yet there may still be a way to deal with both equitably if one chooses the right paradigm or model for the organization of physical reality.

In this chapter, I propose the model of a system (as opposed to the model of substance or individual entity). A system, for example, is basically grounded in bottom-up causality. That is, the energy for change is located in the material constituents as they by their dynamic interrelation from moment to moment sustain the governing structure of the system. Hence, the system is never precisely the same from moment to moment. Within a substance, however, the agency for change is located in an unchanging substantial form. Hence, within a substance, there is only "accidental" change in terms of a change of attributes or properties of the substantial form in given circumstances. Change in the substantial form itself can only come through the intervention of an outside agency (either God or a human craftsman) but this, too, is reductively an instance of unilateral top-down causality.

Yet one must also distinguish here between open-ended and closed systems, that is, systems that evolve in size and complexity and systems that are permanently fixed in their governing structure or persistent mode of operation. Systems at work in physical reality would seem to be open-ended since the cosmic process has clearly evolved in size and complexity since the moment of the Big Bang billions of years ago. Closed systems, on the contrary, are deterministic in their structure and mode of operation. They are designed to work one way and only one way, or they are considered defective. Such closed systems would seem to be the product of a human mind. That is, the components of closed systems are fixed concepts with unchanging meaning and value. For, in a closed system, a concept is valued more for its logical correlation with other concepts in the system than for its correspondence to external reality.[3] When applied in a more general way to physical reality as a whole, the system is tentative or provisional, thus subject to revision in the light of new empirical data.[4]

Given these qualifications, I set forth in this chapter a defense of the notion of system as opposed to substance as a better model or paradigm for a philosophical understanding of the Christian God–world relationship. First, however, I make clear what I see as the strengths and weaknesses of both classical metaphysics and Whitehead's process-oriented approach in dealing with that topic. Afterward, I present a panentheistic systems-oriented approach to the Christian God–world relationship that in my judgment endorses the strengths and compensates for the weaknesses of the other two systems.

THE GOD–WORLD RELATIONSHIP WITHIN CLASSICAL METAPHYSICS

In classical metaphysics, God is both omniscient and omnipotent. There is a master plan for the world of creation from beginning to end, and everything that happens has a predetermined place in that master plan. Hence, even when something seemingly catastrophic happens, human beings should not worry since God has already taken it into account in drawing up the divine master plan and has found a way to eventually produce long-term good out of this short-term evil. For, in the New Testament, God promises to "make all things new," to create a new heaven and a new earth (Rev. 21:1–5). Hence, the cosmic process will not end tragically; the divine plan guarantees a happy ending in which there will be a new heaven and a new earth that will last forever within God's own everlasting life.

The weakness of classical metaphysics, however, lies in its virtually exclusive emphasis on top-down efficient causality as opposed to bottom-up efficient causality (as in a more process-oriented metaphysics). Classical metaphysics, in other words, deals with the problem of the One and the Many by giving clear ontological priority to the One over the Many as their transcendent principle of order and intelligibility.

For example, Thomas Aquinas and other medieval philosophers and theologians applied Aristotle's fourfold explanation of causality (formal, material, efficient, and final) to set forth the Christian understanding of the God–world relationship.[5] In thinking through the relationship of the four causes to one another, Aristotle used the model of a master craftsman giving shape or form to some material object (wood, stone, etc.) in the light of some preconceived idea and with a definite purpose or goal in mind.[6] But he also recognized that this causal scheme had to be adjusted with respect to living things or organisms (as opposed to artifacts made by a human craftsman). For each living thing has its own entelechy or intelligible form quite independent of what the craftsman has in mind for it.[7]

For Aquinas, however, God as Creator of heaven and earth brings into existence all living things as well as all inanimate things. Hence, while a living thing or organism operates in terms of its own divinely given "entelechy" or substantial form, it still functions in subordination to the plan of God for the entire cosmic process.[8] That is, whatever efficient cause the organism exercises is secondary or instrumental to the primary efficient causality exercised by God in producing whatever happens within the cosmic process.[9] Hence, within the Thomistic model for the God–world relationship, efficient causality is always exercised top down not bottom up, as in a process-oriented or evolutionary understanding of reality.

Is God then ultimately responsible for everything that happens within this world, that is, not only for natural disasters like earthquakes, mountain avalanches, hurricanes or tornados, droughts but also for moral evils in which human free choice is likewise involved? Alvin Plantinga and Christopher Southgate have dealt with this issue quite well.[10] Plantinga employs what he calls the "free will defense" to claim that God places such high value on human freedom that he permits human beings to make morally evil choices; he refrains, in other words, from exercising his primary causality to predetermine all the free choices of human beings, whether for good or for evil.[11] For similar reasons, God does not unilaterally exercise his primary causality to prevent natural evils from happening because God would then be undermining the validity of the laws of nature as determined over time by the natural sciences. Southgate, for his part, claims that not only human beings but members of higher-order animal species who experience the pain as well as the joy of life in an evolutionary process that is governed by trial and error should likewise experience together with human beings not only objective immortality in the mind of God but also subjective immortality, albeit to a lesser degree than human beings.[12]

Yet, granted that Plantinga and Southgate have dealt so creatively with the issue of theodicy, that is, human justification of divine goodness in the face of manifest moral and natural evil, classical metaphysics is still problematic in the face of contemporary scientific understandings of physical reality. Matter is not inert (as in classical metaphysics) but in some minimal sense "alive," endowed with energy. For example, water (H_2O) is found in three different forms (ice, water, and steam), depending upon ground-level temperature and the amount of energy required to move from one state to another. But this happens internally as a result of ongoing interaction between hydrogen and oxygen molecules, not externally because of top-down causality exercised by an external agent (God or a human being). Hence, hydrogen and oxygen molecules in dynamic interaction (the Many) produce the One, water at one of its several possible stages of existence and activity. The One is thus the ongoing byproduct of the interaction of the Many with one another, not as in classical metaphysics where the One determines the order and intelligibility of the Many.

THE GOD–WORLD RELATIONSHIP IN PROCESS-ORIENTED METAPHYSICS

Bottom-up causation is, of course, taken for granted in process-oriented metaphysics. But there is an unresolved metaphysical problem with the issue of bottom-up causality that turns up in natural science as well as in speculative philosophy. Terrence Deacon, Professor of Biological Anthropology and Neuroscience at the University of California Berkeley, points to the underlying weakness of classical metaphysics to explain the process of evolution within the world of nature, "The phenomena we are interested in explaining are intrinsically historical and dynamic. Being alive does not merely consist in being composed in a particular way. It consists in *changing* in a particular way."[13] To explain how things change or evolve, Deacon appeals to the notion of constraint. When two or more lower-order systems merge, they each put constraints on one another's customary mode of operation. This conflict is resolved with the emergence of a new higher-order system that coordinates their different modes of operation within the context of its own mode of operation.[14] Thus evolution from a lower-level of existence and activity within physical reality to a higher-order level does not come about from the top down as in Aristotelian metaphysics via a change of substantial form but from the bottom up through the mutual constraints that two or more dynamically interrelated systems place on one another's existence and activity in order to mutually survive and prosper. In the process, a new higher-order system comes into existence that places even more constraints on the mode of operation of each of the lower-order systems in their relation to one another.

Yet a philosophical problem remains in Deacon's explanation of the process of evolution, namely, in his assumption of how constraint works.

Constraints do not exercise any kind of causality on the constituents of a system but merely make it possible for something else to happen.[15] This is very close to philosophical nominalism as Deacon himself admits.[16] But de facto he cannot admit any other possibility. For, in his view, the basic constituents of systems, that is, atoms and molecules, are inanimate or lifeless. How can inanimate constituents bring about the existence of a higher-order system (e.g., a cell) that is at least in some measure alive? Admittedly, Deacon is here expressing the widespread conviction of many natural scientists that atoms and molecules are themselves inert or lifeless.[17] But from a philosophical perspective, this is an anomaly. Deacon and other like-minded natural scientists can only say that under certain circumstances it does happen.[18] But they cannot explain why it happens except by chance.

Whitehead, to his credit, solves that problem by stipulating that "[a]ctual entities—also termed 'actual occasions'—are the final real things of which the world is made up."[19] For, actual entities or actual occasions as momentary self-constituting subjects of experience are alive, responsive to one another and to the world around them. Thus there is a reciprocal causal relation between a society with its pre-given mode of operation or governing structure and its constituent parts or members.[20] The society with its governing structure exercises constraint or formal causality on the activity of its constituent actual entities from moment to moment, but these actual entities at the same time exercise efficient causality in codetermining the specific character of the governing structure of the system from moment to moment. The system as a whole is the objective outcome of this interplay of its parts or members from moment to moment.

Nevertheless, Whitehead in my judgment errs in not thinking through more carefully and stating more clearly the metaphysical status of a society as the physical outcome of the reciprocal interplay of its parts or members. Is a society, as a result, an objective reality in its own right that is greater than and other than its parts or members, or is it simply "the least common denominator" or approximate unity of all the individual patterns of existence proper to the current set of constituent actual entities? Is the governing structure constitutive of a new higher-order reality that has evolved out of the interplay of lower-order constituents from moment to moment, or is it simply the transient unity of the constituents at any given moment?

This ambiguity in Whitehead's thought about the nature of societies is pervasive. I cite two other passages by way of example. The first is likewise from *Process and Reality*: "The point of a 'society,' as the term is here used, is that it is self-sustaining; in other words, that it is its own reason."[21] This, of course, could also be the working definition of an Aristotelian substance. But Whitehead then proceeds to explain how it is not an Aristotelian substance: "To constitute a society, the class name has got to apply to each member, by reason of genetic derivation from other members of that same society."[22] That is, current actual entities derive their individual patterns of self-constitution from "prehending" (incorporating) the patterns of self-constitution of predecessor actual entities in the same society and in the world at large. So something new and different is thereby happening. But Whitehead's focus in this passage from *Process and Reality* is clearly on the constituent actual entities and not on the ontological status of the society as the objective outcome of their dynamic interrelation.

The same ambiguity about the independent ontological reality of a society turns up in a passage out of a later book, *Adventures of Ideas:*

> A society has an essential character, whereby it is the society that it is, and it has also accidental qualities which vary as circumstances alter. Thus a society, as a complete existence and as retaining the same metaphysical status, enjoys a history expressing its changing reactions to changing circumstances. But an actual occasion has no such history. It never changes. It only becomes and perishes.[23]

Here, too, a nominal comparison is made between the mode of operation of a Whiteheadian society and the kindred mode of operation of an Aristotelian substance without any further specification from Whitehead on how they are different. Whitehead concedes as much in a footnote on the same page. I conclude, then, that Whitehead vacillates about the ontological status of "society" in his overall metaphysical scheme. With his antecedent commitment to philosophical atomism,[24] he seems to give ontological priority to ongoing change rather than to permanence of structure and substantial form in his philosophical cosmology.

THE LOGICAL COHERENCE OF A
SYSTEMS-ORIENTED PANENTHEISM

As I argued at the beginning of this chapter, the notion of system does not privilege either the One or the Many, the unity of an entity or the diversity of its parts or members. The system is a qualitative or organically constituted whole that exercises efficient and formal causality vis-à-vis other systems in and through the reciprocal causality of its diverse parts or members on one another. The notion of an organically constituted totality or qualitative whole likewise seems to be involved if one tries to offer a rational explanation for belief in panentheism, namely, that the world of creation exists within God and yet is not absorbed into the reality of God but retains its own finite identity and creaturely mode of operation. That is, the cosmic process as a very large but still finite life-system with innumerable subsystems itself exists within the divine life-system, that is, the community of the three divine persons. God thereby affects the world and the world affects God in virtue of a mutual causal relationship, "Every society must be considered with its background of a wider environment of actual entities which also contribute their objectifications to which the members of a society must conform."[25] Hence, the divine life-system influences but does not control the activity of all the subsystems within the cosmic process. Likewise, the cosmic process with all its subsystems influences but does not control the ongoing mode of operation of the divine life-system. That is, God cannot ignore what happens in the world of creation once God has chosen to create a world that is intrinsically dependent upon God as its first cause and will be incorporated into the divine life as its ultimate goal.

Yet a theoretical hurdle exists. Within an evolutionary process, the topmost system is customarily emergent out of all the finite systems that preexisted it. These lower-order systems are collectively the efficient cause of their coming into existence. Within a Christian or any other theistic understanding of the God–world relationship, however, God preexists the world and is the ultimate cause of the world's existence. The cosmic process came into existence in virtue of a one-time free decision by God to create a finite world. Accordingly, God is transcendent of the world as its first cause. In the *Summa Theologiae*, Thomas Aquinas resolved that theoretical issue by not endorsing Aristotle's notion of God as the Unmoved Mover totally removed from the world of creation.[26] Instead, in keeping with the God–world relationship depicted in the Bible, he claimed that God is actively engaged in the world of creation as its first cause and ultimate goal. But he remained faithful to Aristotle in claiming that God is not internally affected by what happens in the world.[27] Thus for Aquinas and for Aristotle the cause–effect relation between God and the world is strictly unilateral, not bilateral or intersubjective, that is, internally affecting both parties.

But within a process- and systems-oriented approach to panentheism, a bilateral or reciprocal causal relation exists between God and the world of creation. Especially if one thinks of God as Trinity or a community of divine persons, it is easy to envision God as the primordial life-system that brought the world into existence by a free decision on the part of the divine persons and now in virtue of its own internal structure and directionality gives meaning and value to the workings of the cosmic process as a whole and to the internal order and directionality of any single finite process at work within its all-encompassing divine field of activity.

The cosmic process, for example, presumably began with a burst of energy or Big Bang within the all-encompassing field of activity proper to the interaction of the divine persons from moment to moment. Innumerable bits of energy-laden matter simultaneously came into existence and then flew apart

at tremendous speed. Very soon thereafter, however, this initial expansion of
the universe slowed down. Subsequent energy-events began to stabilize in
their relations to one another and through a process of trial and error gradually became different kinds of atoms and molecules. From that point onward,
albeit over billions of years, the universe as we human beings understand it
today has grown in size and complexity. At the same time, the error-prone
character of this process of self-development among all the finite life-systems
within the cosmic process has also imposed inevitable constraints on the
activity of the three divine persons in guiding the cosmic process in creative
rather than in self-destructive directions. So a somewhat tenuous but still very
real bilateral or reciprocal causal relation has existed between God and the
world of creation from time immemorial.

Furthermore, thus understood, a systems-oriented approach to the God–
world relationship stands in sharp contrast to the understanding of the
God–world relationship both in classical Aristotelian-Thomistic metaphysics
and in the philosophical cosmology of Alfred North Whitehead. As already
noted, the basic principles of Aristotelian-Thomistic metaphysics are really
not compatible with an understanding of evolution in terms of a hierarchically
ordered set of systems gradually evolving in size and complexity through
bottom-up causation. That is, within Aristotelian-Thomistic metaphysics the
finite world is hierarchically structured according to descending degrees of
actuality from God or the Prime Mover as infinite actuality to prime matter
as pure potentiality for actuation by a finite substantial form. Thus individual
entities at each level of existence and activity are governed in their mode
of operation by substantial forms that have been introduced into their mode
of operation from the outside by God as the first cause of everything that
exists.[28] Admittedly, Aquinas allows for secondary causality on the part of
finite entities in their immediate dealings with one another, but this secondary causality is strictly subordinate to the primary causality of God in dealing
with creatures.[29]

At the same time, Whitehead's understanding of the God–world relationship is really not compatible with Christian belief in the transcendence of
God to creation. For, thinking as a philosopher of science rather than as a systematic theologian, Whitehead was content with the claim that God exists in
virtue of being a key component in the cosmic process as its necessary principle of unity for the multiplicity of actual entities in existence at any given
moment: "God and the World are the contrasted opposites in terms of which
creativity achieves its supreme task of transforming disjoined multiplicity,
with its diversities in opposition, into concrescent unity, with its diversities
in contrast."[30] As a result, the cosmic process with creativity as its organizing
principle, not the God of biblical revelation, is Ultimate Reality. Whitehead,
therefore, clearly gives ontological priority to the Many over the One, that

is, the reality of unending becoming over the reality of unchanging being. For, even in God the unity of the cosmic process from moment to moment is transient.[31] The consequent nature of God recovers the past of the cosmic process only to see it changed, however subtly, in the next moment of divine self-constitution in virtue of creativity as the principle of novelty within the cosmic process.[32]

A TRINITARIAN SYSTEMS-ORIENTED APPROACH TO THE GOD–WORLD RELATIONSHIP

A third alternative, of course, is my own proposal that, if one substitutes the notion of *system* (as opposed to *substance*) in one's understanding of God, self, and the world, then one will have at the same time found the balance between permanence and change promised at the beginning of this chapter. But this hypothesis should still be tested for its applicability to a Christian understanding of the God–world relationship.[33] In what follows, then, I set forth an explanation of key Christian beliefs about the God–world relationship in terms of the systems-oriented panentheism outlined earlier.

I begin with a quick review of the classical explanation of the doctrine of the Trinity in the *Summa Theologiae* of Aquinas. To guard against the danger of tritheism, namely, that the three divine persons are three separate gods rather than one God in three persons, Aquinas stipulated that each of the divine persons is a *subsistent* relation within the unity of the Divine Being.[34] But to be a subsistent relation (as opposed to a contingent relation) within the Divine Being, each divine person has to be fully God in terms of the divine essence.[35] Hence, each of the divine persons is everything that God is but only from one starting point. From the perspective of the classical understanding of the categories of substance and accident, however, this is logically contradictory; relations are by definition contingent attributes of a substance, not identical with the substance as a thing in its own right.[36] But if God is not a higher-order individual entity but instead a corporate entity, an enduring unity-in-diversity of dynamically interrelated parts or members, then one can say without contradiction that the unity of God is the unity of a corporately organized system composed of three individual subsystems, an enduring community of three divine persons who act toward the world of creation as a unitary entity.

Likewise, the doctrine of the incarnation seems to make more sense if one substitutes *system* for *nature* or *essence* in the definition of the doctrine at the ecumenical Council of Chalcedon in 451 AD: "We confess one and the same Christ, the Son, the Lord, the Only-Begotten, in two natures unconfused, unchangeable, undivided and inseparable."[37] No explanation is offered for how two radically different natures or distinct essences could be conjoined in one person and still function as a unitary reality. But, if one substitutes system for nature in the wording of the decree, then it makes perfect sense to claim that divinity and humanity are conjoined in the personhood and activity of Jesus as two hierarchically ordered systems. The humanity of Jesus serves as the necessary infrastructure for the way that a divine person can function in this world, and the divinity of Jesus serves as the superstructure for the way that Jesus exercises his humanity in this world. The relation of the two natures at work in Jesus would be simultaneous and reciprocal rather than sequential and unilateral as in classical metaphysics (i.e., the divine nature dictating to the human nature how to proceed at every moment).

For example, Jesus was constrained in his human behavior by his obedience to the Father as the higher-order authority in his words and actions. Thus throughout his life on earth, he remained chaste even though in his human nature he likely felt a natural desire for sexual intimacy with a woman. At the same time, as a human being, Jesus was constrained in the exercise of his divinity by his need for food and drink, sleep, and other bodily needs. He also periodically felt disappointed or even angry at the resistance of other people to his message, especially the Scribes and Pharisees who knew better than others what he was talking about. After his death and resurrection, of course, his divinity was much more evident. That is, he appeared and disappeared to the disciples quite unexpectedly even though he ate and drank with them, even prepared food for them, as if he were the same as ever.

It would be intriguing to explore this conjunction of the natural and the supernatural further in the context of the miracles performed by Jesus during his lifetime and by the saints and blessed of the church in the centuries that followed. But it is clearly more important to lay out here a systems-oriented understanding of Christian belief in life after death, specifically the resurrection of the body. For, from the perspective of natural science, this seems to be impossible.

A human being is a strictly time-bound reality. He or she grows in size and strength from infancy, achieves a certain stability in the middle years of life, but then inevitably begins to decline both physically and mentally, and eventually dies. How then can one rationally maintain that a human being as a body-mind unity continues to live in an altered state after earthly life ends? In the context of classical metaphysics, a human being is said to be composed of an immaterial soul and a material body. Thus one can respond that the human soul, given its immateriality, will survive the death of the body and enjoy subjective immortality in union with God afterward. But how the human body with all its physical limitations can also be incorporated into the divine life remains a puzzle.

Within a systems-oriented approach to reality, however, a human being is a hierarchically ordered set of systems. Hence, the self (i.e., the soul of a human being) is a higher-order system emergent out of the ongoing interplay of mind and body over a lifetime as its dynamically interrelated subsystems. But the self or soul is itself a subsystem within the higher-order set of systems characteristic of the cosmic process, and the cosmic process is in turn a subsystem within the divine life-system, the ongoing common life of the three divine persons. The governing structure of each lower-order system is incorporated into the governing structure of the next higher-order system. Hence, when the infrastructure of mind and body for the self decomposes at the moment of death, the governing structure of the self (the personality of the self as it has developed over the years) still survives as woven into the objective structure of the cosmic process and as a participant in salvation history, the divine life-system with its enduring record of the interactions between the divine persons and all their creatures from time immemorial.

This solves the problem of objective immortality for every human being and indeed for all the other finite entities within this world. But what is to be said about the possibility of subjective immortality at least for human beings, that is, subjective awareness of the role that one has played in this grand scheme? At the moment of death, a human being is freed of its infrastructure, the limiting conditions of life in this world. Hence, even though the corpse or physical body of the person is left behind, the system proper to the soul or life-principle of the human being continues to exist but now as a participant within a graded series of increasingly complex life-systems up to and including the divine life-system proper to the divine persons apart from creation.[38]

Yet a human being endowed with freedom of choice still has to decide whether or not to participate in this postmortem higher-level system of existence and activity within the cosmic process and the divine life-system. But then one must accept one's past life in its entirety. That is, one has to admit to other human beings and the divine persons one's faults and failures in dealing with them during one's life in this world and ask for forgiveness, thereby accepting one's status as a forgiven sinner. This may not be easy, given the dominant behavior pattern of one's past life, that is, whether one was basically self-centered or self-giving in dealing with others.

If then a human being rejects participation in the life of the world to come on these terms, what happens to them? One can only assume that the divine persons will never retract their offer of a much richer life in heaven to that individual. Thus they will not banish him or her to hell as a place of everlasting punishment for sin. Instead, they allow him or her to remain within the divine life-system but in isolation from everyone else by one's own choice. One thereby condemns oneself to a personal hell. Under these trying circumstances, possibly everyone will be "saved." That is, even the most obdurate individuals will see the error of their ways in this life and ask for forgiveness from those they have harmed in this life. But that choice must be voluntary to be authentic. As Moses speaking in God's name said to the people of Israel after their escape from captivity in Egypt, "I set before you today life and prosperity, death and destruction. . . . Now choose life, so that you and your children may live and that you may love the LORD your God, listen to his voice, and hold fast to him" (Deut. 30:15–20).

Looking back on the overall argument of this chapter, then, I conclude that this systems-oriented approach to a Christian understanding of the God–world relationship is logically consistent and basically compatible with the full range of traditional Christian beliefs. Likewise, in comparison with scholastic metaphysics and the process-oriented cosmology of Alfred North Whitehead, it seems to offer a better balance between permanence and change. Here everything changes but always in the context of an even greater sense of permanence. Thereby time loses its character of "perpetual perishing" and becomes instead "the moving image of eternity."[39]

At the same time, I should concede that this chapter has been written more from the perspective of rational reflection on purely philosophical issues and as a result makes little reference to its practical meaning and value for a Christian trying to live the gospel message in line with church teaching. But this deficiency can be at least partially resolved if one studies carefully the recent encyclical letter of Pope Francis on the environment, *On Care for Our Common Home (Laudato Si').*[40] For, he uses the language of contemporary systems theory as employed in the life sciences to motivate not only fellow Roman Catholics but all morally upright human beings to take action on remedying the current environmental crisis. Pope Francis, however, immediately adds that the church "has no reason to offer a definitive opinion. She knows that honest debate must be encouraged by experts, while respecting divergent views."[41]

Yet, the church does have its own point of view based on scripture and church documents, notably the encyclical letters of Pope Francis's predecessors on the need for social justice and racial equality (e.g., Popes John XXIII, Paul VI, John Paul II, and Benedict XV1).[42] But, as Pope Francis notes, "There needs to be a distinctive way of looking at things, a way of thinking, policies, an educational program, a lifestyle and a spirituality which together generate resistance to the assault of the technocratic paradigm."[43]

The scientific community responded very favorably to this encyclical letter on the environment, if only because it was so honestly worded and showed an unexpected openness to dialogue which in centuries past was relatively rare among church authorities.[44] The well-known environmentalist Bill McKibben personally commented, "The empirical data about climate change makes it clear that the moment is ripe for this encyclical."[45] Only an appropriate conjunction of religious feeling and sober scientific reflection can motivate human beings to change even at a cost to themselves. Some form of practical theology, accordingly, will flow naturally when thinking along these lines with the Pope.

NOTES

1. Alfred North Whitehead, *Process and Reality: An Essay in Cosmology* (1929), corrected ed., ed. David Ray Griffin and Donald W. Sherburne (New York: Free Press, 1978), 341 (hereafter *"PR"*).

2. Ibid., 338.

3. Cf. Willard V. O. Quine, "Two Dogmas of Empiricism," *The Philosophical Review* 60.1 (1951): 20–43.

4. *PR* 4.

5. Cf. W. T. Jones, *A History of Western Philosophy*, 5 vols., 2nd ed. (New York: Harcourt, Brace & World, 1969), 2:211.

6. Ibid., 1:225.

7. Ibid., 1:226.

8. Cf., e.g., Thomas Aquinas, *Summa Theologiae* (Madrid: Biblioteca de Autores Cristianos, 1951), Ia.22.2 (hereafter *"ST"*).

9. Ibid., Ia.22.2, n. 2.

10. See, e.g., Alvin Plantinga, *God, Freedom and Evil* (Grand Rapids, MI: Wm. B. Eerdmans Publishing Co., 1977); Christopher Southgate, *The Groaning of Creation: God, Evolution and the Problem of Evil* (Louisville: Westminster John Knox, 2008).

11. Plantinga, *God, Freedom and Evil*, 49, 166–67.

12. Southgate, *Groaning of Creation*, 86–90.

13. Terrence W. Deacon, *Incomplete Nature: How Mind Emerged from Matter* (New York: W. W. Norton, 2012), 175 (emphasis in original).

14. Ibid., 182–205.

15. Ibid., 192.

16. Ibid., 191.

17. Ibid., 289. Cf. also Philip Clayton, *Mind & Emergence: From Quantum to Consciousness* (New York: Oxford University Press, 2004), 46.

18. Deacon, *Incomplete Nature*, 237–38. Cf. also Stuart A. Kauffman, *At Home in the Universe: The Search for Laws of Self-Organization and Complexity* (New York: Oxford University Press, 1995), 47–48.

19. *PR* 18.

20. Ibid., 91.

21. Ibid., 89.

22. Ibid.

23. Alfred North Whitehead, *Adventures of Ideas* (1933; repr., New York: Free Press, 1967), 204.

24. *PR* 18, 35.

25. Ibid., 90.

26. Jones, *A History of Western Philosophy*, 2:228–32.

27. *ST* Ia.8.3.
28. Ibid., Ia.2.3.
29. Ibid., Ia.22.3 ad 2.
30. *PR* 348.
31. Ibid., 350.
32. Ibid., 21.
33. Ibid., 3–4, where Whitehead sets out the parameters for a philosophical cosmology.
34. *ST* Ia.29.4.
35. Ibid.
36. Aristotle, *Metaphysics*, 1029a.
37. Josef Neuner, Heinrich Roos, and Karl Rahner, eds. *The Teaching of the Catholic Church*, trans. Geoffrey Stevens (Staten Island, NY: Society of Saint Paul, 1967), 154n2.
38. Cf. John Polkinghorne, *The God of Hope and the End of the World* (New Haven, CT: Yale University Press, 2002), 105–6. Atoms within the human body are regularly replaced, but the "information-bearing pattern that is the soul" survives as the principle of identity for the human being.
39. *PR* 338.
40. Pope Francis, *Laudato Si'* (Washington, DC: United States Conference of Catholic Bishops, 2015).
41. Ibid., 29.
42. Ibid., 1–3.
43. Ibid., 54.
44. Cf., e.g., "Hope from the Pope," *Nature* 522, June 25, 2015, 391.
45. Bill McKibben, "Introduction: On Care for our Common Home," in *For Our Common Home: Process-Relational Responses to Laudato Si'*, ed. John B. Cobb Jr. and Ignacio Castuera (Anoka, MN: Process Century Press, 2015), 8.

BIBLIOGRAPHY

Aquinas, Thomas. *Summa Theologiae*. Madrid: Biblioteca de Autores Cristianos, 1951.
Aristotle. *The Complete Works of Aristotle*. Edited by Jonathan Barnes. 2 vols. Princeton, NJ: Princeton University Press. 1984.
Clayton, Philip. *Mind & Emergence: From Quantum to Consciousness*. New York: Oxford University Press, 2004.
Deacon, Terrence W. *Incomplete Nature: How Mind Emerged from Matter*. New York: W. W. Norton, 2012.
Francis, Pope. *Laudato Si'*. Washington, DC: United States Conference of Catholic Bishops, 2015.
"Hope from the Pope." *Nature* 522, June 25, 2015.
Jones, W. T. *A History of Western Philosophy*. 5 vols. 2nd ed. New York: Harcourt, Brace & World, 1969.

Kauffman, Stuart A. *At Home in the Universe: The Search for Laws of Self-Organization and Complexity*. New York: Oxford University Press, 1995.

McKibben, Bill. "Introduction: On Care for our Common Home." In *For Our Common Home: Process-Relational Responses to Laudato Si'*, edited by John B. Cobb Jr. and Ignacio Castuera, 1–10. Anoka, MN: Process Century Press, 2015.

Neuner, Josef, Heinrich Roos, and Karl Rahner, eds. *The Teaching of the Catholic Church*. Translated by Geoffrey Stevens. Staten Island, NY: Society of Saint Paul, 1967.

Plantinga, Alvin. *God, Freedom and Evil*. Grand Rapids, MI: Wm. B. Eerdmans Publishing Co., 1977.

Polkinghorne, John. *The God of Hope and the End of the World*. New Haven, CT: Yale University Press, 2002.

Quine, Willard V. O. "Two Dogmas of Empiricism." *The Philosophical Review* 60.1 (1951): 20–43.

Southgate, Christopher. *The Groaning of Creation: God, Evolution and the Problem of Evil*. Louisville: Westminster John Knox, 2008.

Whitehead, Alfred North. *Adventures of Ideas*. 1933. Reprint, New York: Free Press, 1967.

Whitehead, Alfred North. *Process and Reality: An Essay in Cosmology*. 1929. Corrected ed. Edited by David Ray Griffin and Donald W. Sherburne. New York: The Free Press, 1978.

Chapter 7

A Process Interpretation
of *Creatio ex Nihilo*

Thomas E. Hosinski, C. S. C.

While there is a great diversity among Roman Catholic theologians in influences and approaches, one thing they virtually all share in common is a deep respect for the doctrinal tradition of Christianity. In fact, the vast majority of Roman Catholic theologians would agree that faithfulness to the heart of the Christian doctrinal tradition is one of the criteria by which we must evaluate and judge theological interpretations. Many would go so far as to say that any theological interpretation that departs from the core doctrinal tradition might be interesting but can be no more than a *personal* theological viewpoint, not a representation of the Christian *community's* understanding.

One of the reasons Roman Catholic theologians have for the most part ignored or rejected process theology, I believe, is the ease with which many process theologians dismiss and reject important Christian doctrines. The doctrine of *creatio ex nihilo* in particular, the heart of the Christian doctrine of creation, is a favorite target of criticism by process theologians. For example, in their introduction to process theology John Cobb Jr. and David Ray Griffin say, "Process theology rejects the notion of *creatio ex nihilo*, if that means creation out of *absolute* nothingness. That doctrine is part and parcel of the doctrine of God as absolute controller. Process theology affirms instead a doctrine of creation out of chaos."[1] Before proceeding, it would be best to understand why process theology rejects *creatio ex nihilo*.

WHY PROCESS THEOLOGY REJECTS
CREATIO EX NIHILO

There are several interrelated reasons for process theology's rejection of the doctrine of *creatio ex nihilo*. These revolve around the notion of God as absolutely controlling and determining the creation. This in turn is involved in the understanding of the problem of evil in the universe. Whitehead addressed this connection when he said:

> Among medieval and modern philosophers, anxious to establish the religious significance of God, an unfortunate habit has prevailed of paying to Him metaphysical compliments. He has been conceived as the foundation of the metaphysical situation with its ultimate activity. If this conception be adhered to, there can be no alternative except to discern in Him the origin of all evil as well as of all good. He is then the supreme author of the play, and to Him must therefore be ascribed its shortcomings as well as its success.[2]

The attractiveness of Whitehead's solution to the problem of evil, I believe, is one of the reasons process theologians reject the doctrine of *creatio ex nihilo*.

The classical problem of (natural) evil can be stated in this way: If God created the universe from nothing, and if God is all-good and all-powerful, then why is there evil in the world? Although the term "natural evil" may not be ideal, it is the classic term for this problem referring to harmful occurrences and events not caused by human freedom. When experiencing any natural evil, people throughout the ages ask, "Why did God allow this to happen?" The assumptions behind such questions are that God alone creates the universe and controls all things that happen in nature and hence must "permit" these "evil" occurrences to happen. Whitehead solves the problem of evil by abandoning the traditional notion that God controls (i.e., determines) all events in nature and history. His solution involves as well a rejection of the traditional doctrine of *creatio ex nihilo* in a way I shall now outline.

In Whitehead's metaphysics, *creativity* is the "universal of universals," the ultimate principle driving the universal process, and therefore the "ultimate activity" of the universe.[3] God is not the *source* of creativity but rather is creativity's "primordial, non-temporal accident"; that is, God is the primordial actualization of creativity.[4] God, in turn, makes possible the creative becoming of all other actual entities by "deciding" the structure and organization of potentiality for the universe.[5] In this sense, God is Creator in Whitehead's metaphysics. Creativity, however, is not present in the universe as a gift from the Creator, but is *inherent* in every actual entity in the universe, present by the very nature of the metaphysical situation. The actual entities of the temporal world depend upon God in several ways, and so God can rightly be called Creator in Whitehead's philosophy.[6] However, the actual entities of the universe are not creative because God allows or enables them to be so; rather, they are creative in their own right. God and the world, Whitehead says, are both "in the grip of the ultimate metaphysical ground, the creative advance into novelty."[7]

Creativity is in this way independent of God, simply inherent in all actual entities. Regarding creativity in this way goes a long way toward resolving the problem of evil. Freedom is a correlate of creativity; that is, the creativity inherent in every actual entity carries with it a freedom in relation to possibility. Although freedom in the temporal world is always constrained (limited by finitude and the various social influences of the situations in which actual entities arise), Whitehead held that freedom is always present, however minimally, in every actual entity. God alone is unconstrained and absolutely free in how God "decides" or organizes all possibility (Whitehead's primordial nature of God, prehending all eternal objects or potentialities and thus ordering them for the possibility of a universe). However, every temporal actual entity enjoys a limited freedom (to one degree or another) with regard to what possibility it chooses to actualize in itself from among those open to it in its situation. There is nothing in the nature of freedom guaranteeing that free choices will be for the good. The possibility an actual entity actualizes might introduce something trivial or degraded or mediocre in comparison to what might have been, and, on the human level, the free choice can be for a moral evil. In addition, the free decisions of actual entities can be mutually obstructive, the product of competing values, introducing discord and conflict into the universal process.

How this resolves the problem of evil seems obvious. God and the actual entities of the universe are both involved in the creative process, reacting to possibilities ("eternal objects") that neither have created. God cannot control what decisions temporal actual entities make with regard to what possibility they will actualize in themselves. God can "lure" their decisions toward the possibility God prefers, but such "lures" can easily be countered and overcome by other, more powerful influences emanating from the actual entity's social situation or its own inclinations. In short, since every actual entity is free in its decision, and the influences of the social environment may outweigh the influence of God's "lure," God cannot control what decisions actual entities make. God's power is limited by the metaphysical situation; God can exercise the power of persuasion, but not control. In short, God is not the "supreme author of the play" and is not responsible for its shortcomings; the "play" has multiple authors and its shortcomings are the result of the free decisions of the actual entities of the universe as well as the conditions of finitude.

THE THEOLOGICAL PROBLEM INVOLVED
IN REJECTING *CREATIO EX NIHILO*

As attractive as Whitehead's solution to the problem of evil is—for it offers a truly persuasive solution to a problem that has plagued Christian thought

for many centuries—it involves a rejection of the notion of *creatio ex nihilo*.
This claim for God as Creator *ex nihilo* has been central to Christianity's
self-understanding since the time of the Christian apologists in the second
century. It is questionable whether a rejection of this doctrine can result in a
theology that can claim to represent the Christian *community's* understanding
of God and God's relation to the universe.

The apologists were aware that *creatio ex nihilo* is not explicitly stated in
scripture.[8] Yet they regarded this doctrine as implied by scripture and understood it as an important corrective to the Greek notion of the coeternity of
God and matter. In the judgment of early Christian theologians, this Greek
notion could lead only to pantheism or to an ultimate dualism of God and
matter. In either case, this seemed to them to compromise monotheism, the
Judeo-Christian belief that God alone is the source of all.[9] Therefore, Cobb
and Griffin's argument that creation out of chaos is preferable to the doctrine
of creation out of nothing seems to ignore what the early church saw as a
dangerous compromise of monotheism. Throughout the centuries, whatever
differences emerged within the Christian church, all Christians affirmed *creatio ex nihilo* as the core of the doctrine of creation. It seems to me that one
can make a very strong case for the doctrine of *creatio ex nihilo* being central
to the Christian community's understanding of reality, of the God–world
relationship.

The difficulty in accepting Whitehead's solution to the problem of evil and
his understanding of God and creativity is precisely that it seems to compromise monotheism. It sets up creativity and the eternal objects as independent
of God and implies that the source of the universe is not solely God but
rather an amalgam of eternal objects (or possibilities), creativity, and God,
all equally eternal and metaphysically ultimate. Furthermore, it seems to me
that Whitehead's claim that creativity has an ultimate independence of God
undercuts one of his own insights regarding the God–world relationship. In
Religion in the Making, Whitehead wrote a sentence that has haunted me
since I first read it many years ago. He wrote: "The world lives by its incarnation of God in itself."[10] This statement rings with truth. It is actually making
a complex claim, but part of its meaning must surely concern the world's
creativity. The *life* of the world—its activity, its ongoing experience—is precisely its creativity, continually responding to the world of the past and to the
possibilities open to the present in order to create the ground of the future. If
the world lives by incarnating God in itself, does this not imply that the world
is creative because it shares in the infinite creativity of God?

In short, in my judgment, it is not compatible with the Christian theological tradition to reject *creatio ex nihilo* and hold that creativity operates independently of God. This compromises what the tradition has held to be the
necessary implications of monotheism and God's absoluteness as Creator, the

source of the universe.[11] Rather, Christian theology affirms that creativity is God's own being or "life," and creatures share in the creativity of the divine life precisely because they *exist by participation* in the Divine Being or "life," an ancient Christian idea. In the remainder of this chapter, I will attempt to show that one can articulate the traditional claim of *creatio ex nihilo* in process categories (despite the necessary revision of Whitehead's own view) and that even important elements of Whitehead's solution to the problem of evil can be retained in this revised view.

A PROCESS INTERPRETATION OF *CREATIO EX NIHILO*

In addition to the revisions of Whitehead's metaphysics that are required and which I will discuss in this chapter, there are two keys to developing a process understanding of *creatio ex nihilo*.[12] The first is to separate the notion of *control* or determination from the idea of creation in general and *creatio ex nihilo* in particular. The second is to accept Whitehead's extension of freedom to all actual entities and to regard that universal freedom of the agents of the universe as a divine gift, the gift of creaturely participation in the Divine Being and freedom. I will begin with the notion of control in relation to creation (and providence).

I believe process theology is correct in criticizing the tradition on the topic of divine control of all things in nature and even history. Anyone acquainted with the tradition knows that until quite recently theologians assumed that God controlled the events of nature and, to some extent, history. The tradition believed that all the events of nature occurred in conformity to God's will (i.e., were controlled by God) because nature was composed of unintelligent things and animals. Humans alone had intelligence and free will and so freedom of action, the tradition assumed, was restricted to human beings. It was therefore quite natural to assume that God's act of creation *ex nihilo* was controlling: God's creative act made things what they are and made them to act the way they do. Creation understood in this way is determining and controlling. One could give many examples, but a particularly clear example is the analysis of Thomas Aquinas in his explication of the fifth way to prove the existence of God.[13]

Even the fact of human freedom is determined because that is how God created humans and determined their nature. The events of human history occur as the result of human free choices, but even here there is some ambiguity in the tradition's understanding. Christian theology recognized that God did not control or determine free human choices—this is, after all, crucial to the doctrine of sin and, consequently, crucial for the doctrine of salvation. Thomas Aquinas, for example, clearly wanted to affirm contingency in the universe and freedom of choice in humans.[14] But his solution, despite Elizabeth Johnson's defense of the distinction between primary (divine) and secondary (creaturely) causation, is problematic.[15]

This topic deserves a more extensive critical analysis than I have space to provide here. However, I offer these critical remarks. Thomas holds that God creates through God's eternal, unchanging knowledge.[16] How does this not impose necessity on all things? Aquinas argues that "eternity, being simultaneously whole, comprises all time."[17] Since God's knowledge is eternal, God knows all contingent events as *present facts*, and this in turn means that God's creative knowledge of all contingent events (and human free choices) is certain and necessary without imposing necessity on them. The events in relation to their proximate causes in the temporal world are truly contingent and free, in that they might have been otherwise, but since God in eternity sees all things as present, God's eternal creative knowledge is certain and necessary. For example, I can know with certainty that 10 minutes ago I was sitting at my computer and that I am presently doing so, although I also know that I was perfectly free 10 minutes ago and am free now to stand up and walk around. In this way, Thomas believes, both contingency and freedom are preserved without violating the necessity, immutability, and perfection of God's knowledge.

Elsewhere Thomas states that things are done in the way God wills, that God "has prepared contingent causes [for certain effects] because He has willed that they should happen contingently."[18] This sounds reasonable. But how can contingent secondary causes truly be contingent in their effects and how can they have any independence and integrity of action of their own, if from all eternity with perfect, unchanging knowledge God wills and creates this outcome? How can I *really* have freedom and independence to do something other than what God from all eternity knows with certain, unchanging knowledge and wills with perfect efficaciousness in the act of creation? The result is indistinguishable from absolute determinism. Thomas's solution of having God "see" in eternity "before" creation what all contingent events and free choices will be and creating them that way is nothing other than metaphysical sleight of hand. The future cannot be known until it is actual, and this means that God cannot *fore*see all events and choices as present facts and create through that knowledge. God has perfect and unchanging knowledge of all *possibilities*, but cannot know events and choices as *facts* until they have become so. The future is actually open in this way, even for God.

The ambiguity in the tradition's understanding of divine determination and human freedom is on full display and even more clear in any discussion of predestination, such as we find in Augustine, Thomas Aquinas, Luther, and Calvin.

The notion that creation necessarily involves control or determination is certainly not the only way to conceive of creation, even creation from nothing. The point of the doctrine of *creatio ex nihilo*, after all, is not to say that God controls everything. Rather, the point, as the ancient tradition makes clear, is to say that nothing stands over against God in the act of creation, that God is not constrained, or limited, or opposed by anything of equal ultimacy (an idea also expressed in the divine attribute of omnipotence). *Creatio ex nihilo* means that God is absolutely free in how God creates. This absolute freedom does not necessarily imply control in the sense of determination. We can affirm God's absolute freedom in creation without affirming that God thereby determines outcomes. Absolute freedom means God can choose to create in any way God wishes and create whatever God wishes. God can create by making things (actual entities) possible and endowing them with freedom to create themselves. God can choose, in other words, not to determine actual entities but *to make them possible and allow and enable them to create themselves* by choosing the possibility they shall actualize in and for themselves. God can influence by "luring" actual entities toward the possibility-value God sees as most beautiful without determining which possibility-value they will actualize. God can choose, in short, to share God's own freedom in a limited way with each temporal actual entity (or agent) as its participation in the divine life, endowing it with all it needs to complete its own becoming. This is very similar to Whitehead's own vision but differs in a very significant way by making the limitation on divine power and control God's own choosing and making the creativity of each actual entity its finite participation in the infinite creativity of God.

Four "categories" or concepts together have an "extreme finality" in Whitehead's metaphysical system.[19] These are creativity, God, "eternal objects" (potentials or infinite possibilities), and actual entities. Each of these notions requires the other three and together they describe the universe in a coherent way.[20] In Whitehead's system, these ideas are on an equal footing. God has a unique role among them and is the most important in the sense that without God creativity and the eternal objects could not bring about a universe of actual entities.[21] God, however, remains "within" the system, requiring the other three, and not "above" or "behind" the system as the ultimate explanation of it all. In Whitehead's philosophy, this system is simply the "given" metaphysical situation: given in the sense that one cannot seek "behind" or "above" the system to find some ultimate explanation of it all, some radically transcendent ground of the system itself. Whitehead believed that to affirm a radically transcendent Creator above or behind the system was to abandon the rational search for metaphysical coherence.[22] As we have seen, this limitation or relativization of God was an essential part of his solution to the problem of evil.

We can affirm *creatio ex nihilo* in process categories or terms by uniting three of the four notions that Whitehead separated or thought of as independent of each other: God, creativity, and the "eternal objects" (or infinite possibilities). I have already discussed how understanding creativity to be the divine life (or Being) itself, instead of regarding it as independent of God, enables us to think of God as Creator in a sense that is compatible with the intent of the doctrine of *creatio ex nihilo*.

I turn now to how we might revise Whitehead's understanding of the relation of the "eternal objects" to God. The term "eternal objects" confuses many of Whitehead's readers. He preferred it, but equated it to the terms "pure potentials" or "forms of definiteness."[23] These terms can also be confusing to many readers. In my view, it is easiest to understand what Whitehead means by thinking of eternal objects as abstract possibilities, that is, pure possibilities in abstraction from the actual world. When you reflect on abstract possibility, its unusual character emerges. Possibilities are real, because we can think of them and mull them over, and even choose among them; in that sense, they are "entities." However, they are not *actual* entities: they are not agents that have the power to make things happen (to actualize some possibility); they are not "things" that can be physically observed or touched. In addition, abstract possibility is infinite.

No contemporary philosopher of whom I am aware reflected more deeply on the nature and importance of possibility than Whitehead. In his metaphysics, the eternal objects (or infinity of pure, abstract possibilities) are extremely important: the creative process of the universe depends on the interaction between possibility and actuality, the actual world continually actualizing new possibilities in its ongoing process of becoming. Yet infinite possibility in abstraction from the actual world is chaotic in the literal sense of that word: if all possibilities are equally possible, as they must be in abstraction from the actual world, then there is no order among them, no relationships that create a scaffolding of order.

One of the necessary roles for God in Whitehead's metaphysics is precisely the *prehension* or grasping of all possibilities in the primordial nature of God, which establishes relationships and thus a limitation among them, ordering them for a world. Whitehead defines the primordial nature of God as, "the unconditioned conceptual valuation of the entire multiplicity of eternal objects."[24] In grasping (or prehending) all possibilities God "valuates" them relative to God's own aim. This not only invests possibilities with value, it necessarily orders them relative to God's valuation and aim.[25] Without this ordering, there could be no universe. The primordial nature of God makes a universe possible by the valuation and ordering of pure abstract possibility.

In Whitehead's metaphysics, however, the eternal objects have no origin; they are simply "there" primordially for God to prehend. Along with creativity, they have an independence from God as ultimate elements of the metaphysical situation. In *Process and Reality*, Whitehead says:

> [T]he differentiated relevance of eternal objects to each instance of the creative process requires their conceptual realization in the primordial nature of God. He does not create eternal objects; for his nature requires them in the same degree that they require him. . . . The general relationships of eternal objects to each other, relationships of diversity and of pattern, are their relationships in God's conceptual realization. Apart from this realization, there is mere isolation indistinguishable from nonentity.[26]

Apart from God, the eternal objects are powerless to bring about a universe and they have no actuality of their own, and so they are "indistinguishable from nonentity," but God does not create them. Whitehead's position on eternal objects as simply "there" for God to prehend primordially creates a problem relative to the doctrine of *creatio ex nihilo*. It seems to set up the eternal objects (or pure abstract possibilities) as coeternal with God, co-ultimate, and this appears to compromise what the tradition has claimed for monotheism: that God alone is the eternal, ultimate source of all that is, that nothing stands alongside God as equally ultimate.

I believe there is a resolution to this problem hinted at in the very quotation I have just considered. Whitehead does not want to say that God creates the eternal objects because that would seem to make God responsible for the very existence of possibilities of evil and make the problem of evil very difficult to resolve. To avoid that difficulty, he treats the eternal objects as an ultimate notion required to understand reality and to understand God's primary action as well. He admits, however, that apart from God's realization of the eternal objects (which fills them with value and orders them so that some universe becomes possible), "there is mere isolation indistinguishable from nonentity." It is *only as they are valuated and ordered by God* that eternal objects are capable of any effective relation to the actual world. My point is that in order for actual process (or creation) to occur, the eternal objects must be *within* God (prehended by God), ordered, and carrying value. Without their presence in God (or, if you prefer, their prehension and conceptual valuation by God), the eternal objects are "indistinguishable from nonentity."

Perhaps, then, we can conceive of God's Infinite Being as necessarily including (or enfolding) infinite possibility so that possibilities are distinguishable from God yet necessarily included within the Divine Being. This may strike one as very strange, yet it is not a new idea in theology. In the fifteenth century, Nicholas of Cusa argued that God may be conceived as "actualized possibility," inclusive of infinite possibility. Nicholas argued in effect that God as Infinite Being must include all possibilities precisely because all that is "unfolds" from God and is "enfolded" by God. He goes so far as to say, "O how great is our God, who is the actuality of every possibility!"[27] Nicholas does not mean that God *actualizes* every possibility (this, if one thinks about it, is impossible); rather, he means that God is the actual source of infinite possibilities. He seems to be claiming that because possibility is infinite and God is absolutely Infinite Being, the infinity of God must encompass or include the infinity of possibilities. If this is a coherent idea, then it would permit a doctrine of *creatio ex nihilo* in process terms or categories, postulating a relation between God and possibilities that does not compromise monotheism and God's absoluteness as Creator.

If creativity is conceived as the divine life (or Being) itself, and if infinite possibilities are understood to spring from the Infinite Being of God, then we can affirm a doctrine of *creatio ex nihilo* in process terms. Instead of holding that God is merely one of the ultimate elements at the base of the very possibility of the universe, both the possibilities that lure the universal process and the creativity that drives it are actually gifts from God. God shares the divine life with the universe in the creative act; the creatures, the temporal actual entities of the universe, participate in a finite way in the freedom and creativity of the Creator. God, in sharing the divine creativity and endowing actual entities with all they require in order to create themselves, does not control or determine what they shall make of themselves, but enables them to be finite instances of creativity, freely completing their own creation in their decision of what possibility to actualize in themselves.

This leads us to the final topic we must consider: the freedom of the temporal actual entities of the universe. There is first the problem of whether one can believe Whitehead's affirmation of some degree of freedom in all actual entities of the universe. I would submit that our knowledge and experience of the universe support Whitehead's view. The universe, as we currently understand it, displays an evolutionary history of amazing novelty. The history of the emergence and evolution of life on our planet displays an astounding novelty of both forms and ways of making a living on this earth. Scientists have a tendency to say that all things are determined by the laws of nature. However, nature really looks like a huge exploration of possibility issuing in the emergence of a wealth of novelty. The occurrence of novelty is really a serious problem for understanding: If all things are determined, if the past entirely determines the present, how can anything new ever emerge? Certainly, there is continuity of form on a massive scale throughout the universe, but there is also an undeniable diversity of forms and the emergence of novel forms also on a massive scale. From the most infinitesimal level of the universe studied by quantum physicists to the most complex forms of life studied by biologists and neurologists, the universe displays astonishing novelty. How is this possible?

This is not the place to rehearse the complexities of Whitehead's answer to this question.[28] To summarize briefly, Whitehead accounts for the occurrence of novelty in the universe by holding that every actual entity in its process of becoming (concrescence) grasps the set of possibilities open to it in its situation, valuates those possibilities relative to its own subjective aim in its situation, and "decides" to actualize one of those possibilities. (Whitehead used "decides" in its root meaning of "cutting off"; he certainly does not mean to imply that all actual entities are conscious.) This implies that actual entities can somehow grasp the value of possibilities open to them in their situations. Whitehead generally refers to this ability as "mentality" and affirms that all actual entities have some degree of mentality, however negligible.[29] In addition, Whitehead's analysis attributes a certain amount of freedom to actual entities, the freedom to "decide." This freedom is present in the actual entity, as we have seen, as a correlate of its inherent creativity. The fact that the actual entity is inherently free, the reader will recall, is part of Whitehead's solution to the problem of evil.

In a process understanding of *creatio ex nihilo*, in contrast, we can understand the freedom of actual entities as the result of God's gift, the sharing in the divine life with which God chooses to endow the creature. The finite creature exists by participating in the Infinite Being of God and this participation includes a finite sharing in the infinite creativity and freedom of the Creator. How specifically can we conceive of this sharing in process terms? Briefly, God enables each temporal actual entity to do in a limited and finite way what God does for the universe as Creator. God creates by grasping all possibilities, valuating them relative to God's aim, thereby setting a limitation or condition upon them and making an actual course of events possible. God endows every actual entity in the universe with the set of possibilities relevant for its situation, with its aim to make something of itself, and with its creativity and freedom to complete its becoming. This is what enables and allows every temporal actual entity to do in a limited way what God does. Every temporal actual entity grasps a set of possibilities relevant to its situation, valuates those possibilities, and selects one to actualize in itself. This establishes a condition that will affect future actual entities, limiting them in some way but perhaps also opening the way for a novel course of events. The creativity and influence of temporal actual entities mirror in a limited, finite way the infinite creativity and influence of God.

We have seen how Whitehead's ideas may be modified and revised to support the aims and intents of affirming the doctrine of *creatio ex nihilo*. This may raise an important objection, however. Does not affirming that God creates *ex nihilo* bring back the problem of evil that has vexed Christian theology for so many centuries? I think that much of Whitehead's solution to the problem of evil remains once one thinks through the implications of existence as participation in the divine life and creativity. Process theology rejects *creatio ex nihilo* because the tradition assumed this meant God's absolute control of the universe and it seems that a God who creates *ex nihilo* ought to be able to avoid or eliminate evil from the world. However, if God chooses to create a universe that shares in God's own creativity and freedom, God thereby must limit God's own power to control what happens. If God chose to prevent all evil, this would destroy the very universe God seeks to create: a universe in which temporal actual entities or agents share in the divine freedom to decide what possibilities are actualized. It would be God acting against God's own freedom. In short, if God wills the universe to be free and empowers every temporal actual entity to share in a limited way in God's own autonomy and freedom, then God must necessarily limit God's own power to control. To remove that limitation on divine power would be to destroy the very thing God wills to create. It would be violating God's own sharing of the divine life with the creature, in effect a violation of God's own creativity. To create a universe of creatures participating in God's own life, God's creative freedom, means that God cannot control or determine what those creatures do in their freedom and autonomy. In this way, the practical result of conceiving of God as Creator *ex nihilo* in process terms is virtually identical with Whitehead's view.

There is, however, a major theological difference. In Whitehead's metaphysics, the limitation on God's power is simply "built into" the system and God is only one of several ultimate realities at the source of the universe. God is not the Creator *ex nihilo*. In the revised understanding of God as Creator *ex nihilo*, God is the sole source of all that is and the limitation on God's power is self-imposed, freely chosen by God. God, in this view, has theoretical omnipotence, but God's decision to create a universe in which the agent-entities composing the universe share in the divine life—the divine creativity, autonomy and freedom—means that God must freely limit God's power to enable the exercise of creaturely freedom. This view of God shares much in common with the Whiteheadian view but is much more in accord with the tradition's conviction that God is the sole source of all, the absolutely free Creator *ex nihilo*.

In sum, I believe that faithfulness to the doctrinal tradition of Christianity requires us to affirm God as Creator *ex nihilo*. While Whitehead himself did not find that claim congenial because of certain assumptions that the tradition made about divine control of nature and history, I believe that his philosophy may be used to express the central meaning of *creatio ex nihilo* if we make the appropriate revisions in his metaphysics. Specifically, instead of regarding creativity as independent of God and God its "primordial accident," we may affirm that creativity is the divine life (or Being). Likewise, instead of regarding the "eternal objects" or multiplicity of infinite possibility as simply "there," outside of God, for God to prehend, we may recognize that the Infinite Being of God, the absolute Infinite, must necessarily include, or encompass, or "enfold" infinite possibility within God's Infinite Being. We can then express the doctrine of *creatio ex nihilo* in process categories and articulate the central claim of that doctrine: God alone is the source of all; nothing stands alongside or over against God in the act of creating. God creates out of nothing other than the fullness of God's own being.

I am convinced that making these revisions in Whitehead's metaphysics makes process philosophy and theology much more available to Roman Catholic theologians precisely because these revisions respect the core claims of the tradition while expressing its aims in a new way. Process thought has a great richness to it and offers a profound analysis of the universe we experience. Christian theology can benefit greatly by employing the riches of this philosophical vision, so compatible with the contemporary scientific understanding of the universe. I only hope that I have shown in a small way and in one respect how process thought and Roman Catholic theology can benefit by their association.

NOTES

1. John B. Cobb Jr., and David Ray Griffin, *Process Theology: An Introductory Exposition* (Philadelphia, PA: The Westminster Press, 1976), 65. See also, David Ray Griffin, "A Naturalistic Trinity," in *Trinity in Process: A Relational Theology of God*, ed. Joseph A. Bracken, S. J., and Marjorie Hewitt Suchocki (New York: Continuum, 1997), 23–5.

2. Alfred North Whitehead, *Science and the Modern World* (New York: Macmillan, 1926), 258 (hereafter "*SMW*").

3. Alfred North Whitehead, *Process and Reality: An Essay in Cosmology* (1929), corrected ed., ed. David Ray Griffin and Donald W. Sherburne (New York: Free Press, 1978), 7 (hereafter "*PR*"); *SMW* 258.

4. *PR* 7.

5. Ibid., 164.

6. Thomas E. Hosinski, *Stubborn Fact and Creative Advance: An Introduction to the Metaphysics of Alfred North Whitehead* (Lanham, MD: Rowman & Littlefield Publishers, 1993), 156–78; idem, *The Image of the Unseen God: Catholicity, Science, and Our Evolving Understanding of God* (Maryknoll, NY: Orbis Books, 2017), 111–22.

7. *PR* 349.

8. Jaroslav Pelikan, *The Christian Tradition: A History of the Development of Doctrine, Vol. 1: The Emergence of the Catholic Tradition 100–600* (Chicago: University of Chicago Press, 1971), 36.

9. J. N. D. Kelly, *Early Christian Doctrines*, 2nd ed. (New York: Harper & Row, 1960), 83–7.

10. Alfred North Whitehead, *Religion in the Making* (New York: Macmillan, 1926), 156 (hereafter "*RM*").

11. See Langdon B. Gilkey, *Reaping the Whirlwind: A Christian Interpretation of History* (New York: The Seabury Press, 1976), 112–4, 248–51, 300–18. Robert C. Neville has also defended *creatio ex nihilo* in his challenge to process theology, but on a more strictly philosophical basis. See his *Creativity and God: A Challenge to Process Theology* (1979; repr., Albany, NY: SUNY Press, 1995) and *God the Creator: On the Transcendence and Presence of God* (1968; repr., Albany, NY: SUNY Press, 1992).

12. Joseph A. Bracken has also developed a process understanding of *creatio ex nihilo*, though in a very different way than I shall. See Joseph A. Bracken, S. J., *Does God Roll Dice? Divine Providence for a World in the Making* (Collegeville, MN: Liturgical Press, 2012), 11, 144; idem, *Christianity and Process Thought: Spirituality for a Changing World* (Philadelphia, PA: Templeton Foundation Press, 2006), 3–13; and idem, *The Divine Matrix: Creativity as Link between East and West* (Maryknoll, NY: Orbis Books, 1995), 52–68.

13. Thomas Aquinas, *Summa theologica*, trans. Fathers of the English Dominican Province (New York: Benziger Brothers, 1911–1925), Ia.2.3 (hereafter "*ST*").

14. Ibid., Ia.19.8.

15. Elizabeth A. Johnson, C. S. J., "Does God Play Dice? Divine Providence and Chance," *Theological Studies* 57 (1996): 3–18.

16. *ST* Ia.14.8.

17. Ibid., Ia.14.13.

18. Ibid., Ia.19.8.

19. *PR* 7, 21–2.

20. Hosinski, *Stubborn Fact and Creative Advance*, 212–14.

21. *RM* 119–20.

22. See *RM* 71 and *PR* 42.

23. *PR* 22.

24. Ibid., 31.

25. Hosinski, *Stubborn Fact and Creative Advance*, 164–72.

26. *PR* 257.

27. Nicholas of Cusa, *De Possest*, in *A Concise Introduction to the Philosophy of Nicholas of Cusa*, by Jasper Hopkins, 2nd ed. (Minneapolis: University of Minnesota Press, 1980), 19.

28. Hosinski, *Stubborn Fact and Creative Advance*, 80–97.

29. Ibid., 92–4.

BIBLIOGRAPHY

Aquinas, Thomas. *Summa theologica*. Translated by Fathers of the English Dominican Province. 3 vols. New York: Benziger Brothers, 1911–1925.

Bracken, Joseph A., S. J. *Christianity and Process Thought: Spirituality for a Changing World*. Philadelphia, PA: Templeton Foundation Press, 2006.

Bracken, Joseph A., S. J. *The Divine Matrix: Creativity as Link between East and West.* Maryknoll, NY: Orbis Books, 1995

Bracken, Joseph A., S. J. *Does God Roll Dice? Divine Providence for a World in the Making.* Collegeville, MN: Liturgical Press, 2012.

Cobb, John B., Jr., and David Ray Griffin. *Process Theology: An Introductory Exposition.* Philadelphia, PA: The Westminster Press, 1976.

Gilkey, Langdon B. *Reaping the Whirlwind: A Christian Interpretation of History.* New York: The Seabury Press, 1976.

Griffin, David Ray. "A Naturalistic Trinity." In *Trinity in Process: A Relational Theology of God*, edited by Joseph A. Bracken, S. J., and Marjorie Hewitt Suchocki, 23–40. New York: Continuum, 1997.

Hosinski, Thomas E. *The Image of the Unseen God: Catholicity, Science, and Our Evolving Understanding of God.* Maryknoll, NY: Orbis Books, 2017.

Hosinski, Thomas E. *Stubborn Fact and Creative Advance: An Introduction to the Metaphysics of Alfred North Whitehead.* Lanham, MD: Rowman & Littlefield Publishers, 1993.

Johnson, Elizabeth A., C. S. J. "Does God Play Dice? Divine Providence and Chance." *Theological Studies* 57 (1996): 3–18.

Kelly, J. N. D. *Early Christian Doctrines.* 2nd edition. New York: Harper & Row, 1960.

Neville, Robert Cummings. *Creativity and God: A Challenge to Process Theology.* 1979. Reprint, Albany, NY: SUNY Press, 1995.

Neville, Robert Cummings. *God the Creator: On the Transcendence and Presence of God.* 1968. Reprint, Albany, NY: SUNY Press, 1992.

Nicholas of Cusa. *De Possest.* In *A Concise Introduction to the Philosophy of Nicholas of Cusa*, 63–153. Edited by Jasper Hopkins. Minneapolis, MN: University of Minnesota Press, 1980.

Pelikan, Jaroslav. *The Christian Tradition: A History of the Development of Doctrine, Vol. 1: The Emergence of the Catholic Tradition (100–600).* Chicago: University of Chicago Press, 1971.

Whitehead, Alfred North. *Process and Reality: An Essay in Cosmology.* 1929. Corrected ed. Edited by David Ray Griffin and Donald W. Sherburne. New York: Free Press, 1978.

Whitehead, Alfred North. *Religion in the Making.* New York: Macmillan, 1926.

Whitehead, Alfred North. *Science and the Modern World.* New York: Macmillan, 1926.

Chapter 8

Whitehead on Incarnation and the Co-Inherence of God and the World

Palmyre Oomen

"The world lives by its incarnation of God in itself."[1] This is how Whitehead introduces the concept of incarnation in his work. His use of the term may be traced back to early Christian theology where, as he sees it, the concept signifies an important metaphysical improvement of Plato's view of the relation between God and the world. For Whitehead, the only way to explain the persuasiveness and effectiveness of the divine ideals in the world is through the notion of incarnation and its connotations of immanence and participation. In this chapter, we will trace the backgrounds of these ideas in Plato and the early Christian theologians, and analyze how Whitehead used the ideas of incarnation and (mutual) immanence to develop his anti-nominalistic organic metaphysics, which he deems necessary for several reasons, including scientific ones. In the concluding section, we will reflect on Whitehead's approach in the perspective of Catholic thought, and one of the observations will be that Whitehead's strongly anti-nominalistic ideas make him more congenial to the Aquinas-informed Catholic tradition than often is recognized.

WHITEHEAD'S SEARCH FOR DIVINE
PERSUASION AND IMMANENCE

In his theological chapter of *Adventures of Ideas* ("The New Reformation"), Whitehead points out three revelatory phases in the conceptions of how God and God's Ideas can be persuasive elements in the world, so that Ideas are effective and forms of order evolve. The middle one he refers to is the life of Christ seen as a revelation of the noncoercive nature of God's agency in the world.[2] Before and after this event, Whitehead discerns two intellectual phases: first, the conviction of Plato concerning the persuasive way of divine agency, and second, the theological interpretation of the Christ event generated in the formative period of Christianity.[3] What is it that makes Whitehead consider these intellectual phases to be revelatory?

Plato

In his metaphysical explorations, Whitehead aligns himself in many respects with the thoughts and questions brought forward by Plato. When he studies Plato with regard to the conception of the divine agency as persuasive or as compulsive, Whitehead ascertains that Plato wavered inconsistently, but that he "does finally enunciate without qualification the doctrine of persuasion."[4] Whitehead considers this "final conviction"[5] of Plato which he summarizes as "the divine element in the world is to be conceived as a persuasive agency and not as a coercive agency" in an extremely positive way, so much so that he characterizes Plato's view as "one of the greatest intellectual discoveries in the philosophy of religion."[6]

The reason why Whitehead so greatly appreciates this view is that, according to him, the doctrine of divine *persuasion* provides the key to the view that the divine ideals are *effective* in the world and allowing for the evolution of forms of order.[7] He considers this as an enormous improvement of the alternative view that the world would be ready-made "out of nothing" as the accidental product of a totally transcendent God, which, according to Whitehead, is the view proposed by the Bible and by Newton.[8]

However, even though Plato (more or less clearly) opts for the view of creation as the victory of persuasion over force,[9] Whitehead argues that Plato fails to explain how the Ideas can be present in the world in order to fulfill their persuasive role, and therefore fails to give a coherent and systematic explanation of the effective link between the Ideas (or Forms) and the evolving transient reality.[10]

Whitehead's major objection pertains to Plato's indecisive interpretation of the relationship between the eternal divine Ideas and their instantiations in the sensible, particular phenomena. In his *Dialogues*, Plato presents several expressions of that relationship between "form" and "particular." Generally speaking, these expressions can be divided into two main clusters, which respectively can be characterized as *mimesis* (duplication, mimicry, or imitation) and *methexis* (participation, sharing) (a term Plato newly introduces into the philosophical terminology).

Whitehead clearly favors Plato's concept of *methexis* (participation, sharing)—to be found in his *Phaedo*[11]—because, so he argues, this notion is the only key to the doctrine of persuasiveness. Taking for granted the standard opinion that the *Timaeus* is a late dialogue, Whitehead deplores that Plato did not maintain this concept of participation in his *Timaeus*. In the *Timaeus*, Plato invariably sees the relationship between the Ideas and their instantiation in terms of "dramatic imitation," while insisting that divine creation occurs through persuasion.[12] It is this combination of imitation and persuasiveness that for Whitehead is simply impossible:

> When Plato turns to the World, after considering God as giving life and motion to the ideas by the inclusion of them in the divine nature, he can find only second-rate substitutes and never the originals. . . . Thus the World, for Plato, includes only the image of God, and imitations of his ideas, and never God and his ideas.[13]

Therefore, according to Whitehead, Plato cannot explain how the divine Ideas can be persuasive and effective in the world, for he leaves a gap between the transient world and the eternal nature of God.[14] So Plato misses an adequate concept to explain a real immanence of God and God's Ideas in the world.[15] This is exactly the concept Whitehead wants to elaborate in his metaphysics.

Early Christian Theologians

At this point, Whitehead turns to the early Christian theologians of the schools of thought mainly associated with Alexandria and Antioch.[16] The theologians of Alexandria (one of them being Athanasius [fourth century] who coined the term "incarnation") emphasized the divine character of Jesus Christ. On the other hand, the theologians of Antioch preferred a historical and moral interpretation and defended more of a distinction between God and Jesus. Next to them the School of Cappadocia (fourth century) should be mentioned, which tried to maintain a balance between those two approaches.

These early theologians tried to find theological answers to the questions pertaining to the relation between Jesus Christ (and the Spirit) and God the Father, as well as to the questions pertaining to the relation between the divine and the human natures within Christ. After considerable debates, they came at the Councils of Nicaea I (325) and Constantinople I (381) to insights and formulations such as that Jesus Christ is *homoousios* (of same substance or essence) as the Father, and that Jesus Christ, the Son of God, for us humans and our salvation was "enfleshed" (*incarnatus est*) and made human (*humanatus est*). The Trinitarian controversies on the relation between Father, Son, and Spirit were settled, mainly under the influence of the Cappadocian Fathers, in the famous formulation, "One *ousia* (being/substance/essence) in three *hupostaseis* (persons)" (Constantinople I). The Christological debate resulted at the Council of Chalcedon (451) in the confession that Jesus Christ is "to be acknowledged in two natures, *inconfusedly, unchangeably, indivisibly, inseparably.*"

Whitehead summarizes these complex theological conclusions as follows:

> [These theologians came to the] solution of a multiplicity in the nature of God, each component being unqualifiedly Divine, [which] involves a doctrine of mutual immanence in the divine nature. . . . They decided for the direct immanence of God in the person of Christ. They also decided for some sort of direct immanence of God in the World, generally. This was their doctrine of the third person of the Trinity.[17]

Here we may add that, while the doctrine of the direct immanence of God in Christ is known as *incarnation*, the doctrine of the mutual immanence in God, that is, the mutual indwelling of Father, Son, and Spirit, goes by the lesser-known name *perichoresis* or *co-inherence*.

Whitehead's enthusiasm for these early theologians pertains primarily to the fact that "in the place of Plato's solution of secondary images and imitations, they demanded a direct doctrine of immanence."[18] And for Whitehead, this concept of immanence is precisely the concept that provides the solution to the question of how to give a rational account of the persuasive agency of God.[19] That is why Whitehead considers the solution given by those theologians as a crucial discovery for metaphysics: "[They] have the distinction of being the only thinkers who in a fundamental, metaphysical doctrine have improved upon Plato."[20]

However, so Whitehead points out, having developed their notion of direct immanence in a theological context, these theologians unfortunately failed to make use of this discovery for a further development of a general metaphysics. This is the task Whitehead sets for himself. He is not interested in the theological doctrines as such, but all the more in a rationally developed doctrine of direct immanence of God in the world.

WHITEHEAD ON IMMANENCE AND MUTUAL IMMANENCE

So far, we saw that in his search for a concept that might bridge the gap between God or God's Ideas and the transient world, Whitehead considers the concept of immanence (as understood by the early Christian theologians) to be a crucial metaphysical discovery which enables him, as will be shown, to conceptualize the Platonic doctrine of the *persuasive presence of the ideal in the actual world.*

Moreover, this concept of immanence enables him to elucidate his general metaphysical view that all reality is inherently relational. As he sees it, no actual entity[21]—God included—stands alone, separate from the other actual entities, but each is a constituent in the constitution of the others.[22] Whitehead develops "immanence" in terms of his notion of prehension (or feeling or absorption): by being prehended, an actual entity becomes immanent in the prehending one. So Whitehead speaks of the "immanence of the past in the present" (by inheritance or reenaction) but also in a slightly different sense of the "immanence of the future in the present" (by anticipation) and even of contemporary occasions in each other (only indirectly, since they are by definition causally independent).[23] By prehending and being prehended, actual entities are interwoven in a web of relations.

From 1932 on (in his lecture entitled "Process and Reality"), Whitehead uses the term *mutual immanence* to signify this specific togetherness: "The key to metaphysics is this doctrine of mutual immanence, each side lending to the other a factor necessary for its reality."[24] In this way Whitehead conceptualizes and expresses his "fundamental thesis . . . that the final actualities of the universe cannot be abstracted from one another because each actuality, though individual and discrete, is internally related to all other actualities," as Nobo aptly phrases.[25] In the same lecture, Whitehead also explicitly uses this expression in the context of the mutual immanence of permanence and transience, and of God and the world.[26]

In *Process and Reality* (1929), Whitehead did not yet use the expression "mutual immanence," but he did express similar insights as follows: "[N]o two actual entities can be torn apart: each is all in all." He continues, "Thus each temporal occasion embodies God, and is embodied in God."[27] The phrase "each occasion embodies God" brings us to the subject of "incarnation."

INCARNATION OF GOD IN THE WORLD

Immanence and Incarnation

How does immanence relate to incarnation? In its strictest theological sense, the term "incarnation" refers to God's direct immanence in Jesus Christ. The Gospel according to St. John proclaims, "The Word became flesh (*sarx*)," and of this Word it states, "The Word was with God and the Word was God."[28]

The meaning of the provocative proclamation that God became flesh has been the subject of intense theological debates, with ramifications for soteriology, and for questions concerning the place of matter in relation to evil, to which we will return shortly.

As stated earlier, Whitehead values the theological doctrine of incarnation, that is, of the direct immanence of God in the person of Christ, as a discovery with a huge *metaphysical* significance that he wants to further develop in his philosophy. Thus, he speaks of the incarnation or embodiment of God in each temporal occasion[29] and writes the intriguing phrase: "[t]he world lives by its incarnation of God in itself."[30] We have now to consider in some more detail how Whitehead conceptualizes in his metaphysics this immanence or embodiment of God in the world, and especially how it relates to persuasiveness and effectiveness.

Incarnation and Persuasiveness: *Eros*

Whitehead's starting point is, what is "really real" must be understood as a process, that is, as an organism. Accordingly, he sees each actual entity as a *process that realizes itself* out of the available material.[31] Whitehead tries to lay out the conditions of the possibility thereof. First, there must be *past events* that are the material from which the novel event forms itself. But since a multitude of materials can be synthesized in many different ways—the one more beautiful than the other—also a limitation by some *standard of value* is required. In *Science and the Modern World*, Whitehead therefore introduces "in the metaphysical situation" a "principle of limitation," which he calls "God."[32] Later on, he will call this more precisely the primordial and abstract aspect of God.[33] In prehending this divine primordial nature, a new event "feels" the most valuable possibility for synthesis of its given past events as its own desire, its initial subjective aim.[34] In this way, God's immutable primordial nature functions as "object of desire." But, immutable though it may be, this divine primordial nature shows itself differently for each and every event. Therefore, God always embodies "a dominant ideal peculiar to each actual entity," which means that God embodies the most attractive possibility of synthesis *relative to each particular givenness*.[35]

Whitehead repeatedly emphasizes that the possibilities offered are not neutral or indifferent: they are working, inciting, luring, because God's relative valuation endows them with attractiveness.[36] Whereas Plato sees the Demiurge as giving "life and motion" to the Ideas, Whitehead in a similar way tells us that in God's primordial nature the Ideas (eternal objects) are felt so as to become attractive and motivating, and therefore (contrary to the *Timaeus*) persuasive. In this way, the occasion's initial aim is the immanence of God in that occasion: "God's immanence in the world in respect to his primordial nature is an urge towards the future based on an appetite in the present."[37]

Here it should be noted that God as "object of desire" is not an impassive object, for it is God's own active longing (the "Divine Eros") that arouses *the attuned longing* or "conformal feeling" of the occasion (like the resonance of a string on a musical instrument).[38] This "co-longing" constitutes the initial subjective aim of the becoming novel occasion which is thereby originated.[39] In this way, Whitehead conceives the divine immanence or the incarnation of God's Ideas in the world as well as their persuasiveness.

Incarnation and Effectiveness: (Self-)Creation

The new occasion originates by its reception of its particular initial aim. So, God's provision of the initial subjective aim is at the same time the "creation" or "origination" of the new actual occasion. However, this "creation" relates to the *beginning of the self-creation* of the new autonomous actual occasion, for it is the point from which the subject's self-causation starts.[40]

One of the consequences of this view is that, although the incarnation of God in the world is a purposive and constitutive *lure*, God also indirectly incarnates in the *facts*, that is, in the results and the outcome of the worldly events: "Every event on its finer side introduces God into the world. Through it [God's] ideal vision is given a base in actual fact."[41]

Thus, God is embodied not merely in value and purpose but also in the facts themselves. Or, to put it differently, to some extent, a fact is not simply something different from value, but it is also the "frozen" result (*factum*) of an earlier *realization of value*, so that in some sense the factual world may be seen as the incarnation of God.

Incarnation and Evil

If, according to Whitehead, the factual world is in some sense the incarnation of God, the question arises how to explain the existence of evil. The question of evil was often connected to a theological judgment about "matter" (out of which things are made, or in Whiteheadian language "out of which new events make themselves"). From the beginning of Christianity, theologians focused on the question whether "matter" should be regarded as a second force apart from and opposed to God. Or phrased differently, they asked the question whether matter explains why there is evil in the world (a vision defended by Marcion [ca. 85–ca. 160] and the later Manichaeism [ca. third–seventh century], and strongly rejected by Tertullian [ca. 155–ca. 225] and Augustine [354–430]).

What is Whitehead's position on this subject? For him, the given facts out of which a new event creates itself constitute "its Actual World," and in this sense this "Actual World" is synonymous with "matter" for the new event. This "matter" is not a factor independent from God nor a force against God, for, as described above, each "factum" is created by itself as well as by God's lure and thus manifests to some extent the incarnation of God in itself.

How then does evil creep in? God's creative activity in the past toward the then becoming entity which (in the meantime) has become fact or matter was at that earlier time (only) an initiation or origination in the need of the subject's subsequent self-creation for the sake of actualization. And, depending on how this self-creation occurred, the result is more or less in conformity to God's ideal: "Every act leaves the world with a deeper or a fainter impress of God. He then passes into his next relation to the world with enlarged, or diminished, presentation of ideal values."[42] And "so far as the conformity is incomplete, there is evil in the world."[43] The conformity *can* be incomplete, since—among other aspects—in addition to the divinely given desire, also the actualization by the new event itself is required, with better or worse result.[44]

Whitehead's view of incarnation, according to which God is present in the world as both lure and fact, keeps him, contrary to old and modern Gnostic views, from holding a negative view on the Actual World as matter. But Whitehead's concept of incarnation also makes him reject a harmonious optimism. God is incarnated in the world, as lure and as fact, *but not every lure or fact is equally and totally an incarnation of God.* This is basically the reason why this world, even though it embodies God in itself, is not the best of all possible worlds.[45] Incarnation does not imply an identity of God with the world.

GOD AND WORLD: MUTUAL INDWELLING (*PERICHORESIS*)

Up to now, we have seen how the notion of "incarnation" found in the Church Fathers allows Whitehead to conceptualize the vision Plato had in mind: the immanence of God's Ideas in the world so as to make them persuasive and by the same token codetermining for the factual result.

But there is much more to be said. Unfortunately, Whitehead obviously was not familiar with the intriguing theological notion of *perichoresis*, which in the seventh or eighth century eventually received its decisive meaning of "mutual indwelling," or "co-inherence," namely the co-inherence of the three divine persons *in* one another "without any coalescence" in spite of their remaining "inseparable."[46] These qualifications clearly indicate that co-inherence is not only *mutual immanence* but *mutual transcendence* too. That is to say, each person has its own individuality, but each is who "he" is by virtue of the inner relations to the others.

When Whitehead in his metaphysical context speaks of the "mutual immanence of actual entities," this language resembles the concept of "co-inherence:" every actual entity is individual and discrete, but no actual entity can be abstracted from the others, because by its prehensions of all others it is internally related to them.[47]

As seen earlier, such mutual immanence applies not only between actual occasions but also between God and the world.[48] In his metaphysics, the concept of what he calls God's consequent nature—that is, God in full concreteness—functions as the mainstay of the conceptualization of the reciprocal immanence of the world in God. Throughout the present chapter, so far we have seen that the worldly actual entities prehend God's primordial nature. But at the end of *Process and Reality*, Whitehead goes a fundamental step further when he argues that "God, as well as being primordial, is also consequent."[49] This means that God not only *is* prehended, but that "by reason of the relativity of all things" God also *prehends* all other actual entities and absorbs them into God's concrete being. Thus the world's ongoing history is forever known and treasured in God and woven upon God's primordial concepts.[50] This is how Whitehead conceives God's consequent nature. And in its turn, this "Great Fact" too has an influence on the world.[51] As Fetz suitably states, "Whitehead thus acknowledges not only a participation of the world in God as Thomas has done, but also a participation of God in the world."[52]

But, mutual though this participation may be, and in spite of the fact that God and the actual occasions pertain to the same metaphysics (God is no exception[53]), Whitehead sees God and the world as opposites.[54] The opposition stems from their reversed polarity: in actual occasions, the physical pole is primordial while the conceptual pole is consequent, whereas in God this order is reversed.[55] And precisely this reversed polarity explains how God and worldly occasions can prehend each other and thereby are instruments of novelty for each other.[56]

This allows Whitehead to express what may be called the "*perichoresis* of God and the world," when he says, "It is as true to say that the World is immanent in God, as that God is immanent in the World. It is as true to say that God transcends the World, as that the World transcends God."[57] In conclusion, Whitehead's philosophical approach allows him to say that "each temporal occasion embodies God" as well as that "each temporal occasion is embodied in God."[58]

PROMISES AND CHALLENGES OF
WHITEHEAD IN CATHOLIC PERSPECTIVE

At this point, it is worthwhile to determine what may be said about Whitehead's approach within the perspective of Catholic thought, here represented by Thomas Aquinas (thirteenth century). In two earlier publications, I compared Aquinas and Whitehead regarding their conceptions of God's power and regarding their use of language about God, respectively.[59] Here I merely want to stress how much Whitehead's thinking is in tune with a fundamental idea of Catholic thought—the idea of participation—which Whitehead expands and dynamizes. We shall see some of its consequences and its background.

Participation and Intimacy—Aquinas

As we have seen, Whitehead developed the Platonic notion of "participation" so as to make conceivable that the divine Ideas are persuasive in the world. He did so by elaborating how God is immanent in the world and incarnates in the world as lure and as fact.

For Aquinas, who also was influenced by Aristotle and Plato, the thought of "the world's participation in God" does not occur through an enlarged concept of *incarnation*—"incarnation" to him applies exclusively to Jesus Christ—but does so by deepening the concept of *being*. In order to describe God's causality with respect to the world Aquinas makes use of the four Aristotelian "causes," but in his account of creation, he adds a fundamentally different kind of causal relationship: God is also and above all *causa essendi*, which means the cause of the *being* of things (not just insofar as they are these-beings or such-beings). Aquinas elucidates this relationship with an example of the sun as illuminator and the air becoming luminous by participating in the light of the sun. Thus, by participating in the light of the sun the air is luminous and has light, but the air is not light by its own nature, which appears all too clearly when the sun fails. Analogously, the world has no being of itself but owes its being and its remaining in existence fully to participation in God's being, that is to God's permanent "influx of *esse*."[60]

Thus, by saying that the creation of the world means participation in God (in God's Being), Aquinas introduces, on top of the Aristotelian elements, a specifically Platonic element. And in this way, Whitehead and Aquinas are very alike. According to Aquinas, the worldly being exists due to its participation in God's *esse*; according to Whitehead, the occasion exists due to its "sharing in the immanent nature of God," whereby it participates in God's Eros.[61] So, both Aquinas and Whitehead agree on the crucial point that the existence of wordly beings fundamentally requires God's *unceasing* active presence (in marked contrast to Deism) and results from their participation therein. For both, God essentially differs from the world and transcends the world, and yet God's presence in the world is of the utmost intimacy.

However, Whitehead and Aquinas differ on one important point. For Whitehead, the participation is reciprocal: the world embodies God and God embodies the world.[62] Whitehead accounts for this in terms of what he calls God's consequent nature. For Aquinas, this idea of reciprocity would be unthinkable because of God's unicity and singularity. And, to some degree, Whitehead goes along with Aquinas when he says that God and the world are fundamentally different to the point of being opposites. However, to him this opposition between God and the world just implies their mutual requirement.[63]

Nominalist Rejection of Participation— Modernity and Protestantism

Both Aquinas and Whitehead were impressed by Plato's attempt to integrate the notion of participation into his thinking. Furthermore, both were obviously influenced by Aristotle. Therefore, it should be of no surprise that, despite all differences, their doctrines show some similar "color," especially on subjects such as participation, relatedness, or finality.

However, it must be noted that the thought of participation, relatedness, finality, and so on, broke down under the influence of crucial theological criticisms and changes in thinking during the thirteenth and fourteenth centuries. Here both the work of Duns Scotus with his *voluntarism* and his doctrine of the *univocity of being* and Ockham's *nominalism* played a decisive role.

The doctrine of univocity does away with any reference to "analogy" or "participation." This implies the rejection of the doctrine of participation in being, which was so crucial to Aquinas. The doctrine of nominalism considers universals (Plato's Ideas) as mere concepts or names, and by the same token it stresses the primacy of individuals which now are seen as "bare" isolated beings not sharing common qualities by participation. Voluntarism for its part stresses the absolute will of God so much so as to declare the will of God unaccountable, so that any reference to God or God's will is duly left out of any intellectual discourse. It emphasizes God's otherness to such a degree that the world takes on an autonomy it never had before in the writings of, for instance, Augustine or Aquinas. The result is that it encourages a thinking in terms of two worlds: a chasm between nature and the supernatural, between creation and Creator, between science and faith, and an "absence of God in the world" that replaces a "sacramentality of the world."

This huge and astonishing reversal in thinking is widely considered to be a key factor in the emergence of modernity in general (the "disenchantment of the world") and of Protestantism in particular.[64] And one of its many and complex consequences is the predominance of naturalism and empiricism, which cleared the way for the rise of modern physics and its characteristic "scientific materialism."

In view of all this, it has to be noted that, by his elaboration of the idea of participation in terms of immanence or mutual immanence, Whitehead has come to occupy a seemingly untimely place in the history of philosophy.

Indeed, his philosophical project shows from beginning to end that his thought is anything but nominalistic. In the next and final section, we will see why Whitehead resists the modern nominalistic trend and develops his "philosophy of organism" for the benefit of science, philosophy, and theology.

Beyond Realism and Nominalism—Whitehead

As mentioned earlier, nominalism involves separate individuals, aimlessness, and a strict separation between the domain of God and the domain of the world. All of these were criticized by Whitehead. Therefore, his metaphysics may be seen as one encompassing attempt to offer an alternative to nominalism.

This makes it quite understandable that Whitehead feels more at home with Plato, the counterpart of nominalism. But his appreciation of Plato never makes him blind to criticism. So, with regard to the status of eternal objects (the Platonic Ideas), Whitehead's view is far more Aristotelian because he insists that the Ideas are not ontologically independent entities but only exist *in* their actualizations (conceptually in God, or physically in the world). Furthermore, he does not value the One higher than the Many, nor God higher than the world. To him these "[o]pposed elements stand to each other in mutual requirement."[65] We must conclude that in fact Whitehead tries to avoid the pitfalls not only of nominalism but of Plato's metaphysical realism as well. Nevertheless, the question may be asked why Whitehead wants to repudiate nominalism and returns to "participation."

Maybe unexpectedly, Whitehead accounts for his rejection of nominalism primarily by reference to the problems faced by contemporary physics. The commonsense concept of nature signified by the expression "scientific materialism" tells us that there are independently existing substances that are only externally related to each other and moved from the outside. For Whitehead, this conception of nature is not only entirely insufficient to justify modern physics, but it is even self-contradictory, for all concepts used in modern physics—such as matter, space, time, substance, order—have fundamentally changed.[66] He summarizes the situation by describing it as "a complete muddle."[67]

In other words, Whitehead tells us that modern science (the science after 1900) needs a better philosophical framework in which justice is done to interdependence, life, emergence, causation, experience, final causality, self-organization, and mind.[68] It is from this heartfelt need to provide a philosophical foundation to modern science, as well as to give in cosmology an intelligible place to the human being, that Whitehead fiercely objects to nominalism and—beyond realism and nominalism—constructs his "philosophy of organism." And it is this organic metaphysics that not only allows for a better understanding of modern science but at the same time offers a splendid opportunity to rethink and express the mutual and intimate relationship between God and the world.

CONCLUSION

This chapter may have shown how, in undertaking his huge project of developing his organic philosophy, Whitehead found essential incentives and tools in the concepts of *incarnation* and *co-inherence* as developed by the early Christian theologians, and how he used those insights in his metaphysics generally as well as explicitly in his thinking about the intimate participative and incarnational relationship between God and the world. All of this puts Whitehead far away from nominalistic ways of thinking and makes him in many respects a congenial as well as refreshing source for Catholic thinking—more so than often is recognized.

NOTES

1. Alfred North Whitehead, *Religion in the Making* (1926; repr., New York: Fordham University Press, 1996), 156 (hereafter "*RM*").

2. Alfred North Whitehead, *Adventures of Ideas* (1933; repr., New York: Free Press, 1967), 167 (hereafter "*AI*").

3. *AI* 166–69; cf. ibid., 129–30.

4. Ibid., 148, 167.

5. Whitehead refers here to the *Sophist* and the *Timaeus* (*AI* 166n), which according to the standard view belong to Plato's later dialogues. The chronology of Plato's dialogues is however a contested issue. See Francisco J. Gonzalez, "Plato's Dialectic of Forms," in *Plato's Forms: Varieties of Interpretation*, ed. William A. Welton (Lanham, MD: Lexington Books, 2002), 31–83. The "persuasion passage" is found in *Timaeus* 48a.

6. *AI* 166.

7. Ibid., 167.

8. Alfred North Whitehead, *Process and Reality: An Essay in Cosmology* (1929), corrected ed., ed. David Ray Griffin and Donald W. Sherburne (New York: Free Press, 1978), 94–96 (hereafter "*PR*").

9. *AI* 83; Plato, *Timaeus* 48a.

10. *AI* 166.

11. Plato, *Phaedo* (100c–d).

12. *AI* 166–67.

13. Ibid., 167–68.

14. Ibid., 168. Plato himself made an effort to bridge the gap between the Ideas and the transient world by introducing a third form, which he calls "*Khōra*" or

"Receptacle." In some passages, this receptacle resembles Aristotle's prime matter, but it is mainly characterized as a space in which the Ideas are connected to the Copies (*Timaeus* 48e–52d). Throughout *Adventures of Ideas*, Whitehead pays a lot of attention to this Receptacle and considers it a "medium of intercommunication" (*AI* 134), but he does not make use of this notion in his search for the persuasiveness of the Ideas.

15. Cf. Ibid., 168.
16. Ibid., 167.
17. Ibid., 168–69.
18. Ibid., 169; cf. ibid., 130.
19. Ibid., 169.
20. Ibid., 167.
21. The term "actual entity" denotes all final real entities (including God as well as the most trivial puff of existence—*PR* 18), whereas the term "actual occasion" (or "occasion" or "event" for short) only denotes *worldly* actual entities (thus God excluded—*PR* 88).
22. Ibid., 22, 148.
23. *AI* 191–97.
24. Alfred North Whitehead, *Essays in Science and Philosophy* (New York: Philosophical Library, 1947), 118 (hereafter "*ESP*"); cf. *AI* 201.
25. Jorge L. Nobo, *Whitehead's Metaphysics of Extension and Solidarity* (Albany, NY: SUNY Press, 1986), 1.
26. *ESP* 117–18.
27. *PR* 348.
28. John 1:14; 1:1.
29. *PR* 348.
30. *RM* 156.
31. Cf. Alfred North Whitehead, *Science and the Modern World* (1925; repr., New York: Free Press, 1967), 152 (hereafter "*SMW*"); and *PR* passim.
32. *SMW* 178. See Palmyre Oomen, "No Concretion without God," in *La science et le monde moderne d'Alfred North Whitehead*, ed. François Beets, Michel Dupuis, and Michel Weber (Frankfurt: Ontos Verlag, 2006), 203–20.
33. *PR* 31–34.
34. Ibid., 85, 224, 244.
35. Ibid., 84.
36. Ibid., 32.
37. Ibid.
38. *AI* 277, 253.
39. *PR* 224, 244; *AI* 198.
40. *PR* 244.
41. *RM* 155–56.
42. Ibid., 159.
43. Ibid., 62.
44. Cf. ibid., 99.
45. *PR* 47.

46. It is in this decisive sense that Pseudo-Cyril and/or John of Damascus (seventh–eighth century) defined the term. See G. L. Prestige, *God in Patristic Thought* (1936; repr., London: S. P. C. K., 1952), chapter fourteen, esp. 296–330, and Charles C. Twombly, *Perichoresis and Personhood: God, Christ, and Salvation in John of Damascus* (Eugene, OR: Pickwick Publications, 2015), chapter two.

47. *PR* 60, 309.

48. Ibid., 348.

49. Ibid., 345.

50. Ibid., 345–46.

51. For an extensive discussion, arguing—against the standard view—in favor of the prehensibility of God's consequent nature, see Palmyre Oomen, "The Prehensibility of God's Consequent Nature," *Process Studies* 27.1–2 (1998): 108–33.

52. Reto Luzius Fetz, "'Creativity'—A New Transcendental?" in *Whitehead's Metaphysics of Creativity*, ed. Friedrich Rapp and Reiner Wiehl (Albany, NY: SUNY Press, 1990), 189–208, esp. 198.

53. *PR* 343.

54. Ibid, 341, 348–49.

55. Ibid., 348.

56. Ibid., 349. For this reversal of God and the world to each other in respect of their process, see Oomen, "The Prehensibility of God's Consequent Nature," and Palmyre Oomen, "Language about God in Whitehead's Philosophy: An Analysis and Evaluation of Whitehead's God-Talk," *Process Studies* 48.2 (2019): 198–218.

57. *PR* 348.

58. Ibid.

59. Palmyre Oomen, "God's Power and Almightiness in Whitehead's Thought," *Process Studies* 47.1–2 (2018): 83–110, and Oomen, "Language about God in Whitehead's Philosophy," respectively.

60. Thomas Aquinas, *Summa Theologiae*, Ia.44.1 co, Ia.44.2 co, Ia.45.5 co; Ia.104.1.

61. Cf. *AI* 130.

62. Cf. *PR* 348. Whitehead is neither the first nor the only thinker who presents the idea of mutual participation between God and the world. It is to be found scattered through Eastern Orthodox and Western Christian thought: for example, in Maximus the Confessor, who refers not only to "incarnation" but also to a reciprocal "*theiosis*" or "deification" (*Ambiguum* 7 [PG 91:1084b]); in Meister Eckhart, Jürgen Moltmann, or Leonardo Boff, who writes that God and world are "related and mutually implicated in one another" (Leonardo Boff, *Cry of the Earth, Cry of the Poor* [Maryknoll, NY: Orbis Books, 1997], 147); or in the interreligious theologian Raimon Panikkar (Raimon Panikkar, *The Rhythm of Being: The Unbroken Trinity* [Maryknoll, NY: Orbis Books, 2010], 403).

63. *PR* 348–49.

64. The crucial impact of voluntarism and nominalism on the rise of modernity has been put forward by Paul Tillich in *A History of Christian Thought* (1956), ed. Carl E. Braaten (London: SCM Press, 1968), 180–91, 198–203. Later prominent accounts are Hans Blumenberg's *Die Legitimität der Neuzeit* (Frankfurt am Main: Suhrkamp,

1966), Louis Dupré's *Passage to Modernity: An Essay in the Hermeneutics of Nature and Culture* (New Haven, CT: Yale University Press, 1933), Marcel Gauchet's *Le désenchantement du Monde* (Paris: Gallimard, 1985), and Charles Taylor's *A Secular Age* (Cambridge, MA: Harvard University Press, 2007). The role of Luther in this development is rather complex. At first, during his education, Luther welcomed the *via moderna* (nominalism), but later on the question of grace changed his attitude. Luther then accuses his nominalistic teacher Gabriel Biel of Pelagianism and takes more distance from the theological positions of the *via moderna*. See Rodney Howsare, *Hans Urs Von Balthasar and Protestantism* (New York: T & T Clark, 2005), 44–53.

    65. *PR* 348.

    66. Alfred North Whitehead, *Modes of Thought* (1938; repr., New York: Free Press, 1968), 127–47.

    67. Ibid., 132.

    68. Ibid., 148–69.

BIBLIOGRAPHY

Aquinas, Thomas. *Summa theologiae*. Leonine edition, Universidad de Navara, 2000, https://www.corpusthomisticum.org/sth0000.html.

Blumenberg, Hans. *Die Legitimität der Neuzeit*. Frankfurt am Main: Suhrkamp, 1966.

Boff, Leonardo. *Cry of the Earth, Cry of the Poor*. Maryknoll, NY: Orbis Books, 1997.

Dupré, Louis. *Passage to Modernity: An Essay in the Hermeneutics of Nature and Culture*. New Haven, CT: Yale University Press, 1993.

Fetz, Reto Luzius. "'Creativity'—A New Transcendental?" In *Whitehead's Metaphysics of Creativity*, edited by Friedrich Rapp and Reiner Wiehl, 189–208. Albany, NY: SUNY Press, 1990.

Gauchet, Marcel. *Le désenchantement du Monde*. Paris: Gallimard, 1985.

Gonzalez, Francisco J. "Plato's Dialectic of Forms." In *Plato's Forms: Varieties of Interpretation*, edited by William A. Welton, 31–83. Lanham, MD: Lexington Books, 2002.

Howsare, Rodney. *Hans Urs Von Balthasar and Protestantism*. New York: T & T Clark, 2005.

Nobo, Jorge L. *Whitehead's Metaphysics of Extension and Solidarity*. Albany, NY: SUNY Press, 1986.

Oomen, Palmyre. "God's Power and Almightiness in Whitehead's Thought." *Process Studies* 47.1–2 (2018): 83–110.

Oomen, Palmyre. "Language about God in Whitehead's Philosophy: An Analysis and Evaluation of Whitehead's God-Talk." *Process Studies* 48.2 (2019): 198–218.

Oomen, Palmyre. "No Concretion without God." In *La science et le monde moderne d'Alfred North Whitehead*, edited by François Beets, Michel Dupuis, and Michel Weber, 203–20. Frankfurt: Ontos Verlag, 2006.

Oomen, Palmyre. "The Prehensibility of God's Consequent Nature." *Process Studies* 27.1–2 (1998): 108–33.

Panikkar, Raimon. *The Rhythm of Being: The Unbroken Trinity.* Maryknoll, NY: Orbis Books, 2010.

Patrologia Graeca. Edited by J.-P. Migne. 162 vols. Paris, 1857–1886.

Plato. *Phaedo.* In *Platonis Opera, Tomus I,* edited by John Burnet, 57–118. Oxford: Clarendon Press, 1899.

Plato. *Timaeus.* In *Platonis Opera, Tomus IV,* edited by John Burnet, 17–105. Oxford: Clarendon Press, 1905.

Prestige, G. L. *God in Patristic Thought.* 1936. Reprint, London: S. P. C. K., 1952.

Taylor, Charles. *A Secular Age.* Cambridge, MA: Harvard University Press, 2007.

Tillich, Paul. *A History of Christian Thought.* 1956. Edited by Carl E. Braaten. London: SCM Press, 1968.

Twombly, Charles C. *Perichoresis and Personhood: God, Christ, and Salvation in John of Damascus.* Eugene, OR: Pickwick Publications, 2015.

Whitehead, Alfred North. *Adventures of Ideas.* 1933. Reprint, New York: Free Press, 1967.

Whitehead, Alfred North. *Essays in Science and Philosophy.* New York: Philosophical Library, 1947.

Whitehead, Alfred North. *Modes of Thought.* 1938. Reprint, New York: Free Press, 1968.

Whitehead, Alfred North. *Process and Reality: An Essay in Cosmology.* 1929. Corrected ed. Edited by David Ray Griffin and Donald W. Sherburne. New York: Free Press, 1978.

Whitehead, Alfred North. *Religion in the Making.* 1926. Reprint, New York: Fordham University Press, 1996.

Whitehead, Alfred North. *Science and the Modern World.* 1925. Reprint, New York: Free Press, 1967.

Chapter 9

The Eucharistic Experience

Process Theology and Sacramental Theology

Thomas Schärtl

It is a widely held view that Catholic sacramental theology after the Second Vatican Council has, fortunately, become decidedly holistic and much more connected to the basic grammar of Christian doctrine. Instead of focusing on the more legal and fine-grained metaphysical problems of how matter and form constitute the sacramental sign as an effective reality, the embeddedness of the sacraments in the overall reality of the church as well as the nature of the church as a mystery—analogous to the mystery of incarnation—serves as a new bedrock to build a more soteriologically oriented theology of the sacraments on:

> The Church, or, in other words, the kingdom of Christ now present in mystery, grows visibly through the power of God in the world. This inauguration and this growth are both symbolized by the blood and water which flowed from the open side of a crucified Jesus, and are foretold in the words of the Lord referring to His death on the Cross: "And I, if I be lifted up from the earth, will draw all things to myself." As often as the sacrifice of the cross in which Christ our Passover was sacrificed, is celebrated on the altar, the work of our redemption is carried on, and, in the sacrament of the eucharistic bread, the unity of all believers who form one body in Christ is both expressed and brought about. All men are called to this union with Christ, who is the light of the world, from whom we go forth, through whom we live, and toward whom our whole life strains.[1]

This marvelously emphasized connection between the mission of Christ, the economy of salvation, the nature of the church and the specific place of the sacraments is equally present when we take a look at one of the other documents that has shaped the message and the impact of the Second Vatican Council. We will find here the very same grammar of sacramental theology:

sacraments are a continuation of the deeds of salvation and, therefore, point to the economy of salvation. They unveil the true meaning of the church as a means to the end of gaining salvation and as a reality-carrying symbol (*Realsymbol*) of the presence of Christ. Their inner constitution has to be aligned at the mystery of incarnation. And the specific impact and meaning of each sacrament are substantially enlightened by one sacramental core, the Eucharist:

> For the liturgy, "through which the work of our redemption is accomplished," most of all in the divine sacrifice of the Eucharist, is the outstanding means whereby the faithful may express in their lives, and manifest to others, the mystery of Christ and the real nature of the true Church. It is of the essence of the Church that she be both human and divine, visible and yet invisibly equipped, eager to act and yet intent on contemplation, present in this world and yet not at home in it; and she is all these things in such wise that in her the human is directed and subordinated to the divine, the visible likewise to the invisible, action to contemplation, and this present world to that city yet to come, which we seek. While the liturgy daily builds up those who are within into a holy temple of the Lord, into a dwelling place for God in the Spirit, to the mature measure of the fullness of Christ, at the same time it marvelously strengthens their power to preach Christ, and thus shows forth the Church to those who are outside as a sign lifted up among the nations under which the scattered children of God may be gathered together, until there is one sheepfold and one shepherd.[2]

SUBSTANTIAL QUESTIONS

However, the metaphysical questions concerning the reality of sacraments have not disappeared despite the more holistic approach and the much stronger connection between sacramental theology, Christology, and ecclesiology.

Famously, Louis-Marie Chauvet has argued against metaphysics as such, seen from a phenomenological angle while basing it on a criticism of onto-theology, and heavily accused the notion of substance as obscuring the true nature of sacramental signs.[3] Reaching back to Heidegger, Chauvet insisted on the givenness of sacramental realities—a signature that will not be captured by substance metaphysics or any metaphysical categories as such. Although Chauvet is at risk to throw out the baby with the bathwater, his suspicions concerning the substance category have a point. For the ontological category of substance does not seem to be suited to unravel the deeper structures of such mysterious "entities" as sacraments: intention-dependent signs of the invisible that are, nevertheless, deeply immersed in the visible side we call liturgy and ritual—which are crucially immersed in events and actions—and would lose their role completely if it wasn't for another layer of reality that consists of meaning, signs, communication, and interaction.

Despite the fact that the ontological category of substance may have some merit in specific theological areas of discourse, it is a burden for sacramental theology. For if we model the hypostatic union and the presence of Christ on a hylomorphic layout, we get stuck with an unfortunate alternative: either the divine nature of Christ and the glorified Christ, respectively, has to be regarded as the forming principle which completely alters the sacramental matter and, literally, annihilates its own ontological constituents or the relationship between the invisible presence of the Lord in the material basis of the sacrament remains purely accidental.

Roger Nutt's summary of scholastic sacramental theology can be considered to be rather the indication of a problem than a convincing solution: sacraments—as the scholastics tell us—are supposed to be causally effective as means to pour divine grace into our hearts. But do we have to introduce some sort of invisible causality which overrides or, at least, overwrites the natural causal effects of the sacramental matter? The metaphysically underpinned concept of transubstantiation leaves us with this puzzle:

> The bread and wine of the Eucharist, for example, are changed and therefore no longer substantially present after the consecration, because when the matter is coupled with the form by a validly ordained priest (with the proper intention) the reality of the sacrament is brought about. Likewise, the regular use of water does not confer the effects of Baptism, because water alone, without the sacramental form, is not the reality of the sacramental sign which contains and confers these effects.[4]

This summary regards sacraments as rather arbitrarily chosen instrumental causes for the transmission of grace. The notion of "transubstantiation"—which Nutt is hinting at—is a description of a concept within a supranaturalistic framework, based especially on a substance metaphysics of everyday objects, but such a rephrasing of the scholastic model is not yet an explanation of how sacramental transformations might take place.[5] The mind of the everyday man and woman might just tell us that the idea of invisible causalities and invisible effects is just too fantastic or far-fetched to be true. It is for this reason that David Grumett calls such strong commitments to purely invisible transactions "exceptionalist":

> The exceptionalism that has been prominent in modern Roman Catholic interpretations, however, has a similar effect, transposing the Eucharist into a realm of faith lying beyond ordinary human experience of the world. This has the effect of separating the Eucharist from the materiality of the created order.

Moreover, it often depends on a background assumption that "ordinary" materiality is plainly and uncontroversially evident. However, this is untenable. From the perspective of contemporary physics, the nature of fundamental forces such as gravitation, electromagnetism, and other quantum interactions, upon which the existence of material objects depends, is not fully understood. Moreover, from a theological perspective the whole material order was created, and is sustained in being, by events and processes that demand a theological account. . . . From a theological perspective, the starting point should be not that materiality requires no explanation, but that everything about it needs explaining.[6]

If we keep in mind what the Nicene Creed may have intended when using the term "invisible," we might have a better impression of the task of sacramental theology: the invisible is the layer of reality that does not meet the immediate sense perception, but which gives meaning and confers truth to what we long for. Therefore, sacramental theology has to emphasize that the invisible is "visible" in the sacramental sign, insofar as the sign calls for our awareness.

But Nutt's reference to a purely instrumental approach also tends to underestimate the sign-element of the sacrament, which is not just an index to indicate the presence of Christ but also a condensed icon of the history of salvation under a certain perspective. Additionally, as Chauvet and others remind us, the event aspect of the sacrament, its reenactment of the history of salvation, gets drowned in an objectified, almost fetish-like constitution of a sacrament as an otherworldly "thing."

MATTER

Sacramental theology needs a convincing story in order to tell us how material signs can truly represent the glorified Christ in time—without turning sacraments into magical objects transcending the mundane realm completely. This very story has to shed light on the fact that our physical universe is capable of taking on an additional layer of meaning, that is, a process of transformation that is not just a matter of interpretation but also alters reality as such. If we *see* bread and wine *as* the body of Christ, this way of perceiving and being aware, however, has to be more than interpreting the arrangement of food in a certain cultural context, using a specific code for our interpretation. Theologically, we want to emphasize that the new way of seeing unveils a deeper and truer reality, although the purely physical constituents of the material substratum remain, apparently, unaltered.

Some more recent debates regarding the concept of transubstantiation have presented us with another, yet parallel, dilemma: either we connect the constitution of the material thing to the transcendental role and identity-defining capacity of a transcendental subject using its "transcendental magic" by means of interpretation[7] or we treat sacraments as *mere signs*, as coincidental arrangements of stuff that can lose their sign-related functions as soon as the eye of the beholder turns its focus toward another direction. The first alternative seems to come awfully close to antirealism, while the second option bows its head before a rather naturalistically attuned realism, while permitting a causally inefficient and, therefore, rather superfluous layer of interpretation. Catholic sacramental theology has always tried to steer clear of both alternatives. Especially the second, unfortunately not uncommon, approach to sacraments as mere signs (in contrast to also being the "floodgates" of Christ's overpouring loving presence) is in serious danger of removing the real presence of Christ from the world:

> To view the Eucharist primarily as a sign, however, is to endorse the fashionable postmodern dissolution of the stability and order given to the world by Christ. According to such interpretations, the body of Christ is not substantially present in the species of bread and wine. Rather, the bread and wine are important because they signify nonmaterial truths and relationships. . . . [A] eucharistic materialism, however, will not ultimately be satisfied with an account of the bread and wine as exceptional containers within which Christ dwells. Rather, it will show how Christ overflows localized presence, or rather, how that presence exemplifies Christ's person and activity in the world.[8]

As the peak example of the Eucharist indicates, we cannot abandon sacramental realism altogether. But such demands vote for a version of realism that cannot be combined with a rather naturalistic account of the material world around us, either.

Most recently, Joanna Leidenhag has given a hint of some ingredients of a more theologically advanced metaphysical story. She is reflecting on Leibniz's panpsychistic notion of living matter as a way to arrive at a more full-blooded concept of sacramental matter. As a matter of fact, Leibniz had developed some parts of his speculative metaphysics to reconcile the more and more separated sacramental theologies of Catholic and Lutheran origins at the time.[9] Leidenhag emphasizes that panpsychism would be the best framework to arrive at a sacramental notion of reality:

> When panpsychism is moulded to serve the theology of a single comprehensive creation, made from nothing but the free and transcendent will of God, the resulting ontology is thoroughly sacramental. That is, all finite substances symbolize, or point beyond themselves, to their transcendent, supernatural source. This final theological aspect of Leibniz's panpsychism arises out of the amalgamation of the indwelling powers that panpsychism posits throughout reality, and

the radical dependency of those powers that the doctrine of creation *ex nihilo* prescribes. The universe is compatible with God's presence and in so doing does not stand in competition to God but is sustained as a panpsychist, sacramental, universe. This combination of statements, bolstered by claims of continuity across the created order, results in the view that all points, bodies or subjects of creation are sacramentally open to the indwelling power of God. Panpsychism facilitates a form of sacramentality by suggesting that it is at the point of inte-riority that all things remain dependent upon and open to the divine presence.[10]

But it is one thing to say that creation is moving toward a goal that can be identified with God, and another thing to commit oneself to the idea that under certain circumstances material things—embedded in events and laden with intentionality—do represent the presence of Christ. Leidenhag's view can open up our perception of the material universe that would be able to take the notion of a cosmic liturgy literally insofar as every proto-consciousness is ultimately directed toward the divine mind and might, therefore, be seen as singing the praises of the Lord. So, this view gives us an underpinning of the idea that the whole material world contains footprints of the Creator and is, seen from a Christian perspective, moving toward him. But it is another thing to claim that some material things represent the presence of Christ in a mediated, yet immediate way.

Leidenhag's Leibnizian interpretation of transubstantiation, that is, that the mind or proto-consciousness inherent in the bread and wine is replaced with the mind of Christ or fused with the mind of God,[11] sounds more like a pan-psychist version of the theory of *impanation*, which is, as some remember, a medieval theory of the eucharistic transformation that was accused of model-ing sacramental theology in too close a proximity to incarnation. Leidenhag's idea also shares the same difficulties with Leibniz's original views (at least, with some interpretations of it). For it presupposes that not only living beings and organisms have proto-consciousnesses or minds, but also artificial things, even at the micro-level. Even if this were true, we, nevertheless, must value a basic axiom of incarnational theology which says that the created nature the eternal Word is related to in the incarnation must share a certain richness and intensity of being—as we paradigmatically find in human beings.

Process thought offers another perspective. If we focus on Charles Hartshorne's notion of divine relativity[12]—and blend it with the idea that the cosmos is, at least *per analogiam*, the body of God—we arrive at the prom-ising layout for a pan-sacramental approach.[13] In this case, we can even use the model of "appropriation"—a key notion to express the relation of the two natures in Christ in virtue of being possessed by the person of the Word—to unfold God's relation to the cosmos as his body. Basically, this idea offers two advantages: (1) in contrast to common hylomorphism, God is not a

forming principle of the cosmos directly and (2) if we want to keep the freedom of the divine creation for the sake of traditional doctrine,[14] we would not
need to explain how a bodiless or matterless form (God) might have existed
and how God may have changed in being the form of the cosmos. Instead,
we can subscribe to the idea that there is an aspect of the divine nature that
is and remains unchangeable and absolute.[15] Nevertheless, the model is not
a blueprint of a God–world dualism, since by means of appropriation, God
contributes to the individuation of the cosmos and supports its identity.

But we still have to be careful here, since it could be an unwelcome derivative of a *pan-sacramental*, cosmo-organic framework to add sacramental
value to everything in the universe. Roger Nutt—approaching sacramental
theology from the point and value of tradition and the formed theological
opinio communis—warns us:

> As signs, therefore, the sacraments ought not to be conflated with the pan-sacra-
> mentality found within the rich and wondrous texture of nature and human cul-
> ture. . . . The exclusive focus on the natural meaning of the food, water, gestures,
> and oil employed in the sacraments ends up closing off the faithful to the divine
> meaning, intention, and agency that the signs are employed to communicate.[16]

Nutt's comment seems to emphasize that sacramental signs do not possess
their meaning naturally. If the meaning of the sign is truly defined by its
point of reference, by its addressee toward whom it is directing us, then Nutt
is correct.

However, in sacramental theology, the texture of the sacramental matter
is not a result of purely arbitrary choices: we don't celebrate the Eucharist
with any kind of nutrition, we don't baptize with any kind of liquid. The
material texture of the sacraments resonates with interpretations that belong
to the deepest level of our culture and have a basic importance that is cross-
culturally accessible. It is, therefore, prudent to follow David Grumett's very
careful reading of the Church Fathers' interpretation of food, food-producing
procedures, and basic human actions to serve as allegories of human life and
as icons of the history of salvation. Therefore, it is their openness to analogy
and allegory that makes some material entities far better suited (than others)
to serve as sacramental signs:

> Natural processes of transformative manufacture have been shown to provide
> analogies for Christ's birth, passion, death, and resurrection. Moreover, by vir-
> tue of the doctrine of creation these processes have been presented as continu-
> ous with the theological mystery of Christ's power over and within the earth.
> This perspective is one in which the created order, rather than being viewed as
> wholly mundane, becomes a site of natural and spiritual transformation in which

all recipients of the Eucharist are taken up . . . The analogy between bread and body is grounded, so to speak, in the milling of the flour to make the bread. The human bodies that receive the Eucharist are also, as it were, put through the mill. From this state of dissolution, the baptismal water furnishes the possibility of reconstitution into a malleable dough. The little oil added to this dough supplies strength of flavour, just as baptism is accompanied by anointing in order to seal this act as a work of the Spirit. . . . Proper attention to the eucharistic elements suggests a theological and pastoral need to become aware of the transformative, spiritual, and sacramental character of all natural objects. . . . [M]aterial objects can no more be purely natural than can the Eucharist be purely natural. Human awareness of the divine presence in particular objects and places is necessarily related to this presence in other objects and places in more veiled form.[17]

In other words, without the pan-sacramental framework, there would be no sign-function and without the more or less naturally and culturally appropriate emergence of meaning, we would not have the possibility of finding the "additional" sacramental meaning—the pointers to the "invisible" reality. There has to be a certain fittingness that makes the natural reality of material texture appropriate to become an equally indexical *and* iconic sign of Christ's presence.

THE EXTENDED BODY

But how could the analogy of embodiment contribute to a more nuanced picture? Let us stay for a minute with the process theological notion of the universe as God's body: as our bodies are signs of our mind-gifted presence, the universe can be a sign of God's salvific presence. Although a living body as such indicates the presence of life, not every part of the body is equally suited to serve as an icon of life and consciousness. It is not a coincidence that human culture was drawn to pictures of the head, the eyes, the mouth, and so on, whenever humans had to picture aspects of mind-gifted while embodied presence. Now if we want to cash in this analogy, we might as well say that certain features of our universe are better suited to serve as the signs of the divine presence than others. Admittedly, we have to be aware of the fact that the notion of a divine body can only serve as an analogy.[18]

Nevertheless, a trinitarian approach can help us to stabilize this very analogy. For if we can agree that the divine Word is the "empirical" side of the divine life—alluding to a revelation-based model of the Trinity that has been around since Origen—and is therefore best suited to serve as the embodiment of the divine in the world, the Holy Spirit would introduce us to the awareness of "behavior" that is the specific perspective and disposition to see meaning in the bodily expressions of the divine. The threefold notion of mind, embodiment, and behavior can serve as an extended analogy for the presence of God in the world.

Once we endorse such an embodiment perspective on the all-encompassing history of salvation, we need to abandon a purely static view of nature. The merits of process theology are precisely here where we need to conceive of divine embodiment as an open system. It is Joseph Bracken who helps us to lead the way. His considerations can support us to connect the idea of divine embodiment with Christology and, ultimately, sacramental theology:

> But the term "nature" seems to imply a self-sufficient and relatively unchanging reality, what is implied by the term "substance" in classical metaphysics. The term "system," on the contrary, implies an ever-changing reality, an ongoing activity rather than a fixed reality or "thing." Likewise, whereas one "thing" can be incorporated into another "thing" only through loss of its own identity (e.g., food and drink become part of me when I eat a meal), systems and other forms of internally or self-organized activity, however, are readily combined to produce a common effect (e.g., the coordinated activity of the nervous system, the circulatory system, and all the other subsystems within the human body from moment to moment). Thus Jesus in and through his human nature was constantly engaged in day-to-day activities, but in and through the workings of his divine nature he presumably performed those activities from a new and unconventional perspective. Consciously or unconsciously he was always responsive to the Will of his Father in heaven even as he retained the freedom to respond to the Father in his own way.[19]

Bracken offers an understanding of nature as a *complex system* for which not only versions of mutual causality are relevant to explain the emergence of new features alongside divine and mundane creativity. He also points out that within a process theological framework, we can understand the fundamental responsiveness of every finite entity toward God who encompasses the initial aims for a multilayered but open and developing reality:

> God, in other words, proposes to each actual occasion an initial aim or lure toward some purpose or goal on a feeling level. The actual occasion, however, remains free to accept that lure from God or to seek satisfaction through some purpose or goal of its own decision, whether conscious or not. . . . This is as true of the actual occasions making up a subatomic particle as it is of the actual occasions that constitute consciousness for us human beings. In the case of the subatomic particle, the amount of spontaneity or freedom it enjoys is very limited, since it tends simply to repeat whatever pattern of activity it finds at work in its environment. Within our human consciousness, on the contrary, each

actual occasion grasps several different possibilities for self-realization, each of which has its own lure for satisfaction. Hence, an actual occasion within the consciousness of a human being enjoys many more options, so to speak, beyond the one offered by God through the divine initial aim.[20]

Bracken's explanation of the spectrum of responsiveness to the divine—ranging from subatomic particles to human consciousnesses—can serve as the foundation to build a sacramental theology on. But since we must not stop with pan-sacramental intuitions only, we have to introduce a decidedly Christological starting point: the presupposition of divine incarnation is the fundamental responsiveness of all creation to God's aims. However, in Christ, we may detect a double orientation which is the blueprint of a reciprocal relation between the subsequent divine nature on the one side and the created realm on the other. For in Christ, we see the reciprocal responsiveness of the "flesh" toward the divine Father, while the divine Father also responds to the human nature of Christ, declaring it—alluding at biblical doxology—the bedrock of the new temple and the seal of the new covenant.

But, as Bracken and others have pointed out, there is also a responsiveness of all created reality around Christ, within Christ, and toward Christ.[21] At the very center, there is the immediate effect of the self-giving and forgiving love of Christ: Christ in his performance as the ultimate Word of God provokes and inspires the response of mind-gifted beings. St. Paul and the gospels use the distinction between faith and faithlessness to illustrate the spectrum of responsive possibilities.[22] Faith, after all, is not just a cognitive situation one finds herself in once she is inspired or provoked by Christ; regarding the divine nature of Christ, faith establishes a robust relation that renders the believer a living organ in the extended body of Christ:

> The gathering of believers, identified by their celebration of baptism and the eucharist, is sent into the world with its own distinctive mission. It thus continues the mission that Jesus himself has received from the Father (Jn 20:21). The primordial love that is the object of Christian witness is inherently bound up with the practical realization of such love in the mutual relationships of the members of the community and in its outreach to the world.[23]

The aforementioned notion of "extension" seems somewhat whimsical because it seems to push our imagination to its limits if we even try to conceive of the extensions of human bodies to encompass other mind-gifted beings. A slightly different angle might let us see that the notion of the extended body of Christ is a theologically important stepstone to understand the immediate framework of sacramental theology. But how can we develop a realistic framework for the extension of the body of Christ?

Paul Ricoeur has introduced the paradoxes and dialectics of selfhood and sameness into the hermeneutical discussions of personal identity.[24] One aspect of the dialectics consists of the fact that our inward orientation toward the true kernel of the self needs the outward orientation toward the other, while our social embeddedness, on the other hand, needs the self as its center of gravity. We can experience the unresolvable dialectics when we contemplate the relevance of narratives—narratives others substantially contribute to—for the perception and content of our very own sameness.[25] We will also encounter the very same dialectics in the awareness of our own embodiment: although *my* body is *my* most intimate companion, it also is the source of my most fundamental experience of passivity—of anything that seems to be out of reach from the self's control—from erotic arousal to the feeling of pain, from hilarious laughter to the trembling of fear. Through the aspects of passivity, our awareness of ourselves is shaped by a drift toward the other:

> How are we to account for the work of otherness at the heart of selfhood? . . . In order to determine our vocabulary here, let us posit that the *phenomenological* respondent to the metacategory of otherness is the variety of experiences of passivity, intertwined in multiple ways in human action. The term "otherness" is then reserved for speculative discourse, while passivity becomes the attestation of otherness. . . . The main virtue of such a dialectic is that it keeps the self from occupying the place of foundation. This prohibition is perfectly suited to the ultimate structure of a self that will neither be exalted, as in the philosophies of the cogito, nor be humiliated, as in the philosophies of the anti-cogito. . . . I spoke of this work of the broken cogito in order to express this unusual ontological situation. I must now add that this situation is the object of an *attestation which itself is broken*, in the sense that the otherness joined to selfhood is attested to only in a wide range of dissimilar experiences, following a diversity of centers of otherness.[26]

Paul Ricoeur mentions different layers of experiencing otherness in the most intimate dimensions of self-consciousness, the experience of bodily passivity being the most immediate—and therefore most affecting—one:

> First, there is the passivity represented by the experience of one's own body—or better . . . of the *flesh*—as the mediator between the self and a world which is itself taken in accordance with its variable degrees of practicability and so of foreignness. Next, we find the passivity implied by the relation of the self to the *foreign*, in the precise sense of the other (than) self, and so the otherness inherent in the relation of intersubjectivity. Finally, we have the most deeply hidden passivity, that of the relation of the self to itself, which is *conscience* in the sense of *Gewissen* rather than of *Bewusstsein*. By placing conscience in third place in

relation to the passivity-otherness of one's own body and to that of other people, we are underscoring the extraordinary complexity and the relational density of the metacategory of otherness.[27]

That the connection between the self and its narrated sameness is pre-echoed in our experience of embodiment should not come as a surprise. For our bodies are not just biological textures but also texts—insofar as even the most rudimentary behavior induces meaning and causes the need for interpretation (even for ourselves and from a mere introspective view). It is, precisely, Ricoeur's metacategory of "otherness" that might help us to understand the "natural" possibility of extending bodily presence. But how can this help us to get to a closer connection between Christology and sacramental theology?

If we can assume that the alignment with the divine nature allows the human nature of Christ to extend and include otherness, while the paradoxes of sameness and otherness are foreshadowing within our very own human experiences what is amplified in the human nature of Christ, it is also possible to include material elements into this very extension of the body. As I have argued elsewhere, this kind of extension presupposes the transfiguration of Christ's human body in the resurrection[28] and the specifics of the ubiquity of the divine nature which is visible in Christ's case in his most radical pro-existence for us:

> The unfathomable solidarity of Jesus with the lost and the dead is a manifestation of limitless mercy. The Son dies for sinners and is dead with them. The farthest realm of ultimate estrangement now knows another presence. It is the only presence that could reach and penetrate it. It can be named only in terms of a love so absolute that it reaches out into what is most distant from itself. The Father so loves the world—and its underworld—as to give his only Son. The sinner lives apart from God in self-imposed isolation. But even that limit of estrangement is enfolded in mercy.[29]

If we dare to establish a process theological framework of a mutual connectedness and a reciprocal responsiveness of any being, this kind of extension is, to say the least, conceivable. But, of course, not any kind of material thing has the same role or meaning within the extended body of Christ. Ricoeur's perspective on narrative identity introduces a rather multilayered picture: those entities that play a predominant role in Christ's narrative sameness are the cornerstones of his extended bodily presence. Anthony Kelly hinted at the very same idea when he outlined that the Eucharist carries Christ's most intimate intention of self-giving existence insofar as it contains his most radical *imagination* of love:

Even the best eucharistic theology tends to hurry on to theoretical considerations of the eucharist as a sacramental sign and symbol. It easily overlooks what is most obvious. The eucharist has its origins in the creative imagination of Jesus himself. His eucharistic gift means not only receiving his body and blood. It is also a matter of being imbued with his imagination. . . . In the parables he told, in the meals shared with his followers and with the sinners and outcasts, Jesus was in effect inviting all these to share his subversive imagination. He imagined the world otherwise.[30]

If Christ in his radical pro-existence for us has imprinted his character as the ultimate embodiment of the divine presence in the world into specific types of material things, we may assume that—based on the continuation of Christ's intention which remains with us thanks to the ubiquitous closeness of the divine nature of Christ—those types of material things become the extended embodiment of the glorified human nature of Christ in our world. But we also have to add that this would not be possible without the process theological picture of nature and our role within it: for if we can state that nature is a mutually responsive system of relational experiences that are echoed in the divine realm, we can offer a foundation for the idea of how the glorified Christ is among us thanks to the responsiveness of our minds and of certain types of material entities that mirror our intentions as well as the self-giving intention of Christ.

THE EUCHARISTIC EXPERIENCE

The process theological notion of nature as a mutually responsive system of relational experiences can also serve as the answer to a quest sketched by David Grumett. He is looking for a robust sacramental ontology that presents a view on sacramental transformation without the need to refer to divine intervention or (invisible) miracles on a point-by-point basis:

> However, the divine governance of the natural order is perhaps not best understood as enacted by a series of discrete interventions. From a theological perspective, this is not primarily because the possibility of such interventions seems unlikely. Rather, the difficulty with such an account is that, by invoking special divine action as a response to specific situations in which order is threatened, a backdrop is supposed of a normally self-sufficient created order. However, this is to posit a realm of pure, self-sustaining nature that exists independently of God. It might be supposed that the belief in miracles effected by a consecrated host within which Christ dwells, or by other bread that has been liturgically associated with this, rests upon a eucharistic ontology that is

too strong to be credible in the present day. In fact, the ontology upon which it rests is, in itself, not ambitious enough. The more radical and constructive step would be to articulate a systematic doctrine of the preservation of the material world that is grounded in a christology in which Christ's action and presence are not restricted to the eucharistic bread, but are nevertheless conceived in a eucharistic context.[31]

The process theological view of nature is not in need of special divine interventions since it assures that all nature is responsive to the divine inspiration at every level. Sacramental signs carry the imprint of Christ and belong to the extended body of the glorified human nature of Christ because their types have become the integral cornerstones of the narrative identity of Christ and because the self-giving identity of Christ is echoed in us—in our faith, in our very own longing for the integration into the body of Christ. Anthony Kelly offers the same diagnostics in his assessment of any attempt to reiterate the scholastics' concept of transubstantiation:

> The transformation of the bread and wine into the body and blood of Christ begs to be related to the larger scope of divine transformation. This is instanced in the incarnation, as the Word was made flesh, and in the resurrection of the Crucified. In other words, the eucharist is primarily a sign of the total mystery of God's redeeming love at work. The transformation of the eucharistic bread and wine is not a strange, even arbitrary, miracle. It cannot be isolated from God's love for all creation. If it is considered outside this larger context, then the bread and wine are simply "the matter of the sacrament," the raw material, as it were. Transubstantiation would be simply a divine replacement of one substance with another—even though, as the scholastics would say, "the accidents" remain. . . . The . . . unnerving aspect of such accounts of transubstantiation is that the real presence of Christ is understood as ousting the reality or substance of the created earthly realities. The heavenly Christ is crudely imagined as coming from the outside, from beyond, our world. The risen Jesus is imagined to replace the "inside" of the realities we know and use. If transubstantiation is thought of in this way, the remaining appearances of the bread and wine seem like a kind of shell, providing temporary camouflage for Christ hidden within them. The implication is that the Lord's presence demands a price: the abolition of some part of created reality. The eucharist contains the heavenly Christ in a mysterious fashion, but the earthly realities of bread and wine are emptied of their substance, that is, their deepest reality.[32]

In other words, we need a greater picture of the presence of Christ in our mundane realities. Our interpretation of sacramental signs as the bodily presence of Christ is, within the process theological framework, not just an accidental layer of reality, it is rather a crucial part of a reality that is regarded as a mutually relational and responsive system. We may as well call the awareness of Christ's self-giving intention that carries the cornerstones of his narrative identity to our present: *the eucharistic experience.* Thus, we do not encounter the sacraments as invisible containers of invisible grace, but we approach types of material entities as the embodiment of Christ because they have been immersed in the narrative identity of Christ and because their responsiveness as participants in an *overall responsive nature* allows them to echo the self-giving intention of Christ. Although the Eucharist is the peak of Catholic sacramental theology, it is also the epitome of all sacramental theology—the bodily presence of Christ in material beings that are a part of our visible world:

> In a larger perspective, we must not imagine Christ "contained" in the eucharistic elements in some way. It is more a matter of the bread and wine being themselves "contained" in Christ in an eschatological and transformative manner. From this point of view, the reality of Christ does not supplant or replace the innermost reality of the bread and wine. Christ's action frees and lifts up these elements of nature and culture to attain their fullest reality in him. By being transformed into his body and blood, they are not less than what they were previously. They attain the full and final reality of what they were meant to be. . . . Familiar elements of our earthly life are constituted in their ultimate significance—food and drink of eternal life.[33]

Now, in taking stock we have to admit that within this picture of sacramental realities we can easily see that this version of sacramental theology requires a view on reality that is ideally met by a process theological approach: at the most fundamental level, we would have to regard nature as the embodiment of the divine so that the incarnation is an organic prolongation of the initial relation between God and the world. At the second level, we need to endorse a view on personal identity that permits the extension of bodily presence which is based on the responsiveness of natural things and persons.

But this view has an additional advantage: Kelly points out that the eschatological transformation of the cosmos should be based on a speculative interpretation of the Eucharist:

> This sacramental reality of the real presence is brought about by the transformation of the shared fruit of the earth and the work of human hands. The bread that is offered becomes for us "the bread of life." The wine we bring becomes "our spiritual drink." In this way, the eucharist anticipates the transformation of

all creation, in which matter, spirit, nature, and culture are connected in the one God-created universe. The fruits of nature and the work of human creativity are integrated in the cosmic scope of God's self-communication in Christ. Nature and the history of human creativity interpenetrate. The produce of the earth is instanced in the wheat and grapes. Human creativity is effective in changing the grain and grapes into bread and wine. The reality of human culture is disclosed in that such food and drink are used in the convivial communication of our meals and festive celebrations. This cultural component enters into the eucharist to constitute the sign of Christ's self-giving on the cross. In its turn, Christ's self-gift incarnates the self-giving love of the Father and the grace of the Holy Spirit.[34]

But in order to cash in the analogy between the sacraments, especially the Eucharist, and the eschatological transformation of the whole cosmos, we need to endorse a *process view on reality*: sacraments are intermediary processes that simultaneously echo the self-giving identity of Christ who continues to inspire the responses of all creation and that foreshadow the ever-growing emergence of the kingdom of God in human culture as well as in all of nature. Sacraments as processes that are entangled with the basic responsiveness of every material being and of every mind-gifted entity are, so to speak, reminiscent of the past and the future framed by God's very own embodiment in the world.

NOTES

1. Vatican Council II, *Lumen Gentium*, 3, in *Vatican II: The Essential Texts*, ed. Norman Tanner, S. J. (New York: Image, 2012).
2. Vatican Council II, *Sacrosanctum Concilium*, 2, in *Vatican II: The Essential Texts*, ed. Norman Tanner, S. J. (New York: Image, 2012).
3. Louis-Marie Chauvet, *Symbole et sacrement. Un relecture sacramentelle de l'existence chrétienne* (Paris: Cerf, 1987).
4. Roger W. Nutt, *General Principles of Sacramental Theology* (Washington, DC: The Catholic University of America Press, 2017), 71.
5. David Grumett has argued that the Catholic "standard" interpretation of the Eucharist does not fit well with orthodox two natures Christology. He points out that the medieval concept of "remanence"—uncovered by Martin Luther as the notion of consubstantiation—might be much more in alignment with Christology (David Grumett, *Material Eucharist* [Oxford: Oxford University Press, 2016], 173–84). The situation would be significantly different, as Grumett admits, if we take bread and wine to become the body and blood as the glorified human nature of Christ. Nevertheless, to him this transformation sounds like another medieval interpretation: the idea of annihilation. In the next section I will, therefore, try to argue that a process

theological framework—using the notion of the extended body of Christ—will offer a different route.

6. Ibid., 103–104.

7. Notger Slenczka, *Realpräsenz und Ontologie. Untersuchung der ontologischen Grundlagen der Transsignifikationslehre* (Göttingen: Vandenhoeck & Ruprecht, 1993).

8. Grumett, *Material Eucharist*, 190.

9. Joanna Leidenhag, *Minding Creation: Theological Panpsychism and the Doctrine of Creation* (New York: T & T Clark, 2021), 88, 100–102.

10. Ibid., 100.

11. Ibid.

12. Charles Hartshorne, *A Natural Theology for Our Time* (La Salle, IL: Open Court, 1989), 100–104.

13. For a pan-sacramental concept, connected to the notion of deep incarnation, see Christopher C. Knight, *The God of Nature: Incarnation and Contemporary Science* (Minneapolis, MN: Augsburg Fortress, 2007).

14. Cf. Philip Clayton, "Kenotic Trinitarian Panentheism," *Dialog* 44.3 (2005): 251.

15. Cf. Santiago Sia, *God in Process Thought: A Study in Charles Hartshorne's Concept of God* (Dordrecht: Kluwer, 1985), 42ff.

16. Nutt, *General Principles of Sacramental Theology*, 64.

17. Grumett, *Material Eucharist*, 69–70.

18. For a critical assessment, see Joseph A. Bracken, S. J., *Christianity and Process Thought: Spirituality for a Changing World* (Philadelphia, PA: Templeton Foundation Press, 2006), 3–13.

19. Joseph A. Bracken, S. J., *The World in the Trinity: Open-Ended Systems in Science and Religion* (Minneapolis, MN: Fortress Press, 2014), 130.

20. Bracken, *Christianity and Process Thought*, 30.

21. Cf. Bracken, *The World in the Trinity*, 130ff.

22. Cf. Bracken, *Christianity and Process Thought*, 21ff.

23. Anthony Kelly, C. Ss. R., *Eschatology and Hope* (Maryknoll, NY: Orbis Books, 2005), 65.

24. Cf. Paul Ricoeur, *Oneself as Another*, trans. Kathleen Blamey (Chicago: University of Chicago Press, 1992), 113–39.

25. Cf. Ibid., 140–63.

26. Ibid., 318.

27. Ibid.

28. Thomas Schärtl, "Die Auferstehung Jesu denken: Ostern zwischen Glaubensgrund und Glaubensgegenstand," *Theologie und Philosophie* 95.1 (2020): 30–37.

29. Kelly, *Eschatology and Hope*, 90.

30. Ibid., 182.

31. Grumett, *Material Eucharist*, 112.

32. Kelly, *Eschatology and Hope*, 192ff.

33. Ibid., 193–94.

34. Ibid., 196.

BIBLIOGRAPHY

Bracken, Joseph A., S. J. *Christianity and Process Thought: Spirituality for a Changing World*. Philadelphia, PA: Templeton Foundation Press, 2006.

Bracken, Joseph A., S. J. *The World in the Trinity: Open-Ended Systems in Science and Religion*. Minneapolis, MN: Fortress Press, 2014.

Chauvet, Louis-Marie. *Symbole et sacrement. Un relecture sacramentelle de l'existence chrétienne*. Paris: Cerf, 1987.

Clayton, Philip. "Kenotic Trinitarian Panentheism." *Dialog* 44.3 (2005): 250–55.

Grumett, David. *Material Eucharist*. Oxford: Oxford University Press, 2016.

Hartshorne, Charles. *A Natural Theology for Our Time*. La Salle, IL: Open Court, 1989.

Kelly, Anthony, C. Ss. R. *Eschatology and Hope*. Maryknoll, NY: Orbis Books, 2005.

Knight, Christopher C. *The God of Nature: Incarnation and Contemporary Science*. Minneapolis, MN: Augsburg Fortress, 2007.

Leidenhag, Joanna. *Minding Creation: Theological Panpsychism and the Doctrine of Creation*. New York: T & T Clark, 2021.

Nutt, Roger W. *General Principles of Sacramental Theology*. Washington, DC: The Catholic University of America Press, 2017.

Ricoeur, Paul. *Oneself as Another*. Translated by Kathleen Blamey. Chicago: University of Chicago Press, 1992.

Schärtl, Thomas. "Die Auferstehung Jesu denken: Ostern zwischen Glaubensgrund und Glaubensgegenstand." *Theologie und Philosophie* 95.1 (2020): 1–37.

Sia, Santiago. *God in Process Thought: A Study in Charles Hartshorne's Concept of God*. Dordrecht: Kluwer, 1985.

Slenczka, Notger. *Realpräsenz und Ontologie. Untersuchung der ontologischen Grundlagen der Transsignifikationslehre*. Göttingen: Vandenhoeck & Ruprecht, 1993.

Vatican Council II. *Lumen Gentium*. In *Vatican II: The Essential Texts*, edited by Norman Tanner, S. J. New York: Image, 2012.

Vatican Council II. *Sacrosanctum Concilium*. In *Vatican II: The Essential Texts*, edited by Norman Tanner, S. J. New York: Image, 2012.

Chapter 10

Babbling on About Pluralism

The Catholicity of Pluralism

John Becker

"A clash of doctrines is not a disaster—it is an opportunity."[1] In 1965, at the close of the Second Vatican Council, Roman Catholicism underwent a spiritual revolution that confronted an array of Catholic experiences in the purview of the modern world, reevaluating Eucharistic prayers, aesthetic susceptibilities, and modes of evangelization. Of these doctrinal and ecclesiastical developments, the Catholic Church's proclamations about other religions have caused much debate due to their cursory yet thought-provoking formulations. This textual ambiguity led to critical explorations into the varying relationships between Christianity and other religions, a confessional theological discipline known as theology of religions, and the later development of comparative theology. Today how to navigate these complex relationships is still a point of contention between Catholics and their neighbors.[2] The official position of the magisterium is the fulfillment or inclusive model where the fullness of truth and salvific efficacy are found in Christ alone and that other religious traditions are efficacious only insofar as Christ is mysteriously operative in their respective traditions. While this model is internally satisfactory, might there be better alternatives to account for the normativity of religious others?

This chapter revisits the universal and unavoidable issue of religious others through a processual Catholic horizon. A process-relational approach does not offer a strictly theological response to pluralism but supplies a provisional metaphysics for the reenchantment of reality through its bewildering relational becoming—a divine-like complexity impenetrable by the finitude of human existence. As such, "complexity" and "relationality" convey a sense of religious mystery and sacredness—we intuit these saturated concepts but never adequately satisfy the premonitions they elicit. Alfred North Whitehead maintained that "mysticism is direct insight into depths as yet unspoken. But the purpose of philosophy is to rationalize mysticism."[3] In this sense, Whitehead is a religiously sensitive thinker who facilitates deeper philosophical and theological reflection. Within this acknowledgment—the synergy between mysticism and rationalism—I present three processual paradigms of pluralisms (unitive, differential, and non-dual).

This chapter consists of (1) a cursory overview of Vatican II and later declarations on non-Christian traditions, highlighting the church's ambivalence concerning religious otherness. This indecision ultimately led Catholicism to develop and advance a qualified fulfillment model that holds all salvific efficacy is found in Christ only and is mysteriously operative in all other religions. (2) Next, I offer an examination of three processual approaches to religious pluralism, two of which are grounded within a Catholic context, albeit not restricted to it: Paul Knitter and Joseph Bracken's unitive pluralism, John B. Cobb Jr. and David Ray Griffin's differential pluralism, and Raimundo Panikkar and Roland Faber's non-dual pluralism. These categories are functional appellations and do not capture the rich complexities between each thinker but convey the spirit of their respective approaches. My goal is to present three processual alternatives to the fulfillment model that, in my opinion, better account for our contemporary context of multiplicity and otherness without diminutive appropriations or radical deviations from the Catholic tradition.

THE SECOND VATICAN COUNCIL AND BEYOND

The Second Vatican Council was groundbreaking in its scope and significance, and some Catholics found its conclusions too progressive, or even worse, sacrilege.[4] The Council fearlessly reenvisioned what it meant to be Roman Catholic in the modern world, a challenging task during challenging times. Of the various pronouncements put forth, those regarding non-Christian religions were most disconcerting. Thomas Bokenkotter perfectly captures the existentially distressing environment that post-Vatican II Catholics found themselves:

> Before the Council, Catholics knew who they were, since they knew who they weren't. They defined themselves over against the non-Catholics—the Protestants, members of other religions, secular humanists, etc . . . but the Council did a 180-degree turn.[5]

Whether the shift was felt as debilitating or liberating, how to encounter "non-Catholics" became a pressing theological and existential inquiry.

Several crucial reasons prompted such a stance by the Council, but one resonates with process thinkers in particular. *Gaudium et Spes* sets the tone for the entire council, stating, "the Church has the duty in every age of examining the signs of the times and interpreting them in the light of the gospel," in the hopes the faith becomes greater attuned to the needs and demands of an ever-changing sociohistorical landscape.[6] The perpetual developments of globalization provide ever new catalysts for revisions and adaptations in a fluid world, technologically, politically, and spiritually. In other words, it is the recognition that the Catholic tradition, including the church, is continually actualizing itself *in the world*, not apart or beyond it. This radical shift in attention—from trying to maintain a purity of essence to embracing a processual becoming—led to a more receptive understanding of faith and belonging. Just as it is "humanity's natural constitution" to be "a social being who cannot live or develop without relations with others," the same applies to the church.[7] Whether individual persons, communities, or institutions, all entities are relational and symbiotic in their self-constitution.

The overarching themes of becoming and reciprocity are evident throughout the Council's documents. Of particular interest, however, is how Catholics are to respond to religious others. How might the newfound truism of mutual interrelatedness be grasped in terms of religious diversity? How might differing religious truth claims be realized in light of a dynamic becoming? This last question remains a point of contention for many participants involved in interreligious dialogue and religious pluralism, who playfully oscillating between the extremes of exclusivism and relativism, between the One and the Many. It is, then, instructive to lay out a general synopsis of the church's relation to other religions before advocating processual approaches.

Nostra Aetate is unsurpassed in its favorable treatment of other religious traditions, and Karl Rahner's central influence is without question.[8] The document, via his Transcendental Thomism, portends a universal spirit of religiosity (broadly construed) that is an integral component of the human condition. This collective human condition acknowledges a universal yearning for meaning, goodness, and truth, albeit being unthematic. Whether this impulse is propelled by *imago Dei*, *atman*, cognitive betterment, or Buddha-nature, the undeniable desire to respond has led to differing perspectives that seek to pacify this longing. Histories and cultures have supplied varying modes of religiosity tackling these all-important existential questions. These varying paths, then, need not appeal to a universal truth but rather evince efficacy in their existential placation, thereby giving a positive perspective outside the Christian domain.

The acknowledgment of humanity's spiritual disposition and existential effectiveness of different religious paths ultimately culminate in the Council's openness to religious diversity. Nevertheless, this openness seemed to require a categorical corrective of particularity—the utter uniqueness of Christ. This ubiquitous tension between the universal and particular is captured in the oft-quoted passage:

> The Catholic Church rejects nothing of those things which are true and holy in these religions. It regards with respect those ways of acting and living and those precepts and teachings which, though often at variance with what it holds and expands, frequently reflect a ray of that truth which enlightens everyone. Yet, without ceasing it preaches, and is bound to preach, Christ who is "the way, the truth and the life" (Jn 14, 6), in whom people find the fullness of religious life and in whom God has reconciled all things to himself.[9]

After maintaining the importance of Christ's centrality, *Nostra Aetate* restates the significance of mutual understanding, promotion of moral values, and social justice. The central tenets are twofold: one is concerned with the cooperation and flourishing between the different religions and cultures of the world, and the second asserts the primacy of Christ.

Exactly how to embody these remarks are unclear. On a liberal reading, the Roman Catholic reformer James Carroll remarks that the church altered its understanding of truth to embrace a form of perspectivism—the theory that all truth is limited to the individual's unique point of view.[10] Carroll's assertion seems to be a gross misappropriation. Dermot A. Lane offers a better appraisal stating that, overall, the Council is deafeningly silent concerning the salvific question of whether other religions offer paths to salvation.[11] Despite the positive language toward other religions, the various documents fail to articulate the ramifications for the church and laity fully, perhaps, intentionally.

Whereas Carroll and Lane find ambiguity in the church's stance regarding religious others and salvation, they seem to neglect the idea clearly stated in *Nostra Aetate,* "Christ who is 'the way, the truth and the life' (Jn 14, 6), in whom people find the fullness of religious life and in whom God has reconciled all things to himself."[12] To dispel ambiguities further, the Pontifical Council for Inter-Religious Dialogue unequivocally proclaim that all salvation is possible through the universal mediator, Jesus Christ:

> From this mystery of unity it follows that all men and women who are saved share, though differently, in the same mystery of salvation in Jesus Christ through his Spirit. Christians know this through their faith, while others remain unaware that Jesus Christ is the source of their salvation.[13]

This was resounded again in the Declaration *Dominus Iesus*, proclaiming that there is but "one salvific economy" revealed through the "One and Triune

God," "the incarnated Son," and "Holy Spirit."[14] The initial kaleidoscopic vision proved to be too ambiguous in the decades following Vatican II, and in its stead, the fulfillment model became orthodoxy.

The flourishing diversified religious landscape welcomes the fulfillment model, especially given the church's former claim to exclusive spiritual hegemony. Although reflecting a ray of truth in a second order, different religious traditions are ultimately refractions gleaned from the orthodox prism that is Christ, who is the criterion and fullness of truth. James Fredericks concludes that other religious paths may be salvific, but their salvific source is "in Christ by the grace of the Holy Spirit."[15] Nevertheless, Christ's centrality is always nuanced with God's universal love, a point of debate for salvific theories going back to the early Church Fathers. All the earth's inhabitants are divine siblings made in God's image, and so there is an undeniable link between humanity and God as between persons, "Whoever does not love, does not know God" (1 John 4:8).

In addressing the fulfillment model in the purview of the previous passage and under the pretense of an inclusive spiritual hegemony, Catholics may ask: Is this love of the other truly genuine? Or are Catholics merely loving themselves and their claim to the truth? If the fullness of reality is found in Christ only via the church, does it truly matter if truths, ultimately illuminated by Christ, are found in other traditions? It does not, and the ramifications are particularly detrimental for Catholics interested in interreligious dialogue or pluralism because there is nothing particularly religious about these fields of inquiry. Everything concerning the "religious" other transmutes into a form of anthropological or cultural studies. This is undoubtedly one of the biggest drawbacks of the fulfillment model.

Nostra Aetate was meant to be the foundational proclamation concerning the church's interpretation of other religions, but obscurities remained. The Pontifical Council on Inter-Religious Dialogue helps clarify some of these uncertainties and proffers a more powerful passage in advocating, at the very least, a more genuine interreligious undertaking. When discussing how missionaries should engage those of other religious traditions, it states, "But Christians too must allow themselves to be questioned. Notwithstanding the fullness of God's revelation in Jesus Christ, the way Christians sometimes understand their religion and practice it may be in need of purification."[16] This passage, while not questioning the ontological fullness of Christ, profoundly situates Catholics and the church as fallible. This passage makes clear the reciprocal dynamic of genuine dialogue, and it overcomes a tacitly unilateral missiology.

Despite these issues, it is easy today to forget the radical nature of the Second Vatican Council, shifting doctrinally from a stringent exclusivism to a form of inclusivism. As Lane put it, the Council signaled a seismic shift in the theological awareness of the church, "God is now understood to be active through grace, through the Spirit, and through the seeds of the Word, not only within Christianity, but also outside the Christian reality within other religions."[17] Despite these changes, how might a process hermeneutic assist in envisioning a mode of pluralism that can be truly Catholic and genuinely pluralistic, whereby overcoming latent hubris and imperialism?

THE CATHOLIC TRADITION AND PROCESS PLURALISM

The disciplines of the theology of religions, interreligious dialogue, and comparative theology seamlessly tie together in constructing a robust process-oriented Catholic pluralism. Notwithstanding these differing typologies, their aims are roughly congruent, that is, to bring logical coherence to the normativity of religious diversity, either confessionally or philosophically. To fruitfully account for the world's religions, moving beyond apologetics, is still an important task, and it has occupied scholars and theologians from the latter half of the twentieth century to today.

So explosive was the field of theology of religions in the last sixty-five years—promulgating Alan Race's typologies of exclusivism, inclusivism, and pluralism[18] or Paul Knitter's replacement, fulfillment, mutuality, and acceptance models[19]—that Fredericks, dissuaded by the theoretical approaches put forth for interreligious engagement but unwavering in his commitment to cross-cultural amity, elevated the praxis of dialogue over any theoretical formulation. He poignantly writes:

> There has been much discussion in the debate over the theology of religions of the need to find a theoretical "foundation" or "basis" for dialogue. The problems attending theologies of religions make clear how dubious this project is . . . Christians should set this project aside, recognizing that a half-century of creativity in this area has firmly established the fulfillment mode, the most suitable of all the alternatives.[20]

While I sympathize with his frustration, I disagree that the paradoxical profundity of the enterprise suggests it is a "dubious" project. I am steadfast in maintaining that it is crucially important to illuminate a foundation if interreligious dialogue is to be more than a form of anthropology or cultural studies. Additionally, and unfortunately, largely missing from his assessment are the processual approaches to religious pluralism, which arguably do not fall victim to the inconsistency plaguing other positions, some of which will be addressed in this chapter.

Here I outline three processual pluralisms for authentically addressing religious diversity. Most notably, all three approaches are able to faithfully provide a Catholic vision in process without implicating *praeparatio evangelica*—a logical necessity of the fulfillment model and evocative of a type of religious Darwinism—or relegating religious otherness to anthropological studies.

Unitive Pluralism

Paul Knitter's *By No Other Name?* provides a brilliant argument for rich interreligious dialogue via a pluralism grounded in a theocentric approach. His unitive pluralistic vision intuitively maintains that there is a wholeness (not singularity) to religious diversity. Yes, "Reality is essentially pluriform: complex, rich, intricate, mysterious" and "there can be no one way . . . nevertheless the 'many' cannot simply exists as many."[21] This recognition does not advocate for a religious confluence into a singular world religion, a vibrant form of syncretism, indifferent tolerance, or religious imperialism:

> Rather, unitive pluralism is a unity in which each religion, although losing some of its individualism (its separate ego), will intensify its personality (its self-awareness through relationship). Each religion will retain its own uniqueness, but this uniqueness will develop and take on new depths by relating to other religions in mutual dependence.[22]

Accordingly and within a Christian context, "losing some of its individualism" equates to faithfully readdressing Christological declarations.

Crucial to Knitter's project is the revisionist principle that advances a nonnormative Christology, not by deviating from the Catholic tradition but rather through critically contextualizing its Christological claims. He exposes the ever-shifting social-historical landscape of biblical interpretation that led to a varying array of Christological pronouncements. These past Christologies are vital discernments of the Christ event but, more importantly, representative of a specific Christian communities' ethos. These doctrinal announcements cannot be dismissed, but they must be understood in and through their historical derivations, influencing present theological reflections but not limited to them. That is, they must be contextualized in their historical-cultural situation, and Catholics must continue to interpret and reinterpret the depths of the Christ event in the church's current environment. This acknowledgment allows him, in conversation with Karl Rahner, process thought, and liberation theology, to envisage a nonnormative, theocentric Christology.[23] Christological language is symbolically profound insofar as "it is undefinable" and "must be understood ever anew."[24] As frequently suggested throughout his numerous works, Christological claims must be taken seriously, not literally. Rejecting strict, absolutizing propositional understandings of the Christ event ("one and only"), Knitter's theocentric proposal proclaims that Christians must be open to the possibilities of other salvific incarnational events.[25] In today's context, where otherness beautifully pervades our existence, what might a pluralistically envisioned Christ event invoke today?

Joseph Bracken's metaphysical acumen nicely compliments Knitter's revisionist project. In *The Divine Matrix*, he tenders a neo-Whiteheadian approach that articulates an ontological scaffolding that accounts for and transcends the problem of the One and the Many through the dual transcendence of God and the world. As predication naturally suggests, "the One and the Many" are built upon static, entitative assumptions. To overcome this Aristotelian-Thomistic rendering, he suggests distinguishing between God's nature and persons.[26] God's immutable nature is the groundless ground—the divine matrix—upon which the divine persons subsist and have their individual *personae*. Within God's nature as the consecrated ground, the divine persons operate through cooperation as *actus purus* in their mutual relationality. Bracken introduces the notion of intersubjectivity to retexture *perichoresis* or *circumincession* to further flesh out the divine activity through deep mutual interaction between the persons of the Trinity. This move signifies that a person's identity is manifest in and through its relations with others (identity-in-difference).[27] In their free act of divine creativity, relationality becomes the divine form of communication, not only between the three *hupostaseis/personae* (immanent Trinity) but God and the world (economic Trinity). Creation, then, shares in the divine nature, albeit in an imperfect, finite manner that affects and contributes to the matrix: "The deeper perception of reality is to recognize the presence of the infinite in the finite and thus to acknowledge the provisional or in any case limited character of the finite."[28] The divine matrix encapsulates both one (God's nature) and many (*personae*/creation), being irreducible to the other. Additionally, it maintains a bilateral engagement between the world and God. In light of his position, he posits that no religion is superior to another, but rather, "they are inseparable dimensions of one and the same august mystery" in their infinitely complex becomings.[29] Although articulated through his Catholic faith, Bracken envisions his conceptual scheme as abstract enough for other traditions to find resonations.

These former colleagues at Xavier University in Cincinnati Paul Knitter and Joseph Bracken provide resounding explorations of religious pluralism while maintaining a resolute faith in the Christian message, albeit differently. Between the One and the Many, Knitter proposes a unitary source (theocentric) of religiosity that allows meaningful dialogue to ensue without diminishing the intensified uniqueness of the religious landscape as heightened through their contrasts. Bracken, on the other hand, proposes a dualistic framework structured within the divine matrix. His position envisions a pantheistic model that sees the One (God/Infinite) and the Many (the Trinity/religious diversity/finite) through irreducible becomings, yet co-constitutive with/in one another in creativity. Whereas Knitter sees promise in intuitive unity, Bracken favors the Many insofar as his argument presupposes the infinite–finite dichotomy. All-in-all, they offer us much in the way of understanding and appreciating religious pluralism with convivial convictions about the "one august mystery."

Differential Pluralism

David Ray Griffin's edited work *Deep Religious Pluralism* structures and vindicates the contributions of John Cobb's pluralistic paradigm, a radical alternative that is often overlooked in pluralism discourses. Griffin argues rightly that most critiques of religious pluralism are directed toward a specific type of pluralism advocated by John Hick, Wilfred Cantwell Smith, and Paul Knitter.[30] Griffin classifies these forms of pluralism as identic pluralism—a form of pluralism that maintains "all religions are oriented toward the same religious object (whether it be called 'God,' 'Brahman,' 'Nirvana,' 'Sunyata,' 'Ultimate Reality,' 'the Transcendent,' or 'the Real') and promote essentially the same end (the same type of 'salvation')."[31] What makes this approach unsatisfactory, according to Griffin and Cobb, is that it is not distinctively Christian. Arguably, the majority of the faithful in any tradition would not assent to the idea that their salvific conduit and goal share a similitude to other religious traditions. In overcoming hegemonic universalizing claims, these identic authors argue to diminish deafening uniqueness in various religious traditions to reveal a ground for dialogue. Accordingly, this simplified version of identist pluralism creates a bland religious landscape. As noted previously, this dissolution of uniqueness is unequivocally denounced in *Dominus Iesus*.[32]

While affirming and admiring much of what identist pluralists strive for, Cobb and Griffin envision a pluralism that better attends to religious differences. Cobb connects three principles that inform a processual horizon, a conviction shared by unitive and non-dual pluralists as well: "1) the world remains complex, always beyond our limits of comprehension, 2) an acknowledgment that throughout human history, people have had profound insights, along with misguided ones, about the totality of reality, and 3) all religious ultimates are valid."[33] Here, Griffin classifies this alternative as *differential pluralism*, which advocates that "religions promote different ends—different salvations—perhaps by virtue of being oriented toward different religious objects, perhaps thought of as different ultimates."[34] The central distinction focuses on contrastive differences as a catalyst for creative advances. Instead of attempting to homogenize religious traditions, a differential approach is pluralistically informed in terms of soteriology and ontology.

Griffin puts forth abstracted categories of different ultimates to help facilitate his argument, namely, God, creativity, and the cosmos.[35] This typology does not suggest conflict or struggle for supremacy (either/or paradigm). Instead, the goal is to find modes of complementariness between different traditions in the creation of a richer appreciation of religious realities (both/and paradigm). The differential approach, as with non-dualism, does not *dismiss* differences but *insists* upon them. It is the difference between "*A* universally valid truth" as opposed to "*the* universal truth." In this context, truth, revealed or otherwise, is not relativized but complexified.

My own rendering of differential pluralism characterizes it as a heno-ontology, not limited to mere theistic conceptions of ultimacy.[36] It maintains that individuals faithfully believe and adhere to a unique facet of reality without rejecting the existence of other possible facets, whether divine or otherwise. The traditional concern for hegemonical exclusivism is replaced by modes of correlation and complementariness between ultimates, always requiring tentative appraisals of truth and being open to modifications. It offers other religious traditions the same qualifications insisted on by Christianity—allowing different traditions to retain their idiosyncratic features: Islam is not looking for God through the incarnate Son, but rather through the Holy Qur'an, the Word of God, as revealed through the prophet Muhammad (peace be upon him). Christ surely is the conduit to God's glory as the Father, but Buddhists are not looking for the Father, but rather "to be extinguished."

Differential pluralism allows religions to preserve their exceptional spiritual intuitions without losing their identity.[37] The faith in the triune God and church is not diminished or threatened in openly accepting the possibility that other religious traditions are genuinely responding to something genuinely other, and to that end, to have faith in Jesus does not logically dictate the rejection of other religious possibilities. However, are they speaking for and structuring too much for that which is not yet? Unitive and differential pluralism, although in agreement with the revisionist principle, seem to hold reifying propensities, either intuitively of the all-inclusive one or many ultimate realities.

Non-Dual Pluralism

The Catholic theologian Raimundo Panikkar holds that every pluralistic agenda ultimately fails from the onset because it considers the issue as something to overcome or rationalize into a superstructure. To be sure, there are varying degrees of mystical threads found in Bracken, Cobb,

Griffin, and Knitter, but Panikkar radically intuits the paradox of pluralistic frameworks:

> I have said that we were dealing with a myth, and a myth is something on which we cannot put our finger without dispelling it. It is something we cannot manipulate. We are not pluralistic by integrating everything in one "pluralistic" worldview. We are pluralistic by believing that none of us possesses the philosophers' stone, the key to the secret of the world . . . by having the restraint not to think through everything lest we destroy the "thought" (*das Gedachte*, not *der Gedanke*) and the thinker. This is not irrationalism. It is intellectual humility or common sense.[38]

He continues to state that reality in its full complexity is "'thought-proof'—viz. resistant to thinking"—but again, in sublating facile renderings of the mystical and apophatic traditions, not irrationalism or anti-intellectualism.[39] Put simply, multiplicity just is, and as such, does not require configuration. Panikkar propounds a pluralism that is eternally open to becoming, without proffering solutions to religious incompatibilities. A genuine plurality demands the acknowledgment of diversity, including perspectives of exclusivism and inclusivism, without ceasing to promote conviviality, ceaselessly "standing between unrelated plurality and a monolithic unity."[40] Ultimacy, in any form, evades any and all classifications, and so he speaks of the cosmotheandric vision that "sees the entire reality as the interaction of a threefold polarity: cosmic, divine, and human."[41] Where Cobb and Griffin propose for the ultimate status of these poles, Panikkar negates this move. Moving away from dialectical dialogue based on logical prescriptions, he promotes dialogical dialogue because humanity is infinitely more than the former approach discloses:

> The dialogical dialogue assumes a radical dynamism of reality, namely that reality is not given once and for all, but is real precisely in the fact that it is continually creating itself—and not just unfolding from already existing premises or starting points.[42]

In line with Panikkar, Roland Faber has written extensively on an emended processual apophatic pluralism, both as a Catholic and now as a Bahá'í. He, too, notes that the various categorizations of the One and Many "are ultimately abstractions from the inaccessible Truth that cannot be formulated in one coherent intellectual system."[43] Pluralism, not dualism, is normative, an inescapable fact sewn into the very fabric of reality, not to be rationalized, overcome, or mollified, but accepted and embraced. The diverse religious voices do not exhaust the divine or reality because it is strictly unknowable (classical apophaticism), but rather precisely because of "the *future* of becoming, as the source of novelty of the not yet."[44] Between the past and the future, the world and God co-inhere within each other in their mutual becoming. Faber arrives at this conclusion after noting mystical patterns of experience and nonnormative logic in the world's religious traditions.

Faber advocates for polyphilic pluralism—a pluralism understood as God's love of the manifold through mutual immanence. Accordingly, any model positing a unitary pluralism is in danger of an implicit power structure of hierarchal subjugation, reminiscent of the chain of being. On the other hand, any pluralism that maintains multiplicity is in danger of religious traditions vying for dominance, either implicitly or explicitly. Both positions are fortified with destructive tensions as necessitated through substantial, hyper-rationalistic thinking. Yet, must it operate under the confines of logical limitations, what Panikkar identifies as dialectical dialogue? To this point, Faber asks us to envision a pluralism that rejects the *power* dynamics of substantial thinking and replaces it with a divine *love* of multiplicity.[45] After all, "the divine element in the world is to be conceived as a persuasive agency and not as a coercive agency" and, "this doctrine should be looked upon as one of the greatest intellectual discoveries in the history of religion."[46] To capture this categorical shift, Faber employs the term "theopoetics," where God is understood as "the *gift* of *self*-creativity" for the world, and when self-creation is concresced or actualized within the world, God evaluates the world and issues the gift anew.[47] This demonstrates the bilateral movement, the coterminous nature of the God–world relationship. It follows that all creaturely significations of ultimacy must be rejected in order to avoid idolatry of the Poet's undifferentiated communication of immanence.[48] Faber upholds multiplicity as grounded upon the divine manifold while maintaining a categorical primacy of God's in/difference or non-duality.[49] He likens this approach to Plotinus's One or Ibn 'Arabi's incipient Sufi concept of the Unity of Existence (*waḥdat al-wujūd*), alluding to the fact that God is concurrently all things (immanent) and none of them (transcendent).[50] The consequence, as with Panikkar, demands a reorientation of the polarities of God–world, ontology–epistemology, and One–Many, an orientation of contrastive becomings: "the apophatic move is one of Reality that/whom religions seek and mediate for experience, that is, one of the Divine Manifold 'itself,' revealing 'its' apophatic Self precisely in polyphilic form."[51]

Panikkar and Faber amplify the import of the apophatic traditions as it pertains to religious pluralism. Panikkar's erudition and fluid religiosity made him suspicious of pluralistic models because they were formed under dialectical logic instead of humanity's existential plurality, thereby detracting interreligious engagement from authentic dialogue as disclosed through cosmothenandric experiences. Unlike differential pluralism's philosophical foundation, Faber seeks to reveal the bewildering array of the complexities of the trifold polarities *without* systematizing them into ultimates while simultaneously revealing a mystical thread to religious unity-in-difference. In this sense, he both embodies and transcends process theology toward a transreligious discourse.

AN INDETERMINATE CONCLUSION

Can these processual foundations be genuine options for Catholics in the twenty-first century? I univocally state yes. Whether unitive, differential, or non-dual, these pluralistic theories understand Christianity and other religious traditions in a web of mutual becoming and offer a radical reorientation from the fulfillment model. While within Catholicism the fulfillment model is internally satisfactory, it is inadequate for our contemporary pluriform environment. To utilize Panikkar further, the fulfillment model is fraught with a dialectical spirit that stifles religiosity, religion, and conviviality. Taken collectively, the processual models thrust Catholicism back into the messy world of relationality, recognizing its limitations and possibilities for the future.

There is a harmony between the multiple divine possibilities and theories about them: between exclusivism, inclusivism, and pluralism. Similarly, reality's full complexities must not be construed as a subjugating hierarchy but as an interpenetrating matrix. The task, then, is to find potential bridges that deepen the profundity of the Christ event through other religious practitioners' lived experiences and beliefs, including secularism. Within a Catholic context, the fullness of the revelation of the Christ event is unquestioned, but the church's discernment of this event must continue in and through the world, most importantly through other religions.[52]

Although I sought to present different pluralistic models in the purview of process thought which are complementary in several ways, my own convictions lie within non-dualism. Humanity may imagine, develop, construct, and reinforce models of mentation concerning the depths of reality, but in the end, it is in their undoing, unstructuring, unbecoming that divinity inebriates us with its depths. This is the oft-neglected side of processual talk of becoming—that is, unbecoming.

As with Panikkar and Faber, I find neatly structured and rationalized ventures to rupture the divine mystery, disenchanting it to the point of *ratio ad absurdum*. Non-dual pluralism best retains the mystery, polarities, and aporias of the ultimacy of things, avoiding what Whitehead refers to as the fallacy of misplaced concreteness. I take Meister Eckhart's paradoxical intuitions seriously when he proclaims: *Sed de natura dei est indistinctio, de natura et ratione creati distinctio* (but God's nature is indistinction, creation's nature and manner are distinction).[53] Normative logic and "dialectical dialogue" are indispensable and necessary modes of reasoning, operating through distinctions yet divine reality, in Eckhart's and other mystical traditions' summation, is qualitatively different: God's sole distinction is indistinction. As with Christ, there is no privileged perspective concerning the divine within the pluriform world: "Foxes have dens and birds have nests, but the Son of Man has no place to lay his head" (Luke 9:58). Concerning religious diversity, how shall humanity proceed except precisely through a non-dual approach that upholds the divine indifferentiation in its manifold of becoming? As genuine exemplifications of this indifferentiation, humanity's rich diversity must faithfully embody their particularity within and between other folds of becoming, allowing for real differences and genuine dialogue.

In conclusion, Catholics are fully aware of the challenges surrounding pluralism, but it seems these processual options are not outside of the realm of possibilities for post-Vatican II or even the more restrictive proclamations of *Dominus Iesus*. The shared convictions of the pluralisms presented here revolve around Cobb's notion of mutual transformation, where authentic dialogue and openness reciprocally transform practitioners, practices, and doctrine. When reconceptualized from dogmatic singularity toward a deep plurality, debilitating "dialectical" aporias are overcome and new interreligious possibilities emerge, from insurmountable differences to dynamic contrasts.

Catholicism can only benefit by engaging authentic interreligious engagements, whereby new possibilities to perennial issues are supplied: What limitations may be said about Catholicism? What prospects are currently excluded from the Catholic vision that can proffer a more vibrant aesthetic unity, for Catholicism and beyond? Instead of insisting on an exclusivist Catholicism (limited monotheism), how might developing these processual models further allow for real contrasts, greater modes of conviviality, and aesthetic unity in our pluralist world? Faithfully answering these questions will lead to creative transformation, both individually and institutionally.

NOTES

1. Alfred North Whitehead, *Science and the Modern World* (1926; repr., New York: Free Press, 1967), 186.

2. For an excellent book on recent interreligious relations in the United States, see Leo D. Lefebure, *Transforming Interreligious Relations: Catholic Responses to Religious Pluralism in the United States* (Maryknoll, NY: Orbis Books, 2020).

3. Alfred North Whitehead, *Modes of Thought* (1938; repr., New York: Free Press, 1966), 174.

4. For example, Traditional or Independent Catholics reject certain aspects of the Second Vatican Council, and in some cases, the Council itself.

5. Thomas S. Bokenkotter, *A Concise History of the Catholic Church* (New York: Doubleday, 2005), 429.

6. Vatican Council II, *Gaudium et Spes*, 4, in *Vatican II: The Essential Texts*, ed. Norman Tanner, S. J. (New York: Image, 2012).

7. Ibid., 12.

8. Dermot A. Lane, *Stepping Stones to Other Religions: A Christian Theology of Inter-religious Dialogue* (Maryknoll, NY: Orbis Books, 2011), 133.

9. Vatican Council II, *Nostra Aetate*, 2, in *Vatican II: Essential Texts*, ed. Norman Tanner, S. J. (New York: Image, 2021).

10. James Carroll, "The Beginning of Change," in *Vatican II: The Essential Texts,* ed. Norman Tanner, S. J. (New York: Image), 24.

11. Lane, *Stepping Stones to Other Religions*, 70.

12. Vatican Council II, *Nostra Aetate*, 2. This proclamation was reaffirmed again in "Dialogue and Proclamation: Reflections and Orientations on Inter-Religious Dialogue and the Proclamation of the Gospel of Jesus Christ" (Pontifical Council for Inter-Religious Dialogue, "Dialogue and Proclamation: Reflections and Orientations on Inter-Religious Dialogue and the Proclamation of the Gospel of Jesus Christ," 1, May 19, 1991, https://www.vatican.va/roman_curia/pontifical_councils/interelg/documents/rc_pc_interelg_doc_19051991_dialogue-and-proclamatio_en.html).

13. Ibid., 29.

14. Congregation for the Doctrine of the Faith, "*Dominus Iesus*: On the Unicity and Salvific Universality of Jesus Christ and the Church," 12, August 6, 2000, https://www.vatican.va/roman_curia/congregations/cfaith/documents/rc_con_cfaith_doc_20000806_dominus-iesus_en.html.

15. James L. Fredricks, *Buddhists and Christians: Through Comparative Theology to Solidarity* (Maryknoll, NY: Orbis Books, 2004), 2. Cf. Congregation for the Doctrine of the Faith, *Dominus Iesus*, 14.

16. "Dialogue and Proclamation," 32.

17. Lane, *Stepping Stones to Other Religions*, 70. James Fredericks establishes the concept of Universal Grace under the influence of Karl Rahner. Fredericks notes that the Council "moved in a Rahnerian direction to the extent that they recognize a supernatural grace to be already operative and efficacious in the lives of people who are not Christians" (Fredericks, *Buddhists and Christians*, 4).

18. See Alan Race, *Christians and Religious Pluralism: Patterns in the Christian Theology of Religions* (Maryknoll, NY: Orbis Books, 1982).

19. See Paul F. Knitter, *Introducing Theologies of Religions* (Maryknoll, NY: Orbis Books, 2002).

20. Fredericks, *Buddhists and Christians*, 26. In the context of the church's 2,000-plus years of spiritual discernments, I find it unusual to claim that the issue of religious pluralism has become a barren discourse after fifty years.

21. Paul F. Knitter, *No Other Name? A Critical Survey of Christian Attitudes Toward the World Religions* (Maryknoll, NY: Orbis Books, 1985), 6.

22. Ibid., 9.

23. Ibid., 172.

24. Ibid., 180.

25. Ibid., 192.

26. Joseph A. Bracken, S. J., *The Divine Matrix: Creativity as Link between East and West* (Eugene, OR: Wipf & Stock, 2006), 145.

27. See Joseph A. Bracken, S. J., *The One and the Many: A Contemporary Reconstruction of the God–World Relationship* (Grand Rapids, MI: Wm. B. Eerdmans Publishing Co., 2001), especially 109–55.

28. Bracken, *The Divine Matrix*, 129.

29. Ibid., 137.

30. David Ray Griffin, "Religious Pluralism: Generic, Identist, and Deep," in *Deep Religious Pluralism*, ed. David Ray Griffin (Louisville, KY: Westminster John Knox Press, 2005), 21.

31. Ibid., 24.

32. Congregation for the Doctrine of the Faith, *Dominus Iesus*, 4.

33. David Ray Griffin, "John Cobb's Whiteheadian Complementary Pluralism," in *Deep Religious Pluralism*, ed. David Ray Griffin (Louisville, KY: Westminster John Knox Press, 2005), 47.

34. Griffin, "Religious Pluralism," 24. In constructing a process pluralism, Whitehead's notions of the fallacy of misplaced concreteness and contrastive intensities are indispensable.

35. Griffin, "John Cobb's Whiteheadian Complementary Pluralism," 49. Cobb suggests only two—creativity and God—but is open to the possibility of other ultimate categories.

36. The number of ultimates is indeterminate (God, creativity, cosmos, etc.) and may be structured to the proclivities of any given thinker.

37. See John B. Cobb Jr., "Beyond 'Pluralism,'" in *Christian Uniqueness Reconsidered: The Myth of a Pluralistic Theology of Religions*, ed. Gavin D'Costa (Maryknoll, NY: Orbis Books, 1990), 92.

38. Raimundo Panikkar, "The Myth of Pluralism: The Tower of Babel—A Meditation on Non-Violence," *Cross Currents* 29.2 (1979): 224–25.

39. Ibid., 225.

40. Raimundo Panikkar, *The Intrareligious Dialogue* (New York: Paulist Press, 1999), 10.

41. Ibid., 24.

42. Ibid., 31.

43. Roland Faber, *The Ocean of God: On the Transreligious Future of Religions* (London: Anthem Press, 2019), loc 1357, Kindle.

44. Roland Faber, "The Mystical Whitehead," in *Seeking Common Ground: Evaluation and Critique of Joseph Bracken's Comprehensive Worldview*, ed. Marc A. Pugliese and Gloria L. Schaab (Milwaukee, WI: Marquette University Press, 2012), 216.

45. Roland Faber, "The Sense of Peace: A Para-Doxology of Divine Multiplicity," in *Polydoxy: Theology of Multiplicity and Relation*, ed. Catherine Keller and Laurel C. Schneider (London: Routledge, 2010), 36–40. Cf. Panikkar, "We [humanity]

are more, not less, than 'rational.' And perhaps the more realistic basis on which to ground human conviviality is not rational knowledge but loving awareness" (*Intrareligious Dialogue*, 11).

46. Alfred North Whitehead, *Adventures of Ideas* (1933; repr., New York: Free Press, 1967), 166. Also, see Roland Faber, *The Becoming of God: Process Theology, Philosophy, and Multireligious Engagement* (Eugene, OR: Cascade Books, 2017), 121–27.

47. Roland Faber, *God as Poet of the World: Exploring Process Theologies* (Louisville, KY: Westminster John Knox Press., 2008), 324.

48. Faber, *The Becoming of God*, 185–86.

49. Faber, *God as Poet of the World*, 254–61.

50. Faber, *Ocean of God*, loc. 1291–1307.

51. Ibid., loc. 1728.

52. See Raimundo Panikkar's "Nine Ways Not to Talk about God," *Cross Currents* 47.2 (1997): 149–53, especially point 8.

53. Meister Eckhart, *Expositio Liber Sapientiae*, no. 154, in *Lateinische Werke Band 2: Expositio Libri Exodi Sermones Et Lectiones Super Ecclesiastici Cap. 24 Expositio Libri Sapientiae Expositio Cantici Canticorum Cap. 1,6*, ed. Josef Koch and Konrad Weiss (Stuttgart/Berlin/Köln: Verlag W. Kohlhammer, 1992), 489.

BIBLIOGRAPHY

Bokenkotter, Thomas S. *A Concise History of the Catholic Church*. New York: Doubleday, 2005.

Bracken, Joseph A., S. J. *The Divine Matrix: Creativity as Link Between East and West*. Eugene, OR: Wipf & Stock, 2006.

Bracken, Joseph A., S. J. *The One and the Many: A Contemporary Reconstruction of the God–World Relationship*. Grand Rapids, MI: Wm. B. Eerdmans Publishing Co., 2001.

Carroll, James. "The Beginning of Change." In *Vatican II: The Essential Texts*, edited by Norman Tanner, S. J., 14–28. New York: Image, 2012.

Cobb, John B., Jr. *Beyond Dialogue: Toward a Mutual Transformation of Christianity and Buddhism*. Eugene, OR: Wipf and Stock, 1998.

Cobb, John B., Jr. "Beyond 'Pluralism.'" In *Christian Uniqueness Reconsidered: The Myth of a Pluralistic Theology of Religions*, edited by Gavin D'Costa, 81–94. Maryknoll, NY: Orbis Books, 1990.

Congregation for the Doctrine of the Faith. "*Dominus Iesus*: On the Unicity and Salvific Universality of Jesus Christ and the Church." August 6, 2000. https://www.vatican.va/roman_curia/congregations/cfaith/documents/rc_con_cfaith_doc_20000806_dominus-iesus_en.html.

Faber, Roland. *The Becoming of God: Process Theology, Philosophy, and Multireligious Engagement*. Eugene, OR: Cascade Books, 2017.

Faber, Roland. *God as Poet of the World: Exploring Process Theologies*. Louisville, KY: Westminster John Knox Press, 2008.

Faber, Roland. "The Mystical Whitehead." In *Seeking Common Ground: Evaluation and Critique of Joseph Bracken's Comprehensive Worldview*, edited by Marc A. Pugliese and Gloria L. Schaab, 213–33. Milwaukee, WI: Marquette University Press, 2012.

Faber, Roland. *The Ocean of God: On the Transreligious Future of Religions*. London: Anthem Press, 2019. Kindle.

Faber, Roland. "The Sense of Peace: A Para-Doxology of Divine Multiplicity." In *Polydoxy: Theology of Multiplicity and Relation*, edited by Catherine Keller and Laurel C. Schneider, 36–56. London: Routledge, 2010.

Fredericks, James L. *Buddhists and Christians: Through Comparative Theology to Solidarity*. Maryknoll, NY: Orbis Books, 2004.

Griffin, David Ray. "John Cobb's Whiteheadian Complementary Pluralism." In *Deep Religious Pluralism*, edited by David Ray Griffin, 39–65. Louisville, KY: Westminster John Knox Press, 2005.

Griffin, David Ray. "Religious Pluralism: Generic, Identist, and Deep." In *Deep Religious Pluralism*, edited by David Ray Griffin, 3–37. Louisville, KY: Westminster John Knox Press, 2005.

Knitter, Paul F. *Introducing Theologies of Religions*. Maryknoll, NY: Orbis Books, 2002.

Knitter, Paul F. *No Other Name? A Critical Survey of Christian Attitudes Toward the World Religions*. Maryknoll, NY: Orbis Books, 1985.

Lane, Dermot A. *Stepping Stones to Other Religions: A Christian Theology of Inter-religious Dialogue*. Maryknoll, NY: Orbis Books, 2011.

Lefebure, Leo D. *Transforming Interreligious Relations: Catholic Responses to Religious Pluralism in the United States*. Maryknoll, NY: Orbis Books, 2020.

Meister Eckhart. *Expositio Liber Sapientiae*. In *Lateinische Werke Band 2: Expositio Libri Exodi Sermones Et Lectiones Super Ecclesiastici Cap. 24 Expositio Libri Sapientiae Expositio Cantici Canticorum Cap. 1,6*, edited by Josef Koch and Konrad Weiss, 302–634. Stuttgart/Berlin/Köln: Verlag W. Kohlhammer, 1992.

Panikkar, Raimundo. *The Intrareligious Dialogue*. New York: Paulist Press, 1999.

Panikkar, Raimundo. "The Myth of Pluralism: The Tower of Babel—A Meditation on Non-Violence." *Cross Currents* 20.2 (1979): 197–230.

Panikkar, Raimundo. "Nine Ways Not to Talk About God." *Cross Currents* 47.2 (1997): 149–53.

Pontifical Council for Inter-Religious Dialogue. "Dialogue and Proclamation: Reflections and Orientations on Inter-Religious Dialogue and the Proclamation of the Gospel of Jesus Christ." May 19, 1991. https://www.vatican.va/roman_curia /pontifical_councils/interelg/documents/rc_pc_interelg_doc_19051991_dialogue -and-proclamatio_en.html.

Race, Alan. *Christians and Religious Pluralism: Patterns in the Christian Theology of Religions*. Maryknoll, NY: Orbis Books, 1982.

Vatican Council II. *Gaudium et Spes*. In *Vatican II: The Essential Texts*, edited by Norman Tanner, S. J. New York: Image, 2012.

Vatican Council II. *Nostra Aetate*. In *Vatican II: The Essential Texts*, edited by Norman Tanner, S. J. New York: Image, 2012.

Whitehead, Alfred North. *Adventures of Ideas*. 1933. Reprint, New York: Free Press, 1967.

Whitehead, Alfred North. *Modes of Thought*. 1938. Reprint, New York: Free Press, 1966.

Whitehead, Alfred North. *Process and Reality: An Essay in Cosmology*. 1929. Corrected ed. Edited by David Ray Griffin and Donald W. Sherburne. New York: Free Press, 1978.

Whitehead, Alfred North. *Science and the Modern World*. 1926. Reprint, New York: Free Press, 1967.

Chapter 11

Aquinas, Whitehead, and the Metaphysics of Morals

The Debate over Intrinsically Evil Acts

Marc A. Pugliese

INTRODUCTION

"In its turn every philosophy will suffer a deposition."[1] Thus wrote Whitehead in a discussion of the limitations of philosophy. Catholic moral theology has always employed the philosophical systems regnant in its various contexts, and notwithstanding the pluralism in contemporary Catholic thought with its variety of philosophical approaches, certain longstanding ones still hold sway. If every philosophy must inevitably be replaced, then whenever this occurs peaceful abdications better preserve the peace of Jesus Christ than violent overthrowals.

This chapter aims to show why Catholic theologians should seriously consider Whitehead's own philosophy to be one of the more desirable hand-maidens of theology in the present moment. It seeks to do so by demonstrating the relevance of Whitehead's philosophy to one contemporary controversy in Catholic fundamental moral theology. This question regards whether certain acts may be qualified as "intrinsically evil" by the "species" of their "object" apart from "intentions" and "circumstances." This debate swelled after *Veritatis Splendor*[2] answered affirmatively and drew more attention when some judged Pope Francis's *Amoris Laetitia*[3] to be in conflict with *Veritatis Splendor*.[4]

THE DEBATE

Beginning in the late Middle Ages, Catholic theology gradually developed a commonplace paradigm for morally assessing human acts. This drew heavily but not exclusively upon Aquinas's highly metaphysical treatment of the human act.[5] Pertinent here are the following aspects:

A "human act" (*actus humanus*) flows from reason and free will and is therefore morally assessable. Morally evaluating a human act[6] requires considering three causes called the "sources of morality" or *fontes moralitatis*: "object," "intention," and "circumstances," and a defect in any makes the act evil.

"Intention" is an interior movement of the will moving toward something reason judges to be good (the "end") as perfective of the human person in the order of reason. The end is the purpose or "why" of the act and specifies the goodness or badness of the agent's intention, giving the will its moral species. It is also the "formal cause" making the act the kind of act it is (species). A good intention cannot make an otherwise evil act good but a bad intention vitiates an otherwise good act.

"Object" refers to a good toward which the will directs itself as the means to the end. It is the external "what" of the act as seen by an objective observer and also the act's "material cause." The object also is or is not rationally ordered to the human person's perfection, and alike specifies the will as good or bad to the extent that reason judges the object to be so.

"Circumstances" are not of the substance of the act but its accidents. Hence circumstances cannot make an evil act good but they can increase or decrease its goodness or evil.

Some objects or external acts can never be ordered to the human person's true good. Always going against reason, they are intrinsically disordered and so always evil without qualification. Consequently, certain acts are intrinsically evil on account of their object alone regardless of intentions and circumstances. *Veritatis Splendor* argues this[7] but a chorus of contemporary Catholic moral theologians disagrees.

SOME REASONS FOR DISSENT

There are numerous reasons for this dissent but just one constellation is summarized here. Dissenters evince numerous examples of acts of evil in species on account of their object being redefined to accommodate instances when they do not seem evil.[8] These redefinitions involve different intentions and circumstances, which problematizes isolating the object in the moral determination of the act. One is how the same physical act of killing may be murder, manslaughter, self-defense, or supposedly for the common good such as capital punishment[9] or executing heretics. Another is how the same physical act of taking another's property without their consent may be theft, sacrilege, the sole means of saving human life, or preventing evil when the owner will use them for injury. Examples could be multiplied.

APPARENT AND REAL ISSUES

Such examples can oversimplify, bypass, and/or misconstrue particularities of the meaning of and relationships between the sources of morality in Aquinas. For instance, they might abstract a pre-moral natural process—sexual intercourse as simply biological—from particular human acts, which in the concrete always have superadded moral conditions.[10] Failing to take into account how one moral act can be considered under multiple, even disparate, species[11] is another example.

In other cases, dissenters do ask valid questions. The issues are numerous and complex, so the focus here will be "circumstances" in relation to only these topics: the categories of "substance" and "accident," causation, universals and particulars, and language.

For Aquinas, circumstances are accidents "outside the substance of the act," and "stand around" the act but still "touch the act."[12] At the same time, circumstances are "in" an act insofar as accidents "inhere" in things.[13] It seems valid to ask more about the "location" of circumstances. How are they both "outside the substance of the act" and "inhering" in it?

Issues correspondingly surround Aquinas's desire to simultaneously say that circumstances cannot make an act evil in species good, only lessen its evil,[14] but also say that circumstances can make an act otherwise good in species evil.[15]

On the one hand, not every circumstance places a moral act in a species of good or evil because not every circumstance is consonant or dissonant with reason.[16] Such circumstances may, though, increase an act's goodness or evil, with "more or less" and "intensity" being examples.[17] These types of circumstances must not possess "in themselves" the goodness or evil necessary to do even this because if they did they would alter the act's species. In order to avoid this, Aquinas argues that circumstances sometimes derive goodness or malice from "some other condition" of the act.[18] Further, this "other condition" may be "another previous circumstance, from which the moral act takes its species of good or evil."[19]

On the other hand, circumstances can make an act good in species evil in species despite how accidents do not give an act its species.[20] Here Aquinas distinguishes between the order of natural things and the order of reason. The species of a natural thing is constituted by its substantial form. Since nature is determinate and finite, a process of nature cannot go on infinitely so there is an ultimate form introducing a specific difference after which no further difference is possible. In this way, what is accidental to a natural thing cannot be taken as a difference constituting its species.

By contrast, the species of a moral act is constituted by its form as conceived by reason, and the process of reason is not fixed to one particular term but can always proceed further. Hence in one act, an accidental circumstance's accordance with or repugnance to reason may not be considered and so it is simply added to the object (which gives the act its species) without affecting the act's species. Reason can then proceed and after considering that same circumstance's accord with or repugnance to reason take it to be the principal condition of the object (again, which specifies the act). Aquinas uses "taking what belongs to another" with the circumstance "from a holy place" to show how in this way one act may be specified by reason as either "theft" or "sacrilege."[21] Interestingly, Aquinas says that when a circumstance is considered a condition of the object it is also considered "as being, as it were (*quasi*), some specific difference of the object placing it in a species."[22]

Several questions come up here. First, do circumstances differ ontologically? Some can make an act's species evil while others can only increase its goodness or malice. Is not a circumstance that is a principal condition of the object more real and does it not possess real causal power, even if vicariously through the object, compared to a merely accidental circumstance with no such power?

Second, does not at least *some* circumstance ultimately determine a moral act's species in either case? If a circumstance considered as introducing an additional repugnance to reason becomes a principal condition altering the act's species through the object is it not a cause of sorts? When a circumstance that only increases an act's goodness or malice takes the goodness or evil required to do so from some other condition of the act, and that other condition is itself "another previous circumstance, from which the moral act takes its species of good or evil,"[23] then is not a circumstance, namely the latter, still essential to the determination of the act's moral species?

Third, how is the order of reason connected to the moral act as concrete fact? Should the process of reason stop at the conception of simple theft with the circumstance as location remaining negligible or with location becoming a principal condition of the object thereby placing the act in the species of sacrilege?[24] In actual fact, theft from a holy place is never simple theft but always sacrilege. When the intellect apprehends the species by which the concrete act is known, is not the concrete act always known to be specifically sacrilege?[25] If so, then is not location always essential to the concrete act?

The last point is connected to the question of predicating universals to particular acts. Here Aquinas assumes the Aristotelian distinction between "what is said of another" and "what is not said" of another,[26] a subject–predicate form of language. Circumstances are accidents precisely because they are "particular conditions" of individual acts, and the particular conditions of an individual thing are called its "individuating accidents."[27]

When reasoning that no particular individual human act is morally indifferent,[28] Aquinas says an act may be morally indifferent in its species but is always moral in the concrete because particular acts always have circumstances. A particular thing considered in its substance is always in one species, but principles other than its species "superadded" to its substance can place the same particular in different, even disparate, species.[29] What is superadded can make the individual particular act actually good or bad.[30] A particular act derives its goodness not only from its object from which it takes its species but also from its circumstances as its accidents, as is the case with other things, like human beings.[31] Further, there is always at least one circumstance by which an individual circumstance is either good or bad, at least on the part of the intention of the end (*individualis actus habeat aliquam circumstantiam per quam trahatur ad bonum vel malum, ad minus ex parte intentionis finis*).[32]

Questions likewise arise here. First, is there a disconnect between knowledge and the description of the act on the one hand, and the actual fact that is the act on the other? Something is known in itself by means of its species, as when a particular human is recognized as a human being through her species.[33] If an individual act is morally indifferent in species, then it would be known as such. However, the same individual act is in actual fact good or bad on account of its circumstances as individuating accidents. Descriptively, an individual act may be described as morally indifferent in species but a factually accurate description would include that it is good or bad due to its circumstances as individuating accidents.

Second, if at least some circumstance as an individuating accident always makes the actual act good or bad, then does not at least one circumstance, even as an accident, make the act what it is? If good and evil are not extrinsic to the act then it would seem that at least one circumstance is really in some way "essential" to the individual act.

Finally, if there is always at least one circumstance making an act good or bad, this is the circumstance "on the part of the intention of the end," and the end makes the act good or evil,[34] then it would seem that the sources of morality are actually inseparable and mutually determinative.

Here we have surveyed some questions regarding the categories of "substance" and "accident," causation, "species," universals and particulars, and language in Aquinas's treatment of the moral act. Since for Aquinas, "[w]e must speak of good and evil in actions as of good and evil in things,"[35] it would seem these would be issues with his metaphysics in general. Next we will consider Whitehead's metaphysics.

SOME ASPECTS OF WHITEHEAD'S METAPHYSICS

There are several caveats before exploring Whitehead's contribution to this debate. First, the presence of a moral philosophy in Whitehead is disputed.[36] The large body of scholarship on Whitehead's moral theory assumes he has one,[37] and it is clear he intended his philosophy to include the moral aspects of our experience. For Whitehead, one aim of speculative philosophy is to construct a system of general ideas in terms of which every element of our experience may be interpreted as a particular instance of the general scheme, and no element of experience is incapable of being thus interpreted.[38] All experience exhibits the philosophic scheme: "The first metaphysical principles can never fail of exemplification. We can never catch the actual world taking a holiday from their sway."[39] We have seen how Aquinas's own interpretation of the moral act is highly metaphysical.

Second, every aspect of Whitehead's philosophy implies every other. Indeed, this is one of his criteria for speculative philosophy: "the fundamental ideas, in terms of which the scheme is developed, presuppose each other so that in isolation they are meaningless."[40] Only a fuller exposition of Whitehead's philosophy than is possible here would afford a deeper appreciation of this important fact.

Third, before explicating his own system, Whitehead identified some key limitations of any philosophical system, beginning with multiple deficiencies of language.[41] One of the ineluctable overstatements of philosophy is taking its abstractions as concrete renderings of fact. Metaphysics aims at ultimate generalizations regarding all the facts of our experience but must begin and end with the ultimate agents of "stubborn fact" in their full concreteness.[42] The "fallacy of misplaced concreteness" entails neglecting the distance between the abstractions involved in considering any particular entity under certain categories of thought and the entity itself.[43] The necessary but tentative abstractions formulated by both philosophy and science stand in need of verification, undergo pragmatic tests, and are always eventually found wanting. Therefore, the only possible *telos* is progress, not finality of statement.[44]

With these caveats, we may now examine aspects of Whitehead's philosophy applicable to the question under consideration.

The first is his rejection of substance–quality ontology. "Substance" has variously denoted independent subsistence requiring nothing else to exist, self-identity across time with merely accidental change, and that in which a being's qualities inhere. The last correlates to linguistic subject–predicate modes of expression as seen again in Aristotle, who defines substance as "that which is neither said of a subject nor in a subject" (*Categories* 2a14–15). The rudiments of Aristotelian logic presuppose a substance–quality ontology. "Men are rational" and "Socrates is mortal" predicate qualities to subjects but this substance–quality assumption falls apart under closer scrutiny: "'Socrates is mortal' is only another way of saying that 'perhaps he will die.' The intellect of Socrates is intermittent: he occasionally sleeps and he can be drugged or stunned."[45] Whitehead outlines a litany of problems that have haunted Western philosophy due to Aristotelian substance ontology.[46]

Whitehead analyzes how we arrive at the ideas of "substances with undifferentiated endurance of essential attributes" and "occasional modification of their accidental qualities and relations."[47] These concepts are practically effective but also high abstractions which can never hope to capture the most ultimate characterizations of fact.[48] Taking them as adequate does violence to immediate experience.[49]

Reality is actually event-like. This is known in immediate raw experience, which again ought to be where philosophy begins and ends. Our subjective experience comes episodically in indivisible drops or quanta. Sense perceptions are always changing, even if imperceptibly, so our integrated subjective experience comes in an incessant succession of punctiliar presentations.[50]

Science corroborates this philosophical analysis thus affording an exemplification of this metaphysical principle. Substance ontology caused modern science through the early twentieth century to see nature as consisting of bits of "stuff" (e.g., particles) retaining their identities and qualities across time along with accidental features that change (e.g., position and charge).[51] Quantum mechanics points to a different conception of reality in terms of events in spatial relations.[52] What we now know about atoms and quantum mechanics is that seemingly passive enduring objects have a discontinuous, vibratory, and active existence.[53] Light and energy come in irreducible quanta. Something as simple as a stone has lost its continuity, unity, and passiveness, and is now instead conceived as a collection of quantum events continuously in active motion.[54] With regard to the substance–quality notion, the physiology of perception now shows that qualities like color do not inhere in objects.

In summary, being is event-like and substantial objects are abstractions from events.[55] The problem then becomes continuity between discrete events. Substance ontology sees entities as independent substances possessing purely accidental external relations nonessential to their being, but merely external relations undermine causation and induction. This grounds Hume's critiques, which still haunt the philosophy of science,[56] but more generally, "[i]t has been usual, indeed, universal, to hold that spatio-temporal relations are external."[57]

Whitehead maintains the opposite: entities' essences consist of "internal relations." The essences of everything from facts to forms to propositions[58] are sets of relations—themselves sets of relations—comprising other relations and lending aspects to other relations: "each relationship enters into the essence of the event; so that, apart from that relationship, the event would not be itself."[59] No independent substances exist. Common sense sees related parts combining into wholes everywhere, and *Process and Reality* demonstrates relational ontology's ubiquitous exemplification across many domains. Modifying "apprehension," Whitehead coined "prehension"[60] to denote how an entity relates to and integrates other existents into its own essence through a complex process.

Internal relations obviate the continuity and causation problems introduced by exclusively external relationships. Causation is real because causes are immanent in their effects: "The only intelligible doctrine of causation is founded on the doctrine of immanence. Each occasion presupposes the antecedent world as active in its own nature."[61] By contrast, for substance ontology: "the cause in itself discloses no information as to the effect . . . it must be *entirely* arbitrary."[62]

Internal relations more broadly ground reality's organic unity, which would be shattered into pieces by nonoverlapping independent substances. No entity can be utterly isolated and abstracted from the entire cosmic process. Particulars are still real because relations are not *exclusively* internal but also external. Particulars with *solely* external relations, however, would be noncontiguous and wholly disparate. Moreover, substance assumptions disconnect time's flow with Euclidean point-like moments, issuing in a sort of temporal version of Zeno's paradox. The result is no connection between past, present, and future. Temporal continuity requires that successive durations are internally related so that the past is contained in the present.[63]

Relativity theory in physics corroborates Whitehead's relational ontology. There are no bits of matter simply located in Newtonian absolute space and time, but every entity's actual world corresponds to its relative space-time reference frame. An emerging entity relates to its world by prehending aspects of settled entities, which are then modally internal to its essence according to its unique perspective.[64]

Whitehead borrows Berkeley's illustration here.[65] Percipients perceive the castle, planet, and cloud differently according to their relative perspectives. How they are experienced (e.g., size, one side only) depends on the percipient's position. Analogously, entity (B) only ever exists as it is related to some perceiver (A). (B) is never simply located "where (B) is" or "where perceiver (A) is." Rather, (B) is "present at (A) with the mode of location (B)" as an aspect of (A). The unity of the aspects of the castle, planet, and clouds as perceived at a certain region of space-time constitutes the unitary experience that is the percipient in that region of space-time.

Substance ontology also contributes to the problem of universals and particulars. Classically, universals denote qualities possessed by particulars placing them in their species. A universal enters into the description of many particulars but a particular does not enter into the description of other particulars. For Whitehead, classical universals cannot describe any particular entity, even inadequately, because other particular entities do enter into any particular's essential description. Every universal describing an entity is a particular since it is derived from another particular, and every particular is a universal because it enters into the constitutions of all other entities.[66] The classifications of genus and species in Aristotelian logic are thus "a halfway house between the immediateness of the individual thing and the complete abstraction of mathematical notions."[67]

Whitehead's "eternal objects" correspond to metaphysical "forms."[68] In Aristotelian terms form is active and matter is passive in a being's generation. For Whitehead, eternal objects are the innumerable potentials for exemplification in the actual world. Every specific way an entity is related to something else corresponds to one eternal object. Every selectively qualified relational aspect of other entities that an emergent entity prehends as part of its relational essence corresponds to an eternal object, as does how it prehends each of these. Although any eternal object is essentially the same in all entities, its gradation of relevance is unique to each entity.[69] As an entity is the togetherness of all its prehensions, an entity's final form is a complex eternal object integrating all other eternal objects entering its constitution in their various degrees of relevance to that entity.

Eternal objects are generally related to the realm of actuality by being pure potentials for the latter. As all things from the purest abstractions of mathematics[70] to the most concrete actual agents of stubborn fact are essentially constituted by internal relations, eternal objects' individual essences are internally related to all other eternal objects. Just as particularity is guaranteed by how other entities do not enter any one entity's essence in their entirety but only under limited aspects according to its private perspective, finite truth is guaranteed by how other eternal objects do not enter into any one eternal object in their fullness but only under one perspectival aspect.[71]

Since eternal objects are internally related as well as externally related, a complete description of any particular is infinite, and isolating one or more of its eternal objects is an abstraction. The abstraction "apple" is simpler and says much less than what the concrete entity actually is in its full complexity. The higher abstraction of "red" is even simpler and says even less. Note here how abstraction from actuality moves from the complex to the simple.

Perhaps counterintuitive is how a complete description of the realm of possibility is likewise always impossible. The one complex eternal object corresponding to any particular actual entity is more abstract and so less descriptive than the simple eternal objects comprising it. The simple eternal object "red" means "red" in all its possible relationships, which includes but is much more than the ways "red" is related in the *relata* constituting the entity's complex eternal object. "Red" in the entity's complex eternal object excludes all other relations into which "red" may enter. Thus "red" in the complex eternal object is more abstract and more descriptively incomplete than the simple eternal object "red."[72]

AN ALTERNATIVE METAPHYSICS OF MORALS

We have seen how Whitehead intended his philosophy to be adequate to interpret every element of our experience. Not only the most infinitesimal constituents of reality but all actual things exemplify the category of "actual entity," which replaces Aristotle's "primary substance" as the first category of existence. Most fundamentally, an "actual entity" is a *res vera* or whatever is truly real, and, as such, any entity.[73]

Entities widely differ, but all final facts are the same in the sense that they all exemplify the same principles that actuality exemplifies. For Whitehead, everything from God to the most trivial puff of existence is an actual entity.[74] In commenting on religion and morality, Whitehead describes organisms in terms of actual entities and the metaphysical principles they exemplify.[75] The moral act is an element of experience and an actual fact. As such, it, too, may be interpreted by the same philosophical scheme and exemplifies the same metaphysical principles. Aquinas agrees, as again, "[w]e must speak of good and evil in actions as of good and evil in things."[76]

When it is so interpreted, the results are different from Aquinas's metaphysical interpretation with its aforementioned difficulties. To begin with, the moral act is not an externally related independent substance with purely accidental circumstances but rather essentially constituted by internal relations. Because circumstances are internal to the act's essence, there is no question of the "location" of circumstances, or whether and to what degree they are causes of the act or relevant to its moral evaluation. Furthermore, the sources of morality themselves are interrelated and necessarily interdependent.

Every act itself is also unique in fact, form, and description. An act is not "simply located" like a bit of matter in Newtonian absolute space-time. Its internal relations to circumstances and indeed everything else are according to its relative and singular perspective. It possesses a sui generis subjective form corresponding to a complex eternal object composed of all eternal objects that specify its relations to and how it relates to its circumstances and everything else. That other entities including circumstances and eternal objects do not enter into an act's essence in their entirety but only under limited perspectival aspects graded in relevance ensure an act's distinctiveness. Wherefore the manner in and degree to which any one circumstance bears upon moral evaluation is idiosyncratic to that act.

Since every moral act possesses its own unique subjective form there is no one common form across multiple concrete acts that would place them all in the same species. Additionally, the hiatus between descriptive universals and particular facts disappears because all other particulars, including circumstances, enter into any one particular act's description as universals. This also means that a complete description of any moral act is impossible.

We have not yet mentioned God's evaluation of the moral act. God's "initial aim"[77] is the ideal outcome for an entity's subjective form specific to that entity. There is not one ideal order all entities should attain but rather an ideal particular to each individual entity:[78] "particular providence for particular occasions."[79] Whitehead uses the phrase "moral judgment" here[80] and later process thinkers have used God's initial aim to conceptualize sin.[81] Applied to the moral act, an individually tailored initial aim makes moral assessment irreducibly particular to each act.

Another implication of Whitehead's relational ontology is that moral assessment must consider a context well beyond the individual agent. Circumstances include much more than what is in relative propinquity to the agent. Morality stretches beyond individual self-interest to the general good.[82]

If metaphysical principles are universally exemplified, then *all* moral acts exemplify the general ideas of a scheme such as Whitehead's. It is difficult to speak in Whiteheadian terms of moral acts that are "per se" and "independently" of circumstances (and intentions) always evil in "species" by reason of their "object alone."[83] This does not necessarily mean the end of the term "intrinsic evil" but does mean reenvisioning it.

EXEMPLIFICATION IN DISSENT

Those who dissent from *Veritatis Splendor* variously make points that correspond to aspects of Whitehead metaphysics discussed earlier. They urge that there is no one philosophical system valid for all times and places.[84] The discourse is replete with references to the complexities and limitations of language, including interlinguistic and interconceptual interdependencies, pinpointed as culprits in spreading confusion and fueling disagreement.[85]

Dissenters identify and roundly reject substance–accident categories.[86] A constant refrain indicates difficulties in distinguishing object, intention, and circumstances in any concrete moral act, averring their internal relatedness and even reciprocal causal influence.[87] They extend this relational ontology to individuals' subjective characterizations and evaluations of moral acts[88] and enlarge causal nexuses to include institutional conventions, historical situations, and sociocultural conditions.[89]

Dissenters raise the problem of universals and particulars by claiming *Veritatis Splendor* abstracts from the concrete agent and concrete moral acts to arrive at disconnected universal descriptors and classifications. They assert how circumstantial particularity involves inherent relativity, warn against too

quickly subsuming concrete acts and their circumstances under general principles, and question applying the same immutable universals to diverse acts
and commands without exception.[90]

A commonplace example adduced in support[91] is where Aquinas admits
that the general moral principles derived from natural law do not necessarily
apply in all cases due to the particularities of specific cases. Attending the
distinction between the necessary truths of speculative reason and the contingencies of practical reason are the facts that "the more we descend to matters
of detail, the more frequently we encounter defects," in matters of action truth
"is not the same for all as to matters of detail," and general moral principles
may be true in the majority of cases but "it may happen in a particular case"
that they "will be found to fail the more, according as we descend further
into detail."[92]

Among the *dubia* cited by the critics of *Amoris Laetitia* is a section citing
the same passage from Aquinas to argue that general moral principles are
insufficient because divine moral standards are particular to each individual
and their life situation:

> It is reductive simply to consider whether or not an individual's actions corre-
> spond to a general law or rule, because that is not enough to discern and ensure
> full fidelity to God in the concrete life of a human being. I earnestly ask that we
> always recall a teaching of Saint Thomas Aquinas and learn to incorporate it in
> our pastoral discernment [a direct quotation from Aquinas, *ST* IaIIae.94.4 co,
> appears here]. . . . It is true that general rules set forth a good which can never be
> disregarded or neglected, but in their formulation they cannot provide absolutely
> for all particular situations. At the same time, it must be said that, precisely for
> that reason, what is part of a practical discernment in particular circumstances
> cannot be elevated to the level of a rule. That would not only lead to an intoler-
> able casuistry, but would endanger the very values which must be preserved
> with special care.[93]

A footnote in the same article quotes another passage from Aquinas: "If
only one of the two is present, it is preferable that it be the knowledge of the
particular reality, which is closer to the act."[94] These passages from *Amoris
Laetitia* appear to approach aspects of Whitehead's metaphysics as they apply
to the moral act.

In summary, there is meaningful evidence that dissenters from *Veritatis
Splendor* as well as a recent relevant papal apostolic exhortation could concur
with Whitehead when he describes

> the difficulty of describing the world in terms of subject and predicate, sub-
> stance and quality, particular and universal. The result always does violence

to that immediate experience which we express in our actions, our hopes, our sympathies, our purposes, and which we enjoy in spite of our lack of phrases for its verbal analysis.[95]

PROGRESS, NOT FINALITY

Is this agreement with aspects of Whitehead's metaphysics important? To be sure, a critical mass of theologians today view metaphysics with suspicion. Some dissenters from *Veritatis Splendor* decry the "metaphysicalization of moral truth"[96] in older frameworks. Others view metaphysics as ineludible, and this author of course joins them. Try as one may, one cannot operate without at least *some* system of "general ideas which are indispensably relevant to the analysis of everything that happens."[97] Metaphysics is done either consciously and hopefully well, or unconsciously and probably not well, but done it is nonetheless.

When surveying the debate over whether certain acts are intrinsically evil "always and per se, in other words, on account of their very object, and quite apart from the ulterior intentions of the one acting and the circumstances,"[98] it is difficult to not see tacit if not explicit metaphysical categories at work. One may legitimately ask if those who critique aspects of longstanding substance-based metaphysical systems like Thomism on individual points still operate by them, recalling Whitehead's observation that

> [M]any philosophers who in their explicit statements criticize the Aristotelian notion of "substance," yet implicitly throughout their discussions presuppose that the "subject–predicate" form of proposition embodies the finally adequate mode of statement about the actual world.[99]

Is a shared system of general ideas now judged to be inadequate partly to blame for the protraction of this debate? Does it undermine the persuasive power of otherwise justifiable points made by those who dissent from *Veritatis Splendor*?

Perhaps in order to overcome the current impasse, a metaphysical paradigm shift is required, one that aims at a more logically consistent system of general ideas in which any one aspect implies every other aspect, and which bears in itself greater warrant by its fuller exemplification throughout all experience.[100] The degree to which any such new metaphysical paradigm meets these criteria would be in direct proportion to how compelling the cases founded upon it are.

A metaphysics more congruous with our individual and collective experience today would by no means be perfect. In its turn, every philosophy will indeed suffer a deposition, and Whitehead would be alacritous to admit this of his own philosophy as much as any other.[101] The limitations of speculative philosophy notwithstanding its inescapability and indeed necessity perdure.

Catholic theologians will also always employ *some* philosophical system. In this contemporary moral theological debate over whether there are some acts that are always evil in species due to their object alone apart from intentions and circumstances, there is a need to move beyond older metaphysical categories now found wanting but still functioning in the debate. This is assuredly equally true of other theological debates. What is needed is not the ever-elusive last word but improvement:

> There remains the final reflection, how shallow, puny, and imperfect are efforts to sound the depths in the nature of things. In philosophical discussion, the merest hint of dogmatic certainty as to finality of statement is an exhibition of folly. . . . The proper test is not that of finality, but of progress.[102]

This chapter has been a bid at taking Whitehead's metaphysics as a serious candidate for this in our present moment.

NOTES

1. Alfred North Whitehead, *Process and Reality: An Essay in Cosmology* (1929), corrected ed., ed. David Ray Griffin and Donald W. Sherburne (New York: Free Press, 1978), 7 (hereafter "*PR*").

2. Pope John Paul II, *Veritatis Splendor* (Washington, DC: United States Conference of Catholic Bishops, 1993).

3. Pope Francis, *Amoris Laetitia* (Washington, DC: United States Conference of Catholic Bishops, 2016).

4. A flurry of literature on *Veritatis Splendor* appeared in its wake. See, for example, Joseph A. Selling and Miranda Jans, eds., *The Splendor of Accuracy: An Examination of the Assertions Made by Veritatis Splendor* (Grand Rapids, MI: Wm. B. Eerdmans Publishing Co., 1994); John Wilkins, ed., *Considering Veritatis Splendor* (Cleveland, OH: Pilgrim Press 1994); Michael E. Allsopp and John J. O'Keefe, eds., *Veritatis Splendor: American Responses* (Kansas City, MO: Sheed & Ward, 1995); and J. A. DiNoia, O. P., and Romanus Cessario, O. P., eds., *Veritatis Splendor and the Renewal of Moral Theology: Studies by Ten Outstanding Scholars* (Huntington, IN: Our Sunday Visitor, 1999). For discussions of *Amoris Laetitia's* and *Veritatis Splendor's* compatibility, see, for example, James F. Keenan, S. J., "Receiving *Amoris Laetitia*," *Theological Studies* 78.1 (2017): 193–212; Nadia Delicata, "*Amoris Laetitia* and *Veritatis Splendor* on the 'Object of the Act,'" *Melita Theologica* 67.2 (2017): 237–65; and James T. Bretzke, S. J., "*Responsum ad Dubia*: Harmonizing *Veritatis Splendor* and *Amoris Laetitia* through a Conscience-Informed Casuistry," *Journal of Catholic Social Thought* 15.1 (2018): 211–22.

5. Thomas Aquinas, *Summa theologica*, 2nd and rev. ed., trans. Fathers of the English Dominican Province (London: Burns, Oates & Washbourne, 1920–22), IaIIae.18.1–21 (hereafter "*ST*").

6. Hereafter simply "act."

7. Pope John Paul II, *Veritatis Splendor*, 76–83.

8. These examples are commonplaces for the dissenters. They are used by multiple contributors in the edited volumes mentioned earlier (n. 4), for example, Allsopp and O'Keefe, *Veritatis Splendor*, 56–57, 68–70, 283–89. Similarly, see Nenad Polgar and Joseph A. Selling, eds., *The Concept of Intrinsic Evil and Catholic Theological Ethics* (Lanham, MD: Lexington Books / Fortress Academic, 2019), 16–24, 29–40, 42–43, 75–76, 89–90, 100–110. Just two of many more appearances of these examples in the literature are Lisa Sowle Cahill, "Accent on the Masculine," *The Tablet* (Brooklyn, NY), December 11, 1993, and James T. Bretzke, S. J., *A Morally Complex World: Engaging Contemporary Moral Theology* (Collegeville, MN: Michael Glazier/Liturgical Press, 2004), 57–58, 61–62, 75–77.

9. Pope Francis changed the *Catechism* to forbid capital punishment without exception.

10. *ST* IaIIae.1.3 ad 3, IaIIae.18.5 ad 3, and IaIIae.18.7 ad 1.

11. Ibid., IaIIae.1.3 ad 3, IaIIae.18.7 ad 1, and IaIIae.18.10 ad 3.

12. For example, ibid., IaIIae.7.1 co, IaIIae.18.3, IaIIae.18.4 co, IaIIae.18.5 ad 4, IaIIae.18.9 co, and IaIIae.18.10 co and ad 2.

13. Ibid., IaIIae.18.3 ad 1. Aristotle defined primary substance as that which is "not present in" a subject and defined that which is "present in" a subject as accidental (*Categories* 1a20).

14. *ST* IaIIae.18.11.

15. Ibid., IaIIae.18.3, IaIIae.18.4 co, and IaIIae.18.5 ad 4.

16. Ibid., IaIIae.18.10 ad 3.

17. Ibid., IaIIae.18.11 sc, co, and ad 1.

18. Ibid., IaIIae.18.11 arg. 2 and ad 2.

19. Ibid., IaIIae.18.11 co.

20. Ibid., IaIIae.18.10 arg. 1.

21. Ibid., IaIIae.18.10 co and ad 2.

22. Ibid., IaIIae.18.10 ad 1.

23. Ibid., IaIIae.18.11 co.

24. Ibid., IaIIae.18.11 sc.

25. Discussing the same example, Pilsner calls this a "seeming paradox" because "one and the same human action can be viewed from two different perspectives" (Joseph Pilsner, *The Specification of Human Actions in St. Thomas Aquinas* [New York: Oxford University Press, 2006], 242–43).

26. Aristotle, *Categories*, 1a20.

27. *ST* IaIIae.7.1 sc. See also, ibid., IaIIae.6.6 co and III.2.2 co. This is Boethius's view of individuation. Elsewhere he takes Aristotle's view that matter individuates (*De Ente et Essentia* 1.23–34, 1.44–47, 4.98).

28. *ST* IaIIae.18.9.

29. Ibid., IaIIae.1.3 ad 3, IaIIae.18.7 ad 1, and IaIIae.18.10 ad 3.

30. Ibid., IaIIae.18.9 ad 1.

31. Ibid., IaIIae.18.9 co.
32. Ibid.
33. Ibid., 1a.14.5 co.
34. Ibid., IaIIae.18.4.
35. Ibid., IaIIae.18.1 co.
36. Positions range from the common "no philosophical ethics in Whitehead," to its indistinguishability from his social philosophy (Richard Slaton Davis, "Whitehead's Moral Philosophy," *Process Studies* 3.2 [1973]: 75–90) to the presuppositions of a philosophical ethics (John W. Lango, "Does Whitehead's Metaphysics Contain an Ethics?" *Transactions of the Charles S. Peirce Society* 37.4 [2001]: 515–36), to a trajectory toward ethical altruism beyond the common view of only ethical egoism and private interest theory (Lynne Belaief, "Whitehead and Private-Interest Theories," *Ethics* 76.4 (1966): 77–86; idem, "A Whiteheadian Account of Value and Identity," *Process Studies* 5.4 (1975): 31–46), and to a robust philosophical ethics pervading his entire system (John Bunyan Spencer, "The Ethics of Alfred North Whitehead" [doctoral dissertation, The University of Chicago, 1966]). For a discussion of possible reasons for the common position that there is no philosophical ethics in Whitehead, see ibid., 1–5.
37. For an example of treatments of a variety of issues surrounding Whitehead and ethics, see Theodore Walker Jr. and Mihály Tóth, eds. *Whiteheadian Ethics: Abstracts and Papers from the Ethics Section of the Philosophy Group at the 6th International Whitehead Conference at the University of Salzburg* (Newcastle: Cambridge Scholars Publishing, 2006).
38. *PR* 3–4.
39. Ibid., 4.
40. Ibid., 3.
41. Ibid., xiii–xiv, 4–7, 13.
42. Alfred North Whitehead, *Science and the Modern World* (1926; repr., New York: Free Press, 1967), 42–44, 135, 145 (hereafter "*SMW*"); *PR* 117.
43. *SMW* 50–51, 55; *PR* 7–8.
44. Ibid., 14.
45. Ibid., 79.
46. For example, *SMW* 155; *PR* 48.
47. Ibid., 77–78.
48. Ibid., 79.
49. For example, *PR* xiii, 7, 13, 30, 49, 51, 54, 56, 77–79.
50. Ibid., 68. See also, *SMW* 135 and *PR* xii–xiii, 50.
51. *SMW* 145; *PR* 78.
52. Alfred North Whitehead, *The Concept of Nature* (1920; repr., Sydney: Wentworth Press, 2016), 14–15, 24 (hereafter "*CN*"). For a sampling of the extensive literature exploring physics and Whitehead, see Marc A. Pugliese, "Quantum Mechanics and an Ontology of Intersubjectivity: Perils and Promises," *Open Theology* 4 (2018): 337n87.
53. *PR* 78–79.
54. Ibid., 78.

55. *CN* 125. Space prohibits exploring this here, but Whitehead accounts for how macroscopic objects endure with his derivative notion of "society" (e.g., *PR* 34–35, 55–57, 89–111).

56. For example, *SMW* 4, 49–51; *PR* 137; Alfred North Whitehead, *Modes of Thought* (1938; repr., New York: Free Press, 1968), 164–65 (hereafter "*MT*").

57. *SMW* 123.

58. That one proposition's complete truth implies a universe of facts is another limitation of language (*PR* 11–12).

59. *SMW* 123.

60. Whitehead's neologisms connote subjective experience. Prescinding from further explanation, we simply note his absolute prioritization of experience as a reason. Except in advanced organisms this experience is *not consciousness* (*SMW* 69).

61. *MT* 164–65.

62. *SMW* 4.

63. Ibid., 49–50, 58, 124–27.

64. Ibid., 70–71.

65. Ibid., 67–70.

66. *PR* 48–50.

67. *SMW* 28.

68. For example, ibid., 157–72; *PR* 22–23, 40–46, 239–41, 290–91.

69. Ibid., 26, 224, 238–40, 244, 248.

70. Mathematical concepts imply other mathematical concepts, and ultimately all of them.

71. F. H. Bradley had difficulty reconciling internal relations with finite truth (ibid., 200).

72. *SMW* 167.

73. *PR* xiii–xiv.

74. Ibid., 18.

75. Ibid., 15–16.

76. *ST* IaIIae.18.1 co.

77. For example, *PR* 83–84, 88, 244, 345.

78. Ibid., 84.

79. Ibid., 351.

80. Alfred North Whitehead, *Religion in the Making* (1926; repr., New York: Macmillan, 1954), 114 (hereafter "*RM*").

81. See, for example, John B. Cobb Jr., "Whitehead's Philosophy and a Christian Doctrine of Man," *The Journal of Bible and Religion* 32.3 (1964): 210–15; W. Norman Pittenger, *The Word Incarnate: A Study of the Doctrine of the Person of Christ* (New York: Harper & Brothers, 1959), 107; and Lewis Ford, *The Lure of God: A Biblical Background for Process Theism* (Philadelphia, PA: Fortress Press, 1978), 22.

82. *PR* 15–16.

83. Pope John Paul II, *Veritatis Splendor*, 80.

84. For example, Bretzke, *A Morally Complex World*, 29. Compare this with McInerny's urging of the precise opposite (Ralph M. McInerny, *Ethica Thomistica:*

The Moral Philosophy of Thomas Aquinas, rev. ed. [Washington, DC: The Catholic University of America Press, 1997], ix–xi).

85. Six different contributors to Polgar and Selling's volume discuss these sorts of linguistic difficulties. See Polgar and Selling, *The Concept of Intrinsic Evil*, 3–4, 16, 21–22, 31–33, 42–43, 67–68, 78, 89–91, 94, 100–2, 110n16, 111n19.

86. For example, Bretzke, *A Morally Complex World*, 36, 133; Polgar and Selling, *The Concept of Intrinsic Evil*, 21.

87. For example, Bretzke, *A Morally Complex World*, 57–61; Allsopp and O'Keefe, *Veritatis Splendor*, 68–70, 283–84, 289; Polgar and Selling, *The Concept of Intrinsic Evil*, 68–69, 74–78, 89–90, 100–102, 110.

88. Ibid., 100.

89. For example, Allsopp and O'Keefe, *Veritatis Splendor*, 75–76, 286.

90. For example, ibid., 232–33, 286–87; Polgar and Selling, *The Concept of Intrinsic Evil*, 16, 31–33, 67–69, 78–80.

91. For example, Bretzke, *A Morally Complex World*, 60–63; Allsopp and O'Keefe, *Veritatis Splendor*, 286–87.

92. *ST* IaIIae.94.4 co.

93. Pope Francis, *Amoris Laetitia*, 304.

94. Ibid., 304n348.

95. *PR* 49–50.

96. Polgar and Selling, *The Concept of Intrinsic Evil*, 50.

97. *RM* 82n.

98. Pope John Paul II, *Veritatis Splendor*, 80.

99. *PR* 30.

100. Ibid., 3–4.

101. Ibid., 7.

102. Ibid., xiv, 14.

BIBLIOGRAPHY

Allsopp, Michael E., and John J. O'Keefe, eds. *Veritatis Splendor: American Responses*. Kansas City, MO: Sheed & Ward, 1995.

Aquinas, Thomas. *Aquinas on Being and Essence (De Ente et Essentia): A Translation and Interpretation*. Translated by Joseph Bobik. Notre Dame, IN: University of Notre Dame Press, 1988.

Aquinas, Thomas. *Summa theologica*. 2nd and Rev. ed. Translated by Fathers of the English Dominican Province. 10 vols. London: Burns, Oates & Washbourne, 1920–22.

Aristotle. *The Complete Works of Aristotle: The Revised Oxford Translation*. Edited by Jonathan Barnes. 2 vols. Princeton, NJ: Princeton University Press, 2014.

Belaief, Lynne. "Whitehead and Private-Interest Theories." *Ethics* 76.4 (1966): 277–86.

Belaief, Lynne. "A Whiteheadian Account of Value and Identity." *Process Studies* 5.4 (1975): 31–46.

Bretzke, James T., S. J. *A Morally Complex World: Engaging Contemporary Moral Theology*. Collegeville, MN: Michael Glazier/Liturgical Press, 2004.

Bretzke, James T., S. J. "*Responsum ad Dubia*: Harmonizing *Veritatis Splendor* and *Amoris Laetitia* through a Conscience-Informed Casuistry." *Journal of Catholic Social Thought* 15.1 (2018): 211–22.

Cahill, Lisa Sowle. "Accent on the Masculine." *The Tablet* (Brooklyn, NY), December 11, 1993.

Cobb, John B., Jr. "Whitehead's Philosophy and a Christian Doctrine of Man." *The Journal of Bible and Religion* 32.3 (1964): 210–15.

Davis, Richard Slaton. "Whitehead's Moral Philosophy." *Process Studies* 3.2 (1973): 75–90.

Delicata, Nadia. "*Amoris Laetitia* and *Veritatis Splendor* on the 'Object of the Act'." *Melita Theologica* 67.2 (2017): 237–65.

DiNoia, J. A., O. P., and Romanus Cessario, O. P., eds. *Veritatis Splendor and the Renewal of Moral Theology: Studies by Ten Outstanding Scholars*. Huntington, IN: Our Sunday Visitor, 1999.

Ford, Lewis. *The Lure of God: A Biblical Background for Process Theism*. Philadelphia, PA: Fortress Press, 1978.

Francis, Pope. *Amoris Laetitia*. Washington, DC: United States Conference of Catholic Bishops, 2016.

Keenan, James F., S. J. "Receiving *Amoris Laetitia*." *Theological Studies* 78.1 (2017): 193–212.

Lango, John W. "Does Whitehead's Metaphysics Contain an Ethics?" *Transactions of the Charles S. Peirce Society* 37.4 (2001): 515–36.

McInerny, Ralph M. *Ethica Thomistica: The Moral Philosophy of Thomas Aquinas*. Rev. ed. Washington, DC: The Catholic University of American Press, 1997.

Pilsner, Joseph. *The Specification of Human Actions in St. Thomas Aquinas*. New York: Oxford University Press, 2006.

Pittenger, W. Norman. *The Word Incarnate: A Study of the Doctrine of the Person of Christ*. New York: Harper & Brothers, 1959.

Polgar, Nenad, and Joseph A. Selling, eds. *The Concept of Intrinsic Evil and Catholic Theological Ethics*. Lanham, MD: Lexington Books/Fortress Academic, 2019.

Pugliese, Marc A. "Quantum Mechanics and an Ontology of Intersubjectivity: Perils and Promises." *Open Theology* 4 (2018): 325–41.

Selling, Joseph A., and Miranda Jans, eds. *The Splendor of Accuracy: An Examination of the Assertions Made by Veritatis Splendor*. Grand Rapids, MI: Wm. B. Eerdmans Publishing Co., 1994.

Spencer, John Bunyan. "The Ethics of Alfred North Whitehead." Doctoral dissertation, The University of Chicago, 1966.

Walker, Theodore, Jr., and Mihály Tóth, eds. *Whiteheadian Ethics: Abstracts and Papers from the Ethics Section of the Philosophy Group at the 6th International Whitehead Conference at the University of Salzburg*. Newcastle: Cambridge Scholars Publishing, 2006.

Whitehead, Alfred North. *The Concept of Nature.* 1920. Reprint. Sydney: Wentworth Press, 2016.

Whitehead, Alfred North. *Modes of Thought.* 1938. Reprint, New York: Free Press, 1968.

Whitehead, Alfred North. *Process and Reality: An Essay in Cosmology.* 1929. Corrected ed. Edited by David Ray Griffin and Donald W. Sherburne. New York: Free Press, 1978.

Whitehead, Alfred North. *Religion in the Making.* 1926. Reprint. New York: Macmillan, 1954.

Whitehead, Alfred North. *Science and the Modern World.* 1926. Reprint. New York: Free Press, 1967.

Wilkins, John, ed. *Considering Veritatis Splendor.* Cleveland, OH: Pilgrim Press 1994.

Chapter 12

The Philosophy of Organism and Integral Ecology

Wisdom, Whitehead, and Pope Francis

Leo D. Lefebure

In his 2015 encyclical *Laudato Si', On Care for Our Common Home*, Pope Francis invites philosophers, scientists, followers of all religious traditions, together with all people of goodwill, to collaborate in shaping and living out the values of an integral ecology, a new worldview supportive of care for the earth as our common home.[1] Pope Francis accuses the reigning economic-technocratic paradigm of objectifying nature as a resource for unlimited exploitation and extraction; as a constructive alternative, he issues a stirring call to Catholics to engage with followers of all religious traditions, representatives of all worldviews, and all persons of goodwill in challenging and revising contemporary views that violate our common home: "We lack an awareness of our common origin, of our mutual belonging, and of a future to be shared with everyone. This basic awareness would enable the development of new convictions, attitudes and forms of life."[2] He cautions us not to look for a technological solution alone:

> Any technical solution which science claims to offer will be powerless to solve the serious problems of our world if humanity loses its compass, if we lose sight of the great motivations which make it possible for us to live in harmony, to make sacrifices and to treat others well.[3]

The integral ecology that Pope Francis calls for requires a new worldview shaped in dialogue with diverse religious practitioners as well as scientists and philosophers in order to inspire respect for the earth and the entire community of life; such a revised worldview needs to be able to guide appropriate uses of technology.[4] Pope Francis views the ecological crisis as a global problem that cannot be solved by any one religious tradition or philosophical school or political movement on its own; accordingly, he invites contributions from a wide variety of differing perspectives.

More recent statements make clear that care for our common home continues to be one of the most pressing concerns of Pope Francis. Both the final statement of the Synod on the Pan-Amazon Region in the fall of 2019 and Pope Francis's Post-Synodal Apostolic Exhortation, *Querida Amazonia*, call attention to the ecological devastation of the Amazon region, which has global implications and issue a worldwide appeal for collaboration.[5] In his encyclical letter *Fratelli Tutti: On Fraternity and Social Friendship*, issued in October 2020, Pope Francis recalls that St. Francis of Assisi "felt himself a brother to the son, the sea and the wind, yet he knew that he was even closer to those of his own flesh."[6] Inspired by the example of St. Francis of Assisi, the Pontiff invites the entire human family:

> Let us dream, then, as a single human family, as fellow travelers sharing the same flesh, as children of the same earth which is our common home, each of us bringing the richness of his or her beliefs and convictions, each of us with his or her own voice, brothers and sisters all.[7]

Recent Vatican statements have developed particular aspects of this invitation in more detail with regard to ecology; the Dicastery for Promoting Integral Human Development issued *Aqua Fons Vitae: Orientations on Water: Symbol of the Cry of the Poor and the Cry of the Earth*,[8] and the Interdicasterial Team of the Holy See on Integral Ecology released *In Cammino per la Cura della Casa Comune: A Cinque Anni dalla Laudato Si'*.[9]

In *Laudato Si'*, Pope Francis mentions the contributions of Pierre Teilhard de Chardin in passing but does not go into detail.[10] While he does not mention the philosophy of organism of Alfred North Whitehead, this philosopher offers significant support for the Pontiff's agenda through his profound meditation on the place of science in the modern world, together with his warning about the dangers of mechanistic materialism and his hopeful evocation of the role of religion and aesthetics in shaping values. Like Pope Francis, Whitehead believes that the underlying assumptions of our worldview shape our decisions and actions: "As we think, we live."[11] This chapter will propose that Whitehead's philosophy of organism offers a cogent critique of the fundamental presuppositions of mechanistic materialism which have dominated modern technocratic societies; this critique, together with Whitehead's views of the roles of religion and aesthetics, can contribute important resources for Pope Francis's integral ecology.

DIAGNOSIS OF THE ECOLOGICAL CRISIS

The most powerful assumptions are those that we take for granted and fail to criticize. One of the most important contributions that Whitehead offers to theologians and religious leaders such as Pope Francis is a set of conceptual tools for criticizing abstractions by making explicit our most fundamental assumptions about cosmology in order to assess and critique them. In his interpretation of the ecological crisis in relation to modern society, Pope Francis draws heavily on the Catholic philosopher Romano Guardini (1885–1968), whose work he had studied in graduate school.[12] Guardini's book *Der Gegensatz* taught the young Bergoglio to think about reality in terms of polarities; Guardini distinguished *Gegensatz* ("polarity") from *Widerspruch* ("contradiction").[13] Bergoglio learned from Guardini to see realities in terms of polar tensions.[14] In dialogue with Guardini and various Jesuit mentors, Bergoglio proposed what he called sineidetic thought that seeks to unite (Greek: *syn*, "with") ideas (Greek: *eidos*, "idea"), a style of thinking about the part and the whole in dynamic tension without claiming to arrive at a Hegelian synthesis: "It could be called *sineidetic thought,* in which the particulars must be considered as a function of the whole. In this way of thinking *unity* and *rhythm* are essential."[15] Bergoglio explains the style of thinking that flows from this approach:

> This method requires of the mind a *sineidetic tension* necessary to see the parts in relation to the whole and the whole in relation to the parts, with the awareness that in every vital whole (and the social-political reality is a vital whole), it is impossible to separate the parts from the whole and vice versa. . . . It is an operation of bringing together, in tension—a sineidetic way of thinking.[16]

After becoming Pope Francis in 2013, he described to interviewer Antonio Spadaro the enduring impact of Guardini:

> He spoke of a polar opposition in which the two opposites are not annulled. One pole does not destroy the other. There is no contradiction and no identity. For him, opposition is resolved at a higher level. In such a solution, however, the polar tension remains.[17]

In *Laudato Si'*, Pope Francis to a large degree follows the lead of Guardini in his assessment of the deleterious effects of modern philosophical perspectives. Guardini viewed modern Western culture as dominated by the will to power as articulated by Friedrich Nietzsche, but Guardini warned that humans have not learned to exercise power over power and thus stand before chaos.[18] Pope Francis cites with approval Guardini's comment that the technological mind sees nature as an insensate order, as a cold body of facts, as a mere "given," as an object of utility, as raw material to be hammered into useful shape; it views the cosmos similarly as a mere "space" into which objects can be thrown with complete indifference.[19]

Pope Francis warns that in the modern world people have often abused technology in a dangerous, one-dimensional paradigm based on manipulation and control:

> This paradigm exalts the concept of a subject who, using logical and rational procedures, progressively approaches and gains control over an external object. This subject makes every effort to establish the scientific and experimental method, which in itself is already a technique of possession, mastery and transformation.[20]

The result is that humanity's relationship with nature has become confrontational, and we humans fail to acknowledge our limits:

> This has made it easy to accept the idea of infinite or unlimited growth, which proves so attractive to economists, financiers and experts in technology. It is based on the lie that there is an infinite supply of the earth's goods, and this leads to the planet being squeezed dry beyond every limit.[21]

While science and technology in themselves are good, Pope Francis sees the danger that humans make technocracy into a paradigm for all relationships: "Decisions which may seem purely instrumental are in reality decisions about the kind of society we want to build."[22] The logic of the paradigm is inexorable:

> Technology tends to absorb everything into its ironclad logic. . . . The technocratic paradigm also tends to dominate economic and political life. The economy accepts every advance in technology with a view to profit, without concern for its potentially negative impact on human beings. Finance overwhelms the real economy.[23]

This leads to lack of respect both for the natural world and for human life. Francis notes that some believe "current economics and technology will solve all environmental problems" and trust in market growth.[24] In contrast, Francis warns:

> Yet by itself the market cannot guarantee integral human development and social inclusion. . . . We fail to see the deepest roots of our present failures,

which have to do with the direction, goals, meaning and social implications of technological and economic growth.[25]

Francis notes that specialization leads to greater power in specific applications, but he cautions that it "often leads to a loss of appreciation for the whole, for the relationships between things, and for the broader horizon, which then becomes irrelevant."[26] According to Francis, the current problems "cannot be dealt with from a single perspective or from a single set of interests."[27] Thus science and technology must be studied in dialogue with philosophy and social ethics. In the absence of this dialogue, there are no "genuine ethical horizons to which one can appeal. Life gradually becomes a surrender to situations conditioned by technology, itself viewed as the principal key to the meaning of existence."[28] This leads not only to degradation of the environment but also to "anxiety, a loss of the purpose of life and of community living."[29]

Whitehead's critique of modern scientific materialism converges in important ways with Guardini's rejection of the technological mindset of modern Western culture and the will to power. Whitehead's appraisal of scientific materialism offers powerful support for Guardini's and Pope Francis's critiques of the worldview of technocracy. In *Science in the Modern World*, Whitehead praises the epochal breakthroughs of seventeenth-century scientists in what he calls "The Century of Genius," but he also laments the damaging consequences of describing nature through the rigid distinction between primary qualities, which are deemed to be objective because science can measure them, and secondary qualities, which are devalued as merely subjective.[30] Even though this worldview facilitated the development of mathematical laws of science, Whitehead describes the result as a caricature of our experience: "Nature is a dull affair, soundless, scentless, colourless; merely the hurrying of material, endlessly, meaninglessly. However, you disguise it, this is the practical outcome of the characteristic scientific philosophy which closed the seventeenth century."[31]

While Whitehead acknowledges that this worldview has dominated most scientific research and university life around the world, he charges that it lacks credibility because it is conceptualized on a very abstract level; the decisive problem is that many people have mistaken the abstractions for concrete realities.[32] One of Whitehead's most important contributions to integral ecology is his analysis of the fallacy of misplaced concreteness. He argues that materialism can be applied to abstractions but not to concrete organisms, which are always shaped by the wholes to which they belong.[33] Whitehead warns that modern mechanism cannot acknowledge any intrinsic values in nature and thus trivializes artistic expressions.[34] Rejecting this mechanistic worldview, Whitehead turns to the romantic poets to learn about our concrete experience of nature.[35] Instructed by their wisdom, he focuses his philosophy of nature on the role of organisms as realizations of intrinsic value everywhere in nature.[36] Whitehead describes philosophy as intimately related to poetry because it seeks alternate phrasing for the intuitions of great poets.[37]

Anticipating Pope Francis's concerns about technocracy, Whitehead warns that it is an evil practice to ignore the relation of an organism to its environment and cautions that yet another evil habit is to deprive the environment of intrinsic importance.[38] For Whitehead, there is no such thing as an isolated fact because all things are connected; this connectedness is not accidental but essential to their reality; the environment of every reality is the entire universe.[39] In accordance with his philosophy of organism, Whitehead denies that anything in the real world is an inert fact because all actual entities without exception exist for feeling.[40] Like Pope Francis, Whitehead laments that the modern mechanistic mentality fails to recognize any ultimate values in nature and as a result devalues social life in favor of material things.[41] By elevating abstractions to the status of the sole reality, the scientific net of materialism fails to capture the world of concrete experience.[42]

Informed by Guardini's notion of polarities, Pope Francis stresses that relationships make things what they are: "Ecology studies the relationship between living organisms and the environment in which they develop. . . . It cannot be emphasized enough how everything is interconnected."[43] In a similar vein, Whitehead cautions that a philosophy based only on external relations leads to a valueless mechanistic materialism in which change has no meaning or purpose.[44] In one of his most significant insights, Whitehead warns against the fallacy of simple location, insisting that every reality is present in every other, even if in only a minimal manner.[45] Each reality is a coming together of the entire universe in a unique way because each entity in some aspect draws upon all of earlier history and manifests both the identity and diversity of things.[46]

Whitehead argues that all entities have internal relationships to their predecessors, and these internal relationships make them what they are.[47] This supports Pope Francis's insistence that "we need to grasp the variety of things in their multiple relationships" and his citation of the *Catechism of the Catholic Church*: "God wills the *interdependence of creatures.* . . . no creature is self-sufficient."[48] Pope Francis rejects the anthropocentrism that has dominated much of Catholic thought, insisting,

> The ultimate purpose of other creatures is not to be found in us. Rather, all creatures are moving forward with us and through us towards a common point of arrival, which is God, in that transcendent fullness where the risen Christ embraces and illumines all things.[49]

At the center of this vision is the acknowledgment of the value of each creature in relation to God, not simply in relation to humans: "Each organism, as a creature of God, is good and admirable in itself; the same is true of the harmonious ensemble of organisms existing in a defined space and functioning as a system."[50] Like Pope Francis, Whitehead rejects anthropocentrism and affirms the intrinsic value of every creature, maintaining that each actual entity realizes a unique, inherent value for its own sake; he finds in nature "a selective activity which is akin to purpose."[51] Whitehead poked fun at scientists who insist that there is no purpose in nature: "Scientists animated by the purpose of proving that they are purposeless constitute an interesting subject for study."[52] Whitehead proposed instead that each actual entity constitutes its own purpose.[53]

From the general principle that no physical object is independent of its environment, Whitehead concludes that every actual entity that damages its environment is in effect committing suicide because the environment and each species develop in tandem.[54] Whitehead praises Charles Darwin for refusing to go beyond the scientific evidence, but he laments that Darwin's "camp followers" developed unwarranted social theories concerning natural selection and the struggle for existence.[55] Whitehead bewails the social scientists who proposed a mechanistic perspective for modern society, dismissing any consideration of ethics in shaping commercial and national policies.[56] To counterbalance those who stress only the role of competition and conflict in development, Whitehead calls attention to the often-neglected aspect of creativeness in organisms who work together to shape their environment in collaboration. Cooperating organisms can create their environment in ways impossible for any single organism. Whitehead's perspective offers strong reinforcement for Pope Francis's call for cooperation.

LISTENING TO THE NATURAL WORLD

To overcome the dangers of mechanistic materialism, both Pope Francis and Whitehead invite us to learn to listen to the voices of the natural world in ways that modern societies have not always acknowledged or valued. Pope Francis begins his encyclical on ecology with the prayer of Saint Francis of Assisi:

> Praised be You (*Laudato Si'*), my Lord, with [*cum*] all creatures, especially Sir Brother Sun, Who is the day and through whom You give us light. . . . Praised be you, my Lord, through [*per*] Sister Moon and the stars, in heaven You formed them clear and precious and beautiful. . . . Praised be You, my Lord, through

our Sister Mother Earth, who sustains and governs us, and who produces varied
fruits with colored flowers and herbs.[57]

In the thirteenth-century Umbrian dialect of the Italian language in which St.
Francis was praying, the word *per* has multiple meanings: it can mean that
God is praised *for* the Sun, the Moon, the Air, the Waters, and Fire. It can
also mean that God is being praised *by* these creatures even though humans
view them as inanimate; this interpretation echoes Psalm 19:1: "The heavens
are telling the glory of God; and the firmament proclaims his handiwork." *Per*
can also mean *through*, a meaning that suggests both the role of creatures in
praising God and also a sense of God's mystical presence in all of creation.[58]
Modern technocratic societies have usually dismissed the notion that all
creatures, including those viewed as non-animate, could in any way be agents
praising God, but Francis of Assisi invites Sir Brother Sun, Sister Moon, the
Stars, Brother Wind, Sister Water, Brother Fire, Sister Mother Earth, and
even Sister Bodily Death to give praise to God.

A generation later the great Franciscan theologian Bonaventure reflected
on the aesthetic implications of the prayer of St. Francis, noting that the
saint saw all creatures as a reflection of the divine beauty through whom we
can glimpse the presence of the goodness of God in creation.[59] Pope Francis
praises Bonaventure's reflection on St. Francis's calling creatures "brother"
or "sister" and stresses the importance of this perspective to skeptics in language that resonates strongly with Whitehead:

> Such a conviction cannot be written off as naïve romanticism, for it affects the
> choices which determine our behavior. If we approach nature and the environ-
> ment without this openness to awe and wonder, if we no longer speak the lan-
> guage of fraternity and beauty in our relationship with the world, our attitude
> will be that of masters, consumers, ruthless exploiters, unable to set limits on
> their immediate needs. By contrast, if we feel intimately united with all that
> exists, then sobriety and care will well up spontaneously.[60]

Pope Francis structures his encyclical around the contrast between the
beauty of creation as given to us by God and the devastation caused by human
actions. After opening the encyclical with the hymn of Francis of Assisi, Pope
Francis immediately issues a dire warning that we are harming the earth:

> We have come to see ourselves as her lords and masters, entitled to plunder her
> at will. The violence present in our hearts, wounded by sin, is also reflected in
> the symptoms of sickness evident in the soil, in the water, in the air and in all
> forms of life.[61]

This sets the stage for the central tension that runs throughout the encyclical. Pope Francis cites the words of the Apostle Paul that the earth "groans in travail" (Rom. 8:22), and he chides us for forgetting that "we ourselves are the dust of the earth (cf. Gen. 2:7); our very bodies are made up of her elements, we breathe her air and we receive life and refreshment from her waters."[62] To care more effectively for our world, Pope Francis calls us to listen to the cry of the earth in conjunction with the cry of the poor who suffer especially from ecological destruction:

> Today, however, we have to realize that a true ecological approach always becomes a social approach; it must integrate questions of justice in debates on the environment, so as to hear both the cry of the earth and the cry of the poor.[63]

Those who embrace a mechanistic materialist view of nature dismiss the notion that inanimate creatures have anything to say, whether in praise of God or in groaning. Like Pope Francis, Whitehead challenges this assumption and listens to the great English romantic poets, especially William Wordsworth and Percy Bysshe Shelley, for wisdom from the voices of the natural world. Whitehead notes that Wordsworth's romantic reaction against the abstract mechanism of the eighteenth century began with close attention to the concrete experience of nature.[64] Whitehead praises Wordsworth for expressing a more concrete experience of nature than modern scientists, who distort nature by mistaking the abstractions of scientific inquiry for the concrete experience of nature. Whitehead's analysis of the fallacy of misplaced concreteness tells us that abstractions have a role to play, but they are misleading if we mistake them for the concrete experience of nature.[65]

In the poetry of Shelley, Whitehead hears a distinct but closely related sensibility that attends to the beauty and color of nature and that presents nature as composed of organisms. Above all, Whitehead emphasizes that Shelley agreed with Wordsworth in expressing an aesthetic intuition of a presence in nature.[66] Whitehead praises both Wordsworth and Shelley for rejecting the abstract materialism of the science of the Enlightenment. Rejecting the materialist mentality, Whitehead accepts the testimony of Wordsworth and Shelley as testifying to aesthetic values in nature that manifest "the brooding presence of the whole on to its various parts."[67] While the underlying assumptions of their respective cosmologies differ in important ways, Whitehead offers persuasive philosophical support for Pope Francis's rejection of the dominant materialistic worldview and his call to listen to the voice of creation for fresh possibilities.

APPEAL OF BEAUTY

After decrying practices that render the earth a giant garbage dump, Pope Francis hopes that the appeal of beauty can break through the reign of a reductionist technocracy and summon us to a fresh, direct experience of the world in which we live and to the acknowledgment of values beyond technical mastery over nature. He trusts that beauty can awaken us to appreciate the intrinsic value of human life and nature.[68] In the experience of beauty, there appears a mysterious power, which Pope Francis describes as:

> a kind of salvation which occurs in beauty and in those who behold it. An authentic humanity, calling for a new synthesis, seems to dwell in the midst of our technological culture, almost unnoticed, like a mist seeping gently beneath a closed door. Will the promise last, in spite of everything, with all that is authentic rising up in stubborn resistance?[69]

Like Whitehead, Francis sees our attitude toward beauty as powerfully shaping our lives for better or worse:

> If someone has not learned to stop and admire something beautiful, we should not be surprised if he or she treats everything as an object to be used and abused without scruple. If we want to bring about deep change, we need to realize that certain mindsets really do influence our behavior.[70]

Once again Whitehead's analysis offers cogent support for Pope Francis's agenda. According to Whitehead, scientific materialism has focused one-sidedly on matter in motion (primary qualities) as constituting reality and thus has excluded aesthetic values (secondary qualities) from serious consideration in shaping modern life; he describes the result as a disaster.[71] To resist the dominance of mechanistic materialism, Whitehead calls for an aesthetic appreciation of our experience, insisting that direct attention to concrete things with their values will disrupt the reign of materialism.[72] Criticizing the mindset that dismisses aesthetics and that reduces truth to scientific assessments, Whitehead proposes that beauty is more fundamental than truth because it expresses the interrelationships among entities as well as the teleology of the universe itself.[73] Whitehead insists that aesthetic, religious, and moral experiences are not marginal "secondary qualities," but rather put us in touch with what is real; he boldly claims, "Art has a curative function in human experience when it reveals as in a flash intimate, absolute Truth regarding the Nature of Things. . . . Art performing this great service belongs to the essence of civilization."[74]

Whitehead's emphasis on the experience of beauty and the intrinsic value of each actual entity strengthens Pope Francis's call for an integral ecological culture:

There needs to be a distinctive way of looking at things, a way of thinking, policies, an educational programme, a lifestyle and a spirituality which together generate resistance to the assault of the technocratic paradigm. Otherwise, even the best ecological initiatives can find themselves caught up in the same globalized logic.[75]

Both Pope Francis and Whitehead relate the appeal of beauty to the dwelling of God in the world. After the extended, technical philosophical discussion of cosmology in *Process and Reality*, Whitehead closes by offering a moving meditation on the providence of God in every moment of experience, believing that all temporal actualities flow into the divine reality, where God perfects whatever is good in them and makes their enduring contributions flow back into the world of time in order to affect other entities. Whitehead sees the judgment of God as "a tenderness which loses nothing that can be saved. It is also the judgment of a wisdom which uses what in the temporal world is mere wreckage."[76] The God envisioned by Whitehead does not create the world out of nothing as in traditional Catholic thought, but God "is the poet of the world, with tender patience leading it by his vision of truth, beauty, and goodness."[77]

Pope Francis closes *Laudato Si'* on a note of hope:

The universe unfolds in God, who fills it completely. Hence, there is a mystical meaning to be found in a leaf, in a mountain trail, in a dewdrop, in a poor person's face. The ideal is not only to pass from the exterior to the interior to discover the action of God in the soul, but also to discover God in all things.[78]

The mystical meditation of the Pontiff resonates deeply with the hope of Whitehead that God is the great companion of our universe.

EDUCATION FOR INTEGRAL ECOLOGY: WHITEHEAD'S PHILOSOPHY OF EDUCATION

Whitehead's philosophy of education offers valuable resources for developing integral ecology. Pope Francis recognizes that new forms of education are crucial for implementing his vision: "There needs to be a distinctive way of looking at things, a way of thinking, policies, an educational program, a lifestyle and a spirituality which together generate resistance to the assault of the technocratic paradigm."[79] Whitehead describes education as "the acquisition of the art of the utilization of knowledge. This is an art very difficult to impart."[80] He warns that much traditional education has become deadened and pedantic because it has inculcated inert ideas, that is, ideas that are merely accepted without being used, tested, and applied in fresh ways.[81] Whitehead charges that such education is not only useless but harmful, and he calls for an educational revolution.[82]

Whitehead proposes a three-stage model of education, beginning with romance, developing through precision, and culminating in generalization.[83] To prevent the danger of a routinized pedagogy, Whitehead wants to attract students to the romantic prospect of learning genuinely new perspectives that they can apply in innovative ways to improve their lives. Whitehead stresses the connection between education and living: *The function of Reason is to promote the art of life*;[84] he reiterates: "There is only one subject-matter for education, and that is Life in all its manifestations."[85] He trusts that students can experience a romance of discovery in exploring what is truly novel and seeing the implications of relationships previously ignored. He hopes that this "ferment already stirring in the mind" can lure students to think beyond their current horizons.[86]

Building upon this initiation, a necessary stage of detailed precision seeks systematic order through exact formulations of the subjects being studied. Aware that much traditional education has remained enclosed in the quest for precision, Whitehead cautions this stage will be barren if it is not grounded in the romance of exploration. With regard to religious education in particular, Whitehead sees premature insistence on precision as deadly.[87] The acquisition of precise knowledge leads to the last stage of generalization, which moves beyond the individual details to the broader scope of learning. Generalization links the achievement of precision back to the initial romance and offers learners a synthesis as a basis for further development. Whitehead believes there is a rhythm of freedom and discipline in education as in life that must be respected.[88] The creative impulse to learn comes from within the student and hinges on the value and importance of life itself. He emphasizes the importance of education in art in order to develop the aesthetic sense of beauty.[89]

One way to explore and apply ideas in innovative ways is to examine them in contexts very different from their original home. In recent years, scholars in Asia have explored Whitehead's philosophy, including his thoughts on education. In 2009, scholars from around the world convened at Christ University, Dharmaram College in Bangalore, India, for the Seventh International Whitehead Conference. The conference, organized in cooperation with Christ University and Dharmaram Vidya Kshetram, focused on "Process, Religion and Society"; among the many topics discussed was

Whitehead's philosophy of education, including how his perspectives could guide education for sustainable development.[90]

Kurian Kachappilly, C. M. I., suggests that Whitehead is the most significant contributor to the philosophy of higher education since John Henry Newman.[91] He praises Whitehead's analysis of the three stages of education, stressing the stage of generalization as the moment of application to life circumstances, uniting young and old.[92] Joseph Murik brings the three stages of Whitehead's model into dialogue with Thomas Aquinas, stressing the points of contact in the concern for engaging students as active learners, for balancing theory and practice, and for respecting the rights of the student.[93]

Robert Regnier also accepts Whitehead's three stages of learning and proposes that:

> education for sustainable development can be created through the design of education programs, structures and processes that develop the intrinsic capacity of individuals and groups to seek a more adequate wisdom which cultivates the moral imagination to discern and achieve what is most important, and in doing so to have the courage to become committed to truth beyond fear.[94]

Regnier praises Whitehead's approach to learning as valuing by encouraging development in the learners through wisdom, moral imagination, and courage.[95]

In the face of entrenched patterns of action, both Whitehead and Pope Francis recognize the many challenges involved in cultivating new insights and behaviors more conducive to living in greater harmony with our environment and the community of life on this planet. While there are significant differences in perspective between Whitehead and Pope Francis, the philosophy of organism offers valuable resources for promoting the vision of an integral ecological culture to which Pope Francis beckons the human community.

NOTES

1. Pope Francis, *Laudato Si'* (Washington, DC: United States Conference of Catholic Bishops, 2015), 164–201.
2. Ibid., 202.
3. Ibid., 200.
4. Ibid., 63, 137.
5. Synod of Bishops for the Pan-Amazon Region, "The Amazon: New Paths for the Church and for an Integral Ecology," Special Assembly of the Synod of Bishops for the Pan-Amazon Region—6 to 27 October, 2019, http://www.synod.va/content /sinodoamazonico/en/documents/final-document-of-the-amazon-synod.html; Pope Francis, *Querida Amazonia* (Vatican City: Libreria Editrice Vaticana, 2020).

6. Pope Francis, *Fratelli Tutti* (Vatican City: Libreria Editrice Vaticana/ Huntington, IN: Our Sunday Visitor Press, 2020), 2.

7. Ibid., 8.

8. Dicastery for Promoting Integral Human Development, *Aqua Fons Vitae: Orientations on Water: Symbol of the Cry of the Poor and the Cry of the Earth* (Vatican City, 2020).

9. Interdicasterial Team of the Holy See for Integral Ecology, *In Cammino per la Cura della Casa Comune: A Cinque Anni dalla Laudato Si'* (Vatican City: Libreria Editrice Vaticana, 2020).

10. Pope Francis, *Laudato Si'*, 83n53.

11. Alfred North Whitehead, *Modes of Thought* (1938; repr., New York: Free Press, 1968), 63 (hereafter "*MT*").

12. Pope Francis, *Laudato Si'*, 105, 108, 115; Romano Guardini, *Der Gegensatz: Versuch zu einer Philosophie der Lebendig-Konkreten* (1925; repr., 3rd ed., Mainz: Matthias Grünewald Verlag, 1985).

13. Ibid.

14. Massimo Borghesi, *The Mind of Pope Francis: Jorge Mario Bergoglio's Intellectual Journey*, trans. Barry Hudock (Collegeville, MN: Liturgical Press Academic, 2018), 57–141.

15. Pope Francis-Jorge Mario Bergoglio, *Pastorale Sociale*, edited by Marco Gallo, trans. A. Taroni (Milan: Jaca Book, 2015); Borghesi, *The Mind of Pope Francis*, 128.

16. Pope Francis-Bergoglio, *Pastorale Sociale*, 302; Borghesi, *The Mind of Pope Francis*, 128.

17. Pope Francis, cited by Borghesi, *The Mind of Pope Francis*, 105.

18. Guardini, *Der Gegensatz*, 91–92; Borghesi, *The Mind of Pope Francis*, 135.

19. Romano Guardini, *The End of the Modern World*, rev. ed. (Wilmington, DE: ISI Books, 1998), 55, quoted in Pope Francis, *Laudato Si'*, 115.

20. Pope Francis, *Laudato Si'*, 106.

21. Ibid.

22. Ibid., 107.

23. Ibid., 108–109.

24. Ibid., 109.

25. Ibid.

26. Ibid., 110.

27. Ibid.

28. Ibid.

29. Ibid.

30. Alfred North Whitehead, *Science and the Modern World* (1926; repr., New York: Free Press, 1967), 53–54 (hereafter "*SMW*").

31. Ibid., 54.

32. Ibid., 54–55.

33. Ibid., 79.

34. Ibid., 196.

35. Ibid., 77–94.

36. Ibid., 194.

37. *MT* 50, 174.

38. *SMW* 196.

39. *MT* 9.

40. Alfred North Whitehead, *Process and Reality: An Essay in Cosmology*, corrected ed., ed. David Ray Griffin and Donald W. Sherburne (New York: Free Press, 1978), 310 (hereafter "*PR*").

41. *SMW* 202–203.

42. *MT* 18–19.

43. Pope Francis, *Laudato Si'*, 138.

44. *SMW* 107.

45. Alfred North Whitehead, *Symbolism: Its Meaning and Effect* (1927; repr., New York: Capricorn Books, 1959), 38 (hereafter "*SME*").

46. *PR* 50–51, 228.

47. *SMW* 104.

48. Pope Francis, *Laudato Si'*, 86.

49. Ibid., 83.

50. Ibid., 140.

51. *SMW* 107.

52. Alfred North Whitehead, *The Function of Reason* (1929; repr., Boston, MA: Beacon Press, 1962), 16 (hereafter "*FR*").

53. Ibid., 30–31.

54. *SMW* 110.

55. Ibid., 111.

56. Ibid.

57. Francis of Assisi, "The Canticle of Brother Son," in *Francis and Clare: The Complete Works*, trans. Regis J. Armstrong and Ignatius C. Brady (New York: Paulist Press, 1982), 38–39.

58. Ibid.

59. Bonaventure, "The Life of St. Francis," in *Bonaventure: The Soul's Journey into God, The Tree of Life, The Life of St. Francis*, trans. Ewert Cousins (New York: Paulist Press, 1978), 262–63.

60. Pope Francis, *Laudato Si'*, 11.

61. Ibid., 2.

62. Ibid.

63. Ibid., 49.

64. *SMW* 81.

65. *SME* 39; *SMW* 84.

66. Ibid., 85.

67. Ibid., 87–88.

68. Pope Francis, *Laudato Si'*, 112.

69. Ibid.

70. Ibid., 215.

71. *SMW* 204.

72. Ibid., 199.

73. Alfred North Whitehead, *Adventures of Ideas* (1933; repr., New York: Free Press, 1967), 265.

74. Ibid., 272.
75. Pope Francis, *Laudato Si'*, 111.
76. *PR* 346.
77. Ibid.
78. Pope Francis, *Laudato Si'*, 233.
79. Ibid., 111.
80. Alfred North Whitehead, *The Aims of Education and Other Essays* (New York: American Library, 1929), 16 (hereafter "*AE*").
81. Ibid., 13.
82. Ibid., 13–14.
83. Ibid., 28–30.
84. *FR* 4 (emphasis in original).
85. *AE* 18.
86. *FR* 29.
87. *AE* 49.
88. Ibid., 39–50.
89. Ibid., 49.
90. Kurian Kachappilly, ed., *Process, Religion and Society: Proceedings of the 7th IWC 2009*, 2 vols. (Bangalore: Dharmaram Publications, 2011).
91. Kurian Kachappilly, "Introduction: Whitehead and Education," in *Process, Religion and Society: Proceedings of the 7th IWC 2009*, 2 vols., ed. Kurian Kachappilly (Bangalore: Dharmaram Publications, 2011), 22.
92. Ibid., 24.
93. Joseph Murik, "Educational Philosophies of Thomas Aquinas and Alfred North Whitehead: Beacons for the Modern Educator," in *Process, Religion and Society: Proceedings of the 7th IWC 2009*, 2 vols., ed. Kurian Kachappilly (Bangalore: Dharmaram Publications, 2011), 63–67.
94. Robert Regnier, "Education for Sustainable Development through Learning as Valuing," in *Process, Religion and Society: Proceedings of the 7th IWC 2009*, 2 vols., ed. Kurian Kachappilly (Bangalore: Dharmaram Publications, 2011), 54.
95. Ibid., 30.

BIBLIOGRAPHY

Bonaventure. "The Life of St. Francis." In *Bonaventure: The Soul's Journey into God, The Tree of Life, The Life of St. Francis*. Translated by Ewert Cousins, 177–327. New York: Paulist Press, 1978.

Borghesi, Massimo. *The Mind of Pope Francis: Jorge Mario Bergoglio's Intellectual Journey*. Translated by Barry Hudock. Collegeville, MN: Liturgical Press Academic, 2018.

Dicastery for Promoting Integral Human Development. *Aqua Fons Vitae: Orientations on Water: Symbol of the Cry of the Poor and the Cry of the Earth*. Vatican City, 2020.

Francis of Assisi. "The Canticle of Brother Son." In *Francis and Clare: The Complete Works*. Translated by Regis J. Armstrong and Ignatius C. Brady, 37–39. New York: Paulist Press, 1982.

Francis, Pope. *Fratelli Tutti*. Vatican City: Libreria Editrice Vaticana/Huntington, IN: Our Sunday Visitor Press, 2020.

Francis, Pope. *Laudato Si'*. Washington, DC: United States Conference of Catholic Bishops, 2015.

Francis, Pope. *Querida Amazonia*. Vatican City: Libreria Editrice Vaticana, 2020.

Francis, Pope-Bergoglio, Jorge Mario. *Pastorale Sociale*. Edited by Marco Gallo. Translated by A. Taroni. Milan: Jaca Book, 2015.

Guardini, Romano. *Der Gegensatz: Versuch zu einer Philosophie der Lebendig-Konkreten*. 1925. Reprint, 3rd ed. Mainz: Matthias Grünewald Verlag, 1985.

Guardini, Romano. *The End of the Modern World*. Rev. ed. Wilmington, DE: ISI Books, 1998.

Interdicasterial Team of the Holy See for Integral Ecology. *In Cammino per la Cura della Casa Comune: A Cinque Anni dalla Laudato Si'*. Vatican City: Libreria Editrice Vaticana, 2020.

Kachappilly, Kurian. "Introduction: Whitehead and Education." In *Process, Religion and Society: Proceedings of the 7th IWC* 2009, 2 vols., edited by Kurian Kachappilly, 2:20–28. Bangalore: Dharmaram Publications, 2011.

Kachappilly, Kurian, ed. *Process, Religion and Society: Proceedings of the 7th IWC 2009*. 2 vols. Bangalore: Dharmaram Publications, 2011.

Murik, Joseph. "Educational Philosophies of Thomas Aquinas and Alfred North Whitehead: Beacons for the Modern Educator." In *Process, Religion and Society: Proceedings of the 7th IWC* 2009, 2 vols., edited by Kurian Kachappilly, 2:57–68. Bangalore: Dharmaram Publications, 2011.

Regnier, Robert. "Education for Sustainable Development through Learning as Valuing." In *Process, Religion and Society: Proceedings of the 7th IWC* 2009, 2 vols., edited by Kurian Kachappilly, 2:29–56. Bangalore: Dharmaram Publications, 2011.

Synod of Bishops for the Pan-Amazon Region. "The Amazon: New Paths for the Church and for an Integral Ecology." Special Assembly of the Synod of Bishops for the Pan-Amazon Region - 6 to 27 October. 2019. http://www.synod.va/content/sinodoamazonico/en/documents/final-document-of-the-amazon-synod.html.

Whitehead, Alfred North. *Adventures of Ideas*. 1933. Reprint, New York: Free Press, 1967.

Whitehead, Alfred North. *The Aims of Education and Other Essays*. New York: New American Library, 1929.

Whitehead, Alfred North. *The Function of Reason*. 1929. Reprint, Boston, MA: Beacon Press, 1962.

Whitehead, Alfred North. *Modes of Thought*. 1938. Reprint, New York: Free Press, 1968.

Whitehead, Alfred North. *Process and Reality: An Essay in Cosmology* (1929). Corrected ed. Edited by David Ray Griffin and Donald W. Sherburne. New York: Free Press, 1978.

Whitehead, Alfred North. *Science and the Modern World*. 1926. Reprint, New York: Free Press, 1967.

Whitehead, Alfred North. *Symbolism: Its Meaning and Effect*. 1927. Reprint. New York: Capricorn Books, 1959.

Afterword

Discovering Process (Again)

Thomas P. Rausch, S. J.

Discovering process philosophy opened a new world for me. As a young Jesuit preparing for the priesthood, my program included the traditional three years of philosophy, a program stressing scholastic philosophy, especially the work of Thomas Aquinas. I was sent to Mount Saint Michael in Spokane, Washington. "The Mount" was a rather imposing set of buildings set on a hill for Jesuit scholastics doing their philosophical studies, accredited through Gonzaga University. One cynical young Jesuit called it "a Neogothic bastion of Visigothic philosophy."

As the Second Vatican Council was drawing to a close and religious communities began updating their lives in keeping with the Council's reforms, our rather monastic Jesuit formation began to loosen up. No longer was it required that the courses be taught in Latin—the better to read the *Summa*—though some of the professors still did their best to use Latin in their teaching. Leaving the sanctuary of the scholasticate, we were able to take some classes with ordinary undergraduate students on the Gonzaga campus. Putting aside our cassocks, we began wearing for class a black shirt over our black pants, but always with a Roman collar. The curriculum also was expanded, with the works of some new thinkers. Especially popular was Bernard J. F. Lonergan's massive tome on epistemology, *Insight: A Study of Human Understanding* (1957),[1] though some of the faculty found his work controversial.

I quickly found myself engaged by my philosophical studies. For some reason, metaphysics appealed to me in a special way, as did Aquinas's treatise on truth in his *De Veritate*. His treatment of the *intellectus agens* was the subject of my first term paper, with his description of the human intellect as a "participated likeness of the uncreated light" (*quaedam participata similitudo luminis increati*).[2] Lonergan's emphasis on insight into the data of experience, moving from experience to understanding and then judgment in the process of appropriating one's process of understanding, made great sense to me. I decided to complete a M. A. in philosophy. The graduate program, besides requiring additional courses in the history of philosophy, was to considerably broaden my philosophical horizons.

At the end of my second year, I took a graduate course in American philosophy from Fr. Walter Stokes, S. J., then teaching at Fordham University. Stokes contributed an article to an early book on the relation between process thought and Christian faith.[3] We read William James, Alfred North Whitehead—a thinker whom I found at first virtually incomprehensible—Charles Hartshorne, and Charles Sanders Peirce. I was also reading Pierre Teilhard de Chardin's nonconventional approach to evolution *The Phenomenon of Man*.[4] Two other courses were to lead me in new directions. One was in contemporary philosophy, with a focus on Whitehead, especially his *Science and the Modern World*[5] and a careful reading of *Process and Reality*.[6] The second was entitled "Space and Time," an introduction to the philosophy of science.

While I took those courses over fifty years ago, they helped me to move beyond a rather static approach to reality to a more dynamic, evolutionary view, with a metaphysics that saw freedom (indeterminacy) and relationality (prehensions) in nascent forms at the very heart of the real. The course on space and time contrasted two opposing cosmologies. One was Laplace's scientific determinism, a mechanistic view that hypothesized that if the location and direction of every atom in the universe could be grasped in a moment of time, the past and future of the entire universe could be determined. Einstein's epigrammatic remark, "God does not place dice" stays with me to this day. The other, based on exploring the philosophical implications of quantum mechanics, suggested a more open cosmology, striving, developing, complexifying, and embracing value.

My growing appreciation for process philosophy also provided a philosophical context for Teilhard's evolutionary vision of a universe developing toward the human and ultimately the divine. His work was controversial for Roman Catholics. In a more repressive age in the life of the church, Teilhard's Jesuit Order had forbidden him to publish his two major works *Le Milieu divin*[7] and *Le Phénomène humain*[8] during his lifetime (1881–1955), and after his death the Vatican's Holy Office issued a *monitum* or warning against certain of his ideas. The guardians of orthodoxy thought his view of human origins was not compatible with the doctrine of original sin, and/or that he did not sufficiently affirm God's agency in creating human beings and the soul. Others objected that his work was more poetry than science.

I was fascinated with Teilhard's view of evolution, something far more cosmic than the development of the phyla and species of the animal kingdom but embracing the fullness of the material. It satisfied my theological concerns, with its sense of an increasing complexity and brain development, leading to the emergence of the human, encompassing an ongoing evolution, now on the level of self-consciousness, the "noosphere," moving humanity toward greater unity, community, and ultimately toward a consummation in the divine which he called the "Omega Point." In other words, not mere chance, but purpose. I have often remarked how Teilhard would have seen the Internet as a global nervous system.

In 1967, I began teaching for two years at Loyola University of Los Angeles (now Loyola Marymount). I taught courses on the human person, called the "Philosophy of Man," and another on Aristotle. But continuing my growing interest in process thought, I also taught a course on Whitehead and developed one on process philosophy. I had already included in my courses Teilhard's *The Phenomenon of Man*, after rescuing it from "Gehenna," a secure room in the basement of the library where books not approved of by the church were stored. Teaching Teilhard to freshmen and sophomores was a challenge, but many appreciated it and still talk about the book years later. And I found myself, without any background in biology, becoming increasingly interested in evolutionary theory, consulting colleagues who taught biology and borrowing charts and graphs on evolution for my class. One semester, to engage the students' creativity, I encouraged them to do a more "creative" final project. I received from one student his final paper done on a roll of toilet paper, partly to tweak me, but when unspooled it traced evolution with pictures and drawings from trilobites and arthropods to various anthropoids, and finally to two rather sexy human figures.

I was still interested in process philosophy. I had been reading John Cobb's natural theology with great interest and began thinking of going to Claremont for doctoral studies. In 1969, I was invited by the philosophy club at UCLA to give a talk on process thought, a break from the analytic philosophy that dominated departments in those days. But as the end of the 1960s mutated from the flower power and hippy culture of its early days to hard drugs and the violence of its more radical elements, my view began to change. The year 1968 was the *annus horribilis*, with the assassinations of Robert F. Kennedy and Martin Luther King Jr., the riot at the Democratic Convention in Chicago, student protests in the United States and Europe, the murder of hundreds of students, perhaps more, in Mexico City, and the ending of the Prague Spring by Soviet tanks. As I moved to the Graduate Theological Union, just off the UC campus in Berkeley in 1969, the Omega Point seemed to be fading into the indefinite future.

It was also a time of considerable confusion in Catholic theology and life as the church struggled to implement the renewal of the Second Vatican Council. Large numbers of priests and nuns were leaving their dioceses and communities, saying cynically, "Last one out, turn off the lights." Popular articles were looking forward to more radical changes, an end to clerical celibacy, for some a church without ordained ministers, a ferment reflected in works like Harvey Cox's *The Secular City* (1965);[9] Charles Davis's *A Question of Conscience* (1967),[10] announcing his departure from the Catholic Church, protesting its authoritarianism and lack of truth; and Hans Küng's *Why Priests: A Proposal for a New Church Ministry* (1972).[11]

As someone preparing for the priesthood, I found myself increasingly drawn to the foundations of the faith, particularly in the areas of Christology and ecclesiology, concerns that I have focused on ever since. Though I continued to explore process theology at the Graduate Theological Union, the more I turned to its theological expression, the less adequate it seemed to the Christian mystery, especially in Christology. Nor did Whitehead's treatment of eschatology as objective immortality in the consequent nature of God seem adequate to Christian belief in the resurrection. Thus, as I moved on to doctoral studies, I moved also beyond process thought, with a new interest in religious experience and systematic theology, especially ecclesiology.

Yet, after more than forty years of teaching, my memories as a beginning scholar of reading John Cobb remained positive and I was delighted to meet him when John Becker brought him, now in his nineties, to campus for a luncheon with a group of us. I have also come to a new appreciation for process theology in the work of scholars like Joseph A. Bracken, S. J., Marjorie Hewitt Suchocki, James Felt, S. J., and others whom I would call "Neo-Teilhardians," among them Elizabeth A. Johnson, C. S. J., John F. Haught, and Ilia Delio.

Joseph Bracken has challenged recent attempts to focus exclusively on the economic Trinity, at the expense of the immanent Trinity. Stressing a metaphysics of becoming rather than one of being, he sees the relationships between the persons of the Trinity as providing a model or archetype for the world of creation. This places relationality as the heart of the divine mystery. Seeking a way between nature as a mechanistic determinism or simply a realm of freedom and self-determination, he argues that Being Itself, or nature, is intersubjective, reaching its fullest expression in the interpersonal.[12]

I have also found the works of the Neo-Teilhardians particularly fruitful, both for theology and for spirituality. While not as specifically metaphysical as Bracken, their focus is always on the divine economy working in and through the process of evolution, thus having a theological vision that moves far beyond an Anselmian soteriology to join a theology of continuous creation with God's ongoing salvific work. In theological terms, creation and eschatology are correlative terms. For Elizabeth A. Johnson, nature remains free and autonomous, yet with God's presence working not "above" but within it, in all its beauty and diversity, with its suffering and failures, even in those chance events that allow novelty to emerge.[13] John Haught, appealing to the work of Teilhard, sees evolution as a drama, as life in all its variety struggles to be and to flourish, not always successfully.[14] He speaks of the hiddenness of God who from the future, yet present in each moment, draws the cosmos forward. Ilia Delio addresses evolution from a Christological perspective, finding Christ at the heart of the evolutionary process, bringing about unity "in the divine, continual act of creation, redemption, and sanctification of the total universe."[15] Christology today must reflect not just on Jesus as truly God and truly human, but also "on how Christ is truly cosmic."[16]

Influenced by process theology, these scholars have developed a cosmology which sees the sustaining and saving presence of the triune God in the drama of the evolutionary process. Their work does justice to Christian faith in the person of Jesus, the Word, not just the revealer of the divine mystery but active in the ongoing work of creation. The divine work of creation is itself salvific.

The emphasis of these scholars on relationality is not far from that of Pope Francis who himself stresses the interconnectedness of all things. In his beautiful encyclical, *Laudato Si'*, he writes:

> The human person grows more, matures more and is sanctified more to the extent that he or she enters into relationships, going out from themselves to live in communion with God, with others and with all creatures. In this way, they make their own that trinitarian dynamism which God imprinted in them when they were created.[17]

NOTES

1. Bernard Joseph Francis Lonergan, *Insight: A Study of Human Understanding* (London: Longmans, Green & Co., 1957).

2. Thomas Aquinas, *Summa theologica*, 2nd and rev. ed., trans. Fathers of the English Dominican Province (London: Burns, Oates & Washbourne, 1920–22), Ia.84.5.

3. Walter E. Stokes, S. J., "God for Today and Tomorrow," in *Process Theology and Christian Thought*, ed. Delwin Brown, Ralph E. James, Jr., and Gene Reeves (New York: Bobbs-Merrill, 1971), 244–63.

4. Pierre Teilhard de Chardin, *The Phenomenon of Man*, trans. Bernard Wall (New York: Evanston, 1959).

5. Alfred North Whitehead, *Science and the Modern World* (1926; repr., New York, Free Press, 1967).

6. Alfred North Whitehead, *Process and Reality: An Essay in Cosmology* (1929), corrected ed., ed. David Ray Griffin and Donald W. Sherburne (New York: Free Press, 1978).

7. Pierre Teilhard de Chardin, *Le milieu divin* (Tientsin: n. p., 1927).

8. Op. cit., note 4.

9. Harvey Gallagher Cox, *The Secular City: Secularization and Urbanization in Theological Perspective* (London: S. C. M. Press, 1965).

10. Charles Davis, *A Question of Conscience* (London: Hodder and Stoughton, 1967).

11. Hans Küng, *Why Priests? A Proposal for a New Church Ministry*, trans. John Cumming (London: Collins, 1972).

12. Joseph A. Bracken, S. J., "Trinity: Economic and Immanent," *Horizons* 25.1 (1998): 7–22.

13. Elizabeth A. Johnson, *Quest for the Living God: Mapping Frontiers in the Theology of God* (New York: Continuum, 2007), 193; idem, *Ask the Beasts: Darwin and the God of Love* (London: Bloomsbury, 2014).

14. John F. Haught, *Making Sense of Evolution: Darwin, God, and the Drama of Life* (Louisville: Westminster John Knox, 2010), 61–65.

15. Ilia Delio, *Christ in Evolution* (Maryknoll, NY: Orbis Books, 2008), 132.

16. Ibid., 126.

17. Pope Francis, *Laudato Si'* (Washington, DC: United States Conference of Catholic Bishops, 2015), 240.

BIBLIOGRAPHY

Aquinas, Thomas. *Summa theologica*. 2nd and Rev. ed. Translated by Fathers of the English Dominican Province. 10 vols. London: Burns, Oates & Washbourne, 1920–22.

Bracken, Joseph A., S. J. "Trinity: Economic and Immanent." *Horizons* 25.1 (1998): 7–22.

Brown, Delvin, Ralph E. James, Jr., and Gene Reeves, eds. *Process Philosophy and Christian Thought*. Indianapolis, IN: Bobbs-Merrill, 1971.

Cox, Harvey Gallagher. *The Secular City: Secularization and Urbanization in Theological Perspective*. London: S. C. M. Press, 1965.

Davis, Charles. *A Question of Conscience*. London: Hodder and Stoughton, 1967.

Delio, Ilia. *Christ in Evolution*. Maryknoll, NY: Orbis Books, 2008.

Francis, Pope. *Laudato Si'*. Washington, DC: United States Conference of Catholic Bishops, 2015.

Haught, John F. *Making Sense of Evolution: Darwin, God, and the Drama of Life*. Louisville: Westminster John Knox, 2010.

Johnson, Elizabeth A. *Ask the Beasts: Darwin and the God of Love*. London: Bloomsbury, 2014.

Johnson, Elizabeth A. *Quest for the Living God: Mapping Frontiers in the Theology of God*. New York: Continuum, 2007.

Küng, Hans. *Why Priests? A Proposal for a New Church Ministry*. Translated by John Cumming. London: Collins, 1972.

Lonergan, Bernard Joseph Francis. *Insight: A Study of Human Understanding.* London: Longmans, Green & Co., 1957.

Stokes, Walter E., S. J. "God for Today and Tomorrow." In *Process Theology and Christian Thought*, edited by Delwin Brown, Ralph E. James, Jr., and Gene Reeves, 244–63. New York: Bobbs-Merrill, 1971.

Teilhard de Chardin, Pierre. *Le milieu divin.* Tientsin: n. p., 1927.

Teilhard de Chardin, Pierre. *The Phenomenon of Man.* Translated by Bernard Wall. New York: Evanston, 1959.

Whitehead, Alfred North. *Process and Reality: An Essay in Cosmology.* 1929. Corrected ed. Edited by David Ray Griffin and Donald W. Sherburne. New York: Free Press, 1978.

Whitehead, Alfred North. *Science and the Modern World.* 1926. Reprint, New York: Free Press, 1967.

Index

abortion. *See* morality

absolute, 37, 39, 53, 54, 56–57, 95, 97, 98, 100–101, 104, 106–7, 121, 135, 140, 174, 176, 196. *See also* God; relation(s), relational

abstract, abstraction, xxii, 4, 10n9, 20, 23, 25, 33–35, 52, 54, 56, 60, 66, 70, 102–3, 115, 116, 119, 154, 156, 157, 169, 172–73, 174, 175–76, 177, 189, 191, 192, 195. *See also* concrete, concreteness, concretion; generalization(s); universal, universals

accident(s), xiv, 34, 36, 52, 79, 84, 87, 96, 106, 112, 131, 142, 168, 169–73, 176, 177, 181n13, 192. *See also* quality, qualities; substance

act, human. *See* morality

activity, action, active, xvi, xxiv, 4, 22, 26, 37–39, 41, 54–55, 66, 69, 74, 82–83, 85–86, 88–89, 90, 96, 98, 99, 100, 103, 116, 118, 120, 130, 133, 137, 139, 141–43, 152, 154, 173–75, 178, 181n25, 193, 197, 199, 209. *See also* creativity; passive, passivity

actual entity, actual occasion, x, xii, xiii, xix, 10n9, 40, 58, 66–75, 83–84, 96–97, 101, 105–6, 115–19, 124n21, 137–38, 175, 176, 193, 197; agent, as, 4, 7, 38, 58, 82, 99, 101–2, 106, 168, 172, 175, 177, 194; aim, initial, 6, 66–69, 116, 117, 137, 138, 177; aim, subjective, ix, 40, 66–70, 73–75, 105, 116, 117; *causa sui*, self-actualizing, self-constituting, self-creating, self-determining, self-realizing, as, 67, 70–71; concrescence, 20, 66–70, 72–74, 105; creative synthesis, as, xvi; novelty, and, 40, 69–71, 73, 75, 96, 104–5, 119; pole, mental, 68; pole, physical, 119; prehend, prehension, 20, 72, 73, 84, 97, 102, 103, 107, 115, 116, 119, 174, 175, 206; relevance, gradation of, 175; *res vera*, as, 176; satisfaction, 6, 70, 137–38. *See also* God; fact, feeling; relation(s), relational

actualization, actuality, xiv, xix, 10n9, 39, 52, 53, 55–59, 66, 70, 71, 73, 74, 86, 96, 102–4, 115, 118, 122, 175, 176. *See also* actual entity; God; possibility

aesthetic, aesthetics. *See* beauty

Aeterni Patris, 17

agency, agent, 4, 7, 38, 58, 82, 99, 101–2, 106, 168, 172, 175, 177, 194. *See also* actual entity; causal, causation, cause(s), cause and effect

agnosticism, 54

213

Contributors

John Becker is assistant professor of Philosophy in the Department of Religion and Philosophy at Lyon College, Batesville, Arkansas. In 2017, he was the recipient of the International Process Network's Young Scholar Award. He is a member of the Society for Buddhist-Christian Studies and a research fellow for The Institute for Postmodern Development of China, USA. His research interests include process thought, constructive theology, Mahayana Buddhism, and interreligious pluralism.

Joseph A. Bracken, S. J., is professor emeritus of Systematic Theology at Xavier University, Cincinnati, Ohio. One of the foremost Catholic process theologians of our time, he has authored thirteen books and close to two hundred articles, book chapters, and essays on a variety of topics at the intersection of revisionist Catholic and Whiteheadian thought. His most recent books are: *The World in the Trinity: Open-Ended Systems in Science and Religion* (2014), *God: Three Who Are One* (2017), *Church as Dynamic Life System: Shared Ministries and Common Responsibilities* (2019), and *Reciprocal Causality in an Event-Filled World* (2022).

David B. Burrell, C. S. C., is Theodore Hesburgh Professor Emeritus in Philosophy and Theology at the University of Notre Dame, Indiana. He has published extensively on Aquinas, comparative theological and philosophical issues in Judaism, Christianity, and Islam, and ethics. In addition to translating classical and contemporary works from Arabic, his monographs include: *Aquinas: God and Action* (1979), *Knowing the Unknowable God: Ibn-Sina, Maimonides, Aquinas* (1986), *Freedom and Creation in Three Traditions* (1993), and *Friendship and Ways to Truth* (2000). He has received an honorary doctorate in theology from Lund University, the Aquinas Medal from the

American Catholic Philosophical Association, and the John Courtney Murray Award from the Catholic Theological Society of America.

John B. Cobb Jr., is one of the foremost process theologians of the past half century. He is Ingraham professor emeritus of Theology at Claremont School of Theology, professor emeritus of Religion and Philosophy at Claremont Graduate University, and founding codirector of the Center for Process Studies. He has written extensively on Christian theology, process theology and philosophy, religious pluralism and interfaith dialogue, religion and science, ethics and economics, and environmental ethics. Among his over fifty books are: *A Christian Natural Theology* (1974), *Whitehead Word Book: A Glossary with Alphabetical Index to Technical Terms in Process and Reality* (2008), *Spiritual Bankruptcy: A Prophetic Call to Action* (2010), *Theological Reminiscences* (2014), and *Jesus' Abba: The God Who Has Not Failed* (2016). His book *Is It Too Late? A Theology of Ecology* (1971) was a ground-breaking work on environmental ethics. In 2014, he was elected to the American Academy of Arts and Sciences.

Ilia Delio, O. S. F., holds the Josephine C. Connelly chair in Christian Theology at Villanova University. Her area of research is systematic-constructive theology with interests in process thought, evolution, quantum physics, artificial intelligence, and the import of these for Christian doctrine and life. She is the author of over twenty books including: *Making All Things New: Catholicity, Cosmology and Consciousness* (2015), which was a finalist for the 2019 Michael Ramsey Prize, and *The Unbearable Wholeness of Being: God, Evolution and the Power of Love* (2013), which won the 2014 Silver Nautilus Book Award and a 2014 Catholic Press Association Book Award in Faith and Science. She is the founder of the Center for Christogenesis, an online educational resource for promoting the vision of Teilhard de Chardin and, more broadly, the integration of science and religion in the twenty-first century.

Daniel A. Dombrowski is professor of Philosophy at Seattle University. He is the author of twenty books and over a hundred and eighty articles in scholarly journals in philosophy, theology, classics, and literature. Among his books are: *Rethinking the Ontological Argument: A Neoclassical Theistic Perspective* (2006), *Contemporary Athletics and Ancient Greek Ideals* (2009), and *Process Philosophy and Political Liberalism: Rawls, Whitehead, Hartshorne* (2019). His main areas of interest are metaphysics and philosophy of religion from a neoclassical or process perspective. He is the editor of the journal *Process Studies*.

Thomas E. Hosinski, C. S. C., is professor emeritus of Theology at the University of Portland, where he has taught for thirty-eight years. He is the author of: *Stubborn Fact and Creative Advance: An Introduction to the Metaphysics of Alfred North Whitehead* (1993) and *The Image of the Unseen God: Catholicity, Science, and Our Evolving Understanding of God* (2017). The latter won the 2018 Catholic Press Association First Place Book Award in the category of Faith and Science.

Leo D. Lefebure is the inaugural holder of the Matteo Ricci, S. J., Chair of Theology at Georgetown University. His book, *True and Holy: Christian Scripture and Other Religions* (2013), received the 2015 Catholic Press Association first-place award for best academic book on scripture, and his coauthored book *The Path of Wisdom: A Christian Commentary on the Dhammapada* (2011) received the 2011 Frederick J. Streng Book Award from the Society for Buddhist-Christian Studies. His most recent book *Transforming Interreligious Relations: Catholic Responses to Religious Pluralism in the United States* (2020) received the 2021 Catholic Media Association first-place book award in the category of Ecumenism and Interfaith Studies. He is past president of the Society for Buddhist-Christian Studies, research fellow of the Chinese University of Hong Kong, and trustee emeritus of the Council for a Parliament of the World's Religions.

J. J. Mueller, S. J., is retired associate professor of Theological Studies at Saint Louis University. His research and writing have been primarily in theological method, Christology, social justice, and practical theology with a special focus on the American context. His books include: *Practical Discipleship: A United States Christology* (1992), *Valuing Our Differences: A History of African-American Catholics in the United States* (1993), and *Theological Foundations: Concepts and Methods for Understanding Christian Faith* (2007). The latter two have become popular textbooks.

Palmyre Oomen is Thomas More Professor Emeritus of Philosophy at the Eindhoven University of Technology, the Netherlands, and retired senior researcher in Theology at the Radboud University of Nijmegen, the Netherlands, where she directed the Heyendaal Research Group on Theology and Science. Her main areas of research are metaphysics and theology with a specific interest in divine agency, self-organization, biological evolution, freedom of the will, and the thought of Whitehead and of Aquinas. She has written many books and articles on these topics. These include: *Does God Make a Difference?: An Interpretation of Whitehead's Philosophy as a Contribution to a Theology of God's Agency* (in Dutch) (1998), which was awarded the

Legatum Stolpianum Prize in 2001, a contribution on Aquinas's view of free will as anchored in God for *Homo sapiens: Thomas van Aquino en de vraag naar de mens* (2017), and articles on Aquinas and Whitehead on divine power and almightiness (*Process Studies* 2018) and their use of language about God (*Process Studies* 2019). Please visit www.palmyreoomen.nl.

Marc A. Pugliese is associate dean of the College of Arts and Sciences at Saint Leo University. His research interests include fundamental and philosophical theology, the doctrine of God, comparative theology, interdisciplinary research, and the scholarship of teaching and learning. He is author of: *The One, the Many and the Trinity: Joseph A. Bracken and the Challenge of Process Metaphysics* (2010) and coauthor of *Beyond Naïveté: Ethics, Economics and Values* (2012). He coedited the *Festschrift* for Joseph A. Bracken, S. J. (2012) and *Teaching Interreligious Encounters* (2017). He is cofounder and cochair of the Religious Conversions Unit in the American Academy of Religion, has been a Luce Foundation Fellow, has been a faculty member of Saint Leo University's Center for Catholic-Jewish Studies, and is a faculty expert in religion for Saint Leo University's Polling Institute.

Thomas P. Rausch, S. J., is T. Marie Chilton Professor Emeritus of Catholic Theology at Loyola Marymount University, Los Angeles. Christology, ecclesiology, and ecumenism have been among his broad academic and practical theological interests. His over twenty-four books and three hundred essays and articles have been translated into ten different languages, and they include: *Catholicism in the Third Millennium* (2003), *Eschatology, Liturgy, and Christology: Toward Recovering an Eschatological Imagination* (2012), *Systematic Theology: A Roman Catholic Approach* (2016), and *Global Catholicism: Profiles and Polarities* (2021). He has also written books on Pope Benedict and Pope Francis and has published several widely used theology textbooks. He was appointed by the Secretariat for Christian Unity as Catholic Tutor to the World Council of Churches' Ecumenical Institute at Bossey, Switzerland, has served on the Roman Catholic / World Evangelical Alliance Consultation, and serves on the Anglican-Roman Catholic Consultation in the United States

Thomas Schärtl is chair of Fundamental Theology in the Catholic Theological Faculty of Ludwig Maximilians Universität, Munich. His research interests include theological language and hermeneutics, religious epistemology, the doctrine of God in Christian and non-Christian traditions, trinitarian theology, and theological anthropology. His books include: *Jenseits von Innen und Außen: Ludwig Wittgensteins Beitrag zu einer nichtdualistischen Philosophie des Geistes* ("Beyond Inside and Outside: Ludwig Wittgenstein's Contribution to a Non-dualistic Philosophy of Mind," 2000), *Theo-Grammatik. Zur Logik der Rede vom trinitarischen Gott* ("Theo-Grammar: Toward a Logic of Trinitarian God Talk," 2003), *Glaubens-Überzeugung: Philosophische Bemerkungen zur Erkenntnistheorie des christlichen Glaubens* ("Belief-Conviction. Philosophical Remarks on the Epistemology of Christian Faith," 2007), and *Gott Glauben–Gott Denken: Philosophisch-Theologische Grenzfragen* ("To Believe in God–To Think God: Philosophical-Theological Questions," 2022). He is a member of the editorial boards of the *European Journal for Philosophy of Religion* and of the *Journal of Theology and Philosophy* and is coeditor in chief of the *Studies on Systematic Theology, Ethics and Philosophy* (STEP) series, published in Münster.

Maria-Teresa Teixeira currently researches at Universidade de Coimbra, Portugal, and holds a PhD in contemporary philosophy. Her publications include *Ser, Devir e Perecer: A criatividade na filosofia de Whitehead* ("Being, Becoming, and Perishing: Creativity in Whitehead's Philosophy," 2011) and *Consciência e Acção: Bergson e as neurociências* ("Consciousness and Action: Bergson and the Neurosciences," 2012), in addition to numerous book chapters and journal articles. She has also translated Whitehead's *Process and Reality* into Portuguese. She has served as the International Process Network executive director and was the organizer of the 2017 International Whitehead Conference.